MARCONI

W. P. JOLLY

In the early hours of July 20, 1937, Guglielmo Marconi died.

"Wireless carried the news of Marconi's death all over the world, and the most eminent scientists and men of affairs paid tributes and attended memorial services. But, unique, for this man only, was the most impressive gesture of all: wireless stations everywhere closed down, and for two minutes the ether was as quiet as it had been before Marconi."

The inventor of wireless communication—radio—was not only a creative genius but a man capable of founding and managing the companies which developed and exploited radio systems. He lived a colorful life, enjoying his scientific fame, relishing other pleasures, acquiring influential friends: the Pope, Mary Pickford, Queen Victoria, King George V and Queen Mary of England, Mussolini, d'Annunzio, and more than one President of the United States.

This biography is the first to separate fact rom rumor about this genius who inspired as much hatred as admiration. Here are the complete stories of:

nic   —the accusations surrounding Marconi's development of the wireless.

(continued on Back Flap)

MARCONI

MARCONI

W. P. Jolly

STEIN AND DAY/*Publishers*/New York

First published in 1972

Copyright © 1972 by W. P. Jolly

The excerpts from *My Father Marconi* by
Degna Marconi, copyright © 1962 by
McGraw-Hill Book Company, are used with
permission of McGraw-Hill Book Company.

Library of Congress Catalog Card No. 72-79746

Printed in the United States of America

Stein and Day/*Publishers*/7 East 48 Street, New York, N.Y. 10017

ISBN 0-8128-1507-6

ACKNOWLEDGEMENTS

I am indebted to many friends and to those in charge of public and private collections of historical material who have so kindly given encouragement and help in the preparation of this book. Items are acknowledged individually in the text but I must especially thank Vivian Summers, Tom Woodward, Christopher Browne, Susan Williams and Graham Nicholson, and the staff of the libraries of the Italian Institute, India Office, Public Record Office, Beaverbrook Foundation, Royal Institution, Morrab Library, Penzance, Patent Office, Institution of Electrical Engineers, and the National Maritime Museum. For permission to quote from private letters I am grateful to Lord Baden-Powell, Lord Mountbatten, Sir Geoffrey Harmsworth, Mr Mark Bonham-Carter, Mr Nancarrow, and Mrs Noble.

I would like to acknowledge the following for permission to quote extracts from books, journals, and articles in their copyright: American Institute of Electrical Engineers; the Right Honourable Julian Amery M.P., *My Political life* by L. S. Amery; Cassell & Company Ltd., *Letters from Sir Oliver Lodge* by J. Arthur Hill; The Cornishman Newspaper Co. Ltd; *The Daily Telegraph*; Gerald Duckworth & Co. Ltd., *Economic Development of Radio* by U. C. L. Sturmey; *Electrical Review*; *Electrical Times*; Faber & Faber Ltd., *Life and letters of Rupert Brooke* by Christopher Hassall; *The Guardian*; William Heinemann Ltd., and Farrar, Straus & Giroux Inc., *Lord Reading* by Montgomery Hyde; Hutchinson Publishing Group Ltd., *Marconi – Master of Space* by Jacot and Collier; the Jellicoe Papers; Mr Oliver Lodge, *Past Years* by Sir Oliver Lodge; the McGraw-Hill Book Co., and Frederick Muller Ltd., *My Father, Marconi,* by Degna Marconi; *Nature*;

ACKNOWLEDGEMENTS

The New York Times; A. D. Peters & Co., *Into the wind* by G. C. W. Reith; Public Record Office, Crown Copyright; Routledge & Kegan Paul Ltd., *Wireless over thirty years* by R. N. Vyvyan; *The Times*. For use of illustrations I gratefully acknowledge: Beken of Cowes; John Lawrence; The Marchesa Degna Paresce Marconi; The Marconi Company Ltd; the National Maritime Museum.

Finally, I thank The Marconi Company for permission to consult and quote from material in their historical archives, and in particular Dick Raikes and Betty Hance of that company whose interest and help were most valuable and who, with other colleagues, demonstrated the continuity of the Marconi corporate spirit.

WPJ

CONTENTS

ILLUSTRATIONS

ILLUSTRATIONS

MARCONI

CHAPTER 1

THE UNCERTAIN ITALIAN BOY

On 26 April 1864, Giuseppe Marconi, a widower, was married at Boulogne to Annie Jameson, a spinster. He was thirty-eight, his bride twenty-one. His journey, by horse-drawn coach from Bologna, had been the longer, but hers, from her native Wexford, had involved two sea crossings, and was the successful outcome of many months' plotting to outwit and defy her parents.

The second child of this marriage was to become the Marchese Guglielmo Marconi, Nobel prizewinner, world-famous pioneer of wireless communication, and founder of rich and powerful companies for the development and exploitation of radio systems. Scientific fame, a taste for high life, and a flair for acquiring influential friends were to give him a spectrum of acquaintances which ranged from the Pope to Mary Pickford, and included Queen Victoria, a handful of other monarchs, Mussolini, and more than one President of the United States. Business and social activities on the grand international scale inevitably led into politics, and although his first involvement was unintentional – in the 'Marconi Scandal' which almost destroyed Lloyd George just before the 1914–18 war – he later became Italy's emissary at the 1919 Peace Conference, and served on other diplomatic occasions before and after the rise of Fascism.

The pattern of characteristics inherited by Marconi from his enterprising and unconventional parents produced a single-minded, almost obstinate, determination, and enabled him methodically to pursue and bring off scientific and business coups even when 'responsible' opinion dismissed them as airy day-dreams. The offspring of a daring and romantic runaway marriage, he rarely felt obliged by the married state to limit the attentions he paid to attractive and responsive women, even when his affairs excited public gossip which would obviously distress his family.

Annie Jameson had travelled abroad before her elopement to Boulogne, and the notion of emigration had always been a familiar part of her upbringing. Her father had left his native Scotland and gone with his brothers to Ireland, where he had built his own distillery, and the brothers had set up the Dublin Brewery. During her babyhood the potato crop, which barely supported the Irish peasants, was destroyed by blight. The peasants had been scandalously oppressed by English land-lords for generations, and the Great Famine which followed the failure of the potato crop now set off a tremendous flood of hopeful emigrants to fresh chances in America. The Jameson family in their comfortable mansion surrounded by moat and park did not feel the pangs of hunger, but Annie could not have been unaffected by the distress and injustice falling upon the Irish people, nor by the way in which many of them were driven to pack up and leave their homeland during all the years of her childhood and adolescence.

The first time Annie left home to go abroad she was not so much driven away as offered the opportunity of going by her parents, who believed themselves to be acting for her good. A certain strain had developed in the family because Annie's excellent singing voice, coupled no doubt with her good looks, had secured for her the offer of an engagement at Covent Garden where the eighteenth-century theatre had quite recently become exclusively an opera house. It was the age of first performances of works by Verdi and Wagner. But what-ever revolutions might be taking place in musical and dramatic form, traditional views about the respectability of the stage still held. The very proper Jamesons could not think of permitting Annie to accept the Covent Garden engagement. But they did not wish it to be thought that they were dis-pleased with their daughter or insensitive to her musical ability, and so they sought to soften her disappointment by arranging for her to go to Italy to extend her singing studies.

The Jamesons had considerable doubts and anxieties about sending their youngest daughter abroad, but they could not expect to find a safe colourless alternative which would be accepted by their wilful child as compensation for the forbidden glamour of Covent Garden. On the whole they were satisfied with their chosen scheme, largely because Annie was to stay in Bologna at the home of a family of bankers with whom the Jamesons had business connections. She would go by day to music classes at the Conservatoire, and her social life would be controlled by her hosts, the de Renolis, who were solid and respectable people, as much like themselves as her father and mother could hope to find in a foreign country.

Annie liked the historic old town of Bologna with its narrow streets and romantic buildings. She settled in well with the worthy de Renolis and was introduced to the friends and relatives who visited them. One such visitor was a little boy, Luigi, whose mother, the daughter of the house, had died almost as soon as he was born. Luigi was brought to see the grandparents by his father Giuseppe Marconi who had been a widower for several years.

At the very centre of the ramparts of respectable family life which the Jamesons had intended to protect their daughter, Annie fell in love with the widower Giuseppe. She threw over her studies at the Conservatoire and came home to ask her parents for permission to marry.

To the Jamesons their daughter's choice of suitor sounded disastrous. He was too old, he was foreign, and he was second-hand, with an Italian son to emphasise the point. Once again father and mother had to enforce a parental veto, and this time there was not much hope of a counter-attraction to offer. Annie was sedulously introduced into all the functions where she would meet the young and eligible men of her own country. She was complaisant as a good daughter should be. She went to the functions, she met the young men, and she ate out her heart for Giuseppe. Notes and messages were smuggled between them, and as soon as she was of age the rendezvous in Boulogne was made and kept, and Annie Jameson returned across the Alps to Italy as Signora Marconi.

Giuseppe took his new young wife to the Palazzo Marescalchi, his town house in Bologna, a great solid building with shutters at the windows. In front was a private square, shared with several other houses, and at the back was an enclosed courtyard and garden. Bologna was not the family home of the Marconis: they had long been established as landowners in the Apennines about fifty miles to the south-west. There in the mountains the Marconis stood high on the social scale although they were certainly not wealthy by city standards. As a young man Giuseppe had helped his father run the farm, but he was not content with a life which offered such small rewards, and he became the first of the family to quit the mountains for the town. The modest affluence of his own upbringing in a home surrounded by poor peasant country was in many ways like that of his wife Annie, and national oppression and unrest had been part of his youthful background just as it had for her. Ever since he was a boy there had been political and military struggles under Cavour, Garibaldi, and Mazzini to expel the French and the Austrians from the Italian peninsula and weld into a single kingdom the separate regions of Piedmont, Lombardy, Sicily, and the Papal States. The conflict and upheaval went on for over twenty years until in 1870 the French garrison left Rome and so allowed King Victor Emmanuel II to enter and declare it the capital of a united Italy seven years after Annie and Giuseppe were married.

On 25 April 1874 at the Palazzo Marescalchi in Bologna, Guglielmo Marconi was born, and Annie nearly died bringing him into the world. He was not the first fruit of the runaway romance – his elder brother, Alfonso, had been born the year after the elopement and was now aged nine. Perhaps to a man now forty-eight a new baby in the house was tiresome, and little more than yet another son. For whatever reason, Annie was much more concerned than her husband with bringing up Guglielmo. Such an arrangement was perhaps natural, but as the baby became a child, and the child became a boy with a precocious interest in electricity, the difference in his parents' attitudes towards him sharpened into unhappy partisanship. During his early struggle to establish wireless telegraphy as a practical system Marconi had the constant assistance of a doting mother, and endless humiliating obstruction from a father who was always antagonistic to his scientific studies and experiments.

4

Guglielmo Marconi's parents were comfortably off, and his early childhood was privileged. But the little unhappinesses which haphazardly mar every child's life seem to have visited him more than usually often, and many of them fitted a pattern suggesting that his family life lacked the comfortable, unquestioned stability which was provided for their children by most well-to-do parents in the late nineteenth century.

The Marconis owned a town house in Bologna where Guglielmo was born, and a country estate just outside the town called the Villa Grifone. It was at this estate that Guglielmo's father, Giuseppe, felt most at home. Giuseppe's own father had bought the Villa Grifone after selling up and leaving his land in the Apennines in order to be near Giuseppe when he moved to Bologna. City life had not suited the old man and he had soon bought this country place where he could practise his yeoman's skills. Giuseppe had enjoyed helping his father there with the fields and the vineyards and the raising of silkworms. When eventually he inherited the estate he took a pride in looking after and improving the house and the land. He loved the peace of his country home; the quiet satisfaction of inspecting well-tended crops, and the scholarly seclusion of his library.

By the time Guglielmo was born the romantic elopement of his parents was ten years in the past and they had each settled down in their own way to married life. Nearing fifty, Giuseppe was well past the brief period of middle age allowed to nineteenth-century men, while Annie was only just into her thirties and was an attractive woman with a taste for fashionable clothes and a liking for social life. Certainly Annie did not share her husband's lasting contentment with the simple life at Villa Grifone, and once it became established that she was 'delicate' she always escaped during the bleak winter months, taking Guglielmo and Alfonso across to the milder Mediterranean side of the Apennines.

Florence and Leghorn provided for Annie the winter warmth that her constitution was said to need, and the opportunity for the sort of social life she was determined not to forgo. Both cities contained colonies of British residents who entertained in the English style. They welcomed the society of the vivacious young matron who was an interesting part of the 'real' Italy but who loved the chance of drawing-room talk in her native tongue. Leghorn was especially attractive to Annie because one of her sisters, now married to an Indian Army officer called Prescott, had set up house there with her young daughters, who were of an age to be good companions for Annie's sons while the two mothers exchanged sisterly confidences and gossip.

The bustle of packing and journeys and the confusion of waking in a strange bedroom were common experiences for young Guglielmo from earliest babyhood. As well as the regular long stays in Leghorn and Florence, Annie made frequent trips to take the waters at Porretta, a little village spa which was very close to the original home of the Marconi family in the Apennines. Because of this her husband occasionally accompanied her and the boys and called upon his friends in the neighbourhood while she went to the baths. But much more often it was Annie, Alfonso, and Guglielmo who were the travellers, while Giuseppe stayed at home to look after his business and estate.

The longest of the trips was to England, and Guglielmo was three years old when Annie took him there for the first time. This visit lasted three years, so that by the time they returned to Italy the child had spent half his life away from his native land, and considerably more than half his life away from the family home.

There was not much opportunity for lessons during the visit to England, and for Guglielmo who was less than six years old there was little need. His mother and his nurse had been able to give him a certain amount of simple instruction, but as soon as Annie took the boys back to Italy their father, Giuseppe, decided that it was time for a more systematic education. A schoolroom was set up at the Villa Grifone and a local schoolmaster installed with the particular task of making the boys fluent in Italian, and of providing some continuity in their education when they went off to Florence or Leghorn for the winter. After three years in England Alfonso's Italian must certainly have been very rusty, and Guglielmo's almost non-existent, so their father's concern about this aspect of their education was understandable.

Annie had no wish to see her sons growing more fluent in Italian than they were in her own language so the English lessons, which she herself gave, were not neglected. She was equally determined that the boys should be brought up in her own Protestant religion, in spite of them both having been baptised Roman Catholics. This did not create as much family upset as might have been expected because there was no active opposition from her husband. Giuseppe had been educated by priests with the idea of at some time taking Holy Orders himself. But the call had never come to him and as he grew up in the political and social upheaval of Italian nationalism he had moved further away from the Church to a position of little religious commitment and less concern. There was no serious objection when Annie took the boys away each evening for Bible reading and religious instruction, or when their public devotions were confined to attending Anglican services in Florence and Leghorn with Annie and her English friends.

Young Guglielmo did not relish the schoolroom work, or the religious instruction. He was an irritating pupil, often playing truant from the hired tutor's lessons and making the wretched man's life something of a misery. But although an indulgent mother was prepared to overlook if not condone a certain amount of such behaviour, she came down heavily on any slackness in her own classes.

Perhaps the troublesome Guglielmo might have been more like his pleasant, well-behaved older brother if he had not so early in life been a rolling stone and if he had known the joint love and concern of a mother and father devoted to him and to each other. His early scholastic path might also have been easier if he had not been offered two very different native tongues and had not been aware of two largely incompatible religious faiths. But at least he was not lulled into the un-thinking acceptance of authoritarian views. Later in life he refused to be put off by the uncompromising opposition of established scientific theory and instead he pressed on with the experiments which led to his most spectacular successes in wireless communication.

The visits to Florence and Leghorn meant social life in the English style for Annie. For her sons there were the sophisticated amusements of the big city, the companionship of girls and boys of their own age, and above all freedom from fixed routine and constant surveillance. But Florence was spoiled for Guglielmo when his father decided to send him for a first taste of real school. It was not a success. The school did not take to Guglielmo, and he in turn loathed almost everything about the school.

The other boys found him reserved, not readily dropping into any of the loose groups which make up the community of the classroom. He was partly foreign, and he was different, and this alone would have been a fault difficult to forgive, but worst of all he was judged to be 'stuck up'. His teachers found him backward for his age and were continually telling him off in class for bad work. At this stage of the development of educational practice, much of a lesson would be taken up with pupils standing up to recite work which they had learned. When Guglielmo's turn came the class bubbled with the expectation of hearty entertainment to relieve the tedium of the day. As soon as he spoke there would be sniggers because his Italian was bad, and his accent worse. Only too often he would say something wrong or stupid that provoked a rebuke from the teacher, and when the rebuke was stiffened with sarcasm or other teacher's wit, the class would sense at once that authority was with them and they would explode into uproarious derision.

When at last lessons did end for the day, poor Guglielmo's spirits could not soar and he could not run wildly with friends through the gates and away from the hated confinement, thinking, as schoolboys do, only of the immediate freedom, with no foreboding of tomorrow's misery to damp that effervescent rush to liberty. He knew that waiting to greet him outside the school would be his doting mother, and should that greeting differ in any detail from the conservative standards of the schoolboy pack then it would be noticed and probably criticised by classmates. His mother was far from unobtrusive, she was obviously foreign, and the hats she wore were considered daringly chic even by fashion-conscious society. A mother's hat is accepted universally by schoolboys as a guide to the worth of her son, and Annie's millinery confections, so blatantly paraded outside the school, only confirmed that Guglielmo justly deserved to be the target for mob ridicule and contempt.

But Guglielmo did at least gain one advantage from that first school in Florence, in spite of all the failure and the misery. He met an older boy, Luigi Solari, and they formed a friendship which was to last for many years. He became Marconi's lieutenant, friend and confidant. He assisted him with experiments all over the world, he persuaded the King of Italy to lend him a warship for wireless trials, he walked by his side to the operating theatre when one of his eyes was removed, and Solari was with him on the last busy day of his crowded life. A profit and loss statement for Guglielmo's time at that inhospitable school would show a multitude of entries on the debit side but the single entry – Solari – in the other column would close the account with a handsome credit.

The memories of Leghorn were much more pleasant. The Prescotts lived near, and Daisy, the youngest of his four girl cousins, was a very special favourite of Guglielmo's. Then there was another family of friends, the Camperios, with a boy of Guglielmo's own age, a very pretty older daughter, and another son who was a most superior person because he was training to be a naval officer. Most important of all, though, there was the sea.

Leghorn was the main port of central Italy. Here the Regia Marina, the naval pride of the new united Italy, had its Academy and the inner harbour was busy with pinnaces fetching stores and mail for the warships anchored outside in the bay. Sometimes the boats would be crowded with excited sailors looking forward to their shore leave, and sometimes there would be just two or three officers sitting nonchalant and self-confident in the stern. Each boat would usually be commanded by a young midshipman in a glamorous uniform. Here was something for an ambitious boy to aim at, and here too was a rare case of harmony between Guglielmo and his father. Giuseppe liked the idea of his son becoming a naval officer and encouraged him to direct his studies towards securing entry into the Naval Academy.

He even went as far as buying the boy a sailing boat, and

9

Giuseppe was not a man to spend money lightly. He was careful to the point of meanness, and proud of it. He liked to tell the story of how he had once outmanœuvred a fund-raising deputation of citizens of Bologna who were anxious to have the town's ancient cathedral restored.[1] He magnanimously assured them that when the restoration work was complete he would provide a magnificent and expensive cross to top it off. As he had expected, the work was never started in his lifetime, so his generous gesture cost him nothing.

When Annie wanted her sons taught music she was able to coax the money for lessons out of Giuseppe who may have thought back to the magic that music had meant to the two of them when they were first married. The old man saw a good return for his money in this case because both the boys did well: Alfonso at the violin and Guglielmo at the piano which well suited both his dexterity and his contemplative spirit. Often in the years to come he would sit and play the piano for an hour or more at a time, sometimes for the entertainment of family and friends, but more often for his own relaxation.

Success with the music lessons was particularly welcome to Guglielmo who had so rarely earned praise in any form of learning. His Italian improved tremendously, too, in the gay young Leghorn society, where he began to enjoy the stimulating company of attractive girls and to take a pride in his growing confidence in mild flirtation. His expertise in handling a small boat also increased rapidly, and with his cousin Daisy crewing for him he would show off by pressing his nippy little sailing boat too close to the paths of bigger craft in the harbour.

There was not so much progress to show in the duller subjects which would be needed to gain entrance to the Naval Academy, but life in Leghorn was very pleasant and it was sad to have to leave. The end of the winter meant return to the country and to the Villa Grifone where all the family were in such close and inescapable contact with each other that the various abrasive incompatibilities – especially between Guglielmo and his father – produced harsh friction and some violent rows during the hot summer days.

The Villa Grifone was Giuseppe's kingdom. It was his favourite place and he ran it precisely as he thought proper, which was autocratically with an inflexible routine suited to an old man's idea of good manners, and with a hierarchical domestic structure which put him a long way clear at the top, and the children below the servants at the bottom. The arrangement did not suit Guglielmo and he was always in trouble.

Family meals at the Villa Grifone were presided over by Giuseppe and were as free and easy as the ceremony of Trooping the Colour. The first hazard for the childen was unpunctuality. When the bell was sounded for the meal there was only just time for them to wash and tidy themselves to withstand the parental scrutiny at the table. Guglielmo was not the type to have half an ear cocked for the bell, ready to drop whatever he was doing and rush to lunch. He was often out alone fishing, or exploring in the woods and investigating wildlife. Too often his intense concentration on the interest of the moment would cause him to forget to allow time to get back to the house. Even when he was in the house he would sometimes be so immersed, perhaps in a story of Ancient Greece in his father's library, that he would not even hear the bell. Then there would be the inevitable scene with Giuseppe who believed that to be late for a meal was inexcusable.

A punctual, tidy arrival was only the first sacrifice a child had to make to the gastronomic ritual. The order of service, the manner of passing the dishes, and even the method of transferring food from plate to mouth, were all rigidly pre-scribed. Then, as accompaniment to the stylised circulation of the dishes, Giuseppe liked to conduct the family in discussion of subjects he considered fitting. Each would be called upon in turn to contribute to the general theme, and Guglielmo would again and again displease his father by being caught in boorish introspective silence or irrelevant uninvited outburst during this conversational pass-the-parcel. Meals, which are an hour of joyful stuffing for most growing boys, provided a stiff daily examination which Guglielmo often failed.

Ever since he was a young child with his first mechanical toys Guglielmo had been interested in the way things were put together. During boyhood he was always making some

11

gadget that he had seen or read about, and he liked the Villa Grifone because in the large house and the estate buildings it was usually possible to find the bits and pieces he needed to construct his latest device.

He made a miniature still which actually produced crude spirits, he converted cousin Daisy's sewing machine temporarily into a turnspit, and he rigged up wires and a battery for an electric bell. But growing skill with his scientific toys was not matched by improvement in his general scholastic ability. It was a blow to him and to Giuseppe when he failed to qualify for entry into the Naval Academy. From that moment his father was absolutely confirmed in his earlier belief that the scientific experiments were dilettante rubbish, and that Guglielmo, encouraged by his mother, had frittered away the irrecoverable time when he should have been studying to take the first step towards a proper profession. Money had been thrown away buying materials, and valuable household property had been appropriated for the equipment. The last straw was when Guglielmo smashed a large number of plates in full view of the neighbours in a particularly harebrained experiment. Giuseppe was affronted and humiliated by this public display of stupidity and waste, and from then on if he came across anything which he thought was a piece of his son's scientific nonsense he destroyed it.

Guglielmo had failed to prepare himself for any sort of career, he was despised as feckless by Giuseppe, and he was forced to conspire with his mother against his father to try to conjure some fruitful occupation out of his scientific hobby. This was the position, no longer to be disguised, into which his nature and curious upbringing had led him. The less obvious effects of this upbringing upon his character and personality were probably also firmly established.

By the time he was twelve or thirteen he had the brittle self-reliance of a child who had grown used to a mobile life lacking the security provided by familiar objects with which the ordinary child surrounds himself. Still further complicating the pattern of imprints on the developing character was the uncertain emotional climate in the family, with father and mother separated by a growing gulf, and young Guglielmo receiving from Annie a flood of affection which might better have been shared more evenly among Giuseppe, Alfonso and her step-son Luigi.

The years of his teens were to be the nadir of Guglielmo's life. He had returned to Italy from the long visit to England as little more than a baby, unusually independent, used to his own company, his own amusements, and his own way. But what is amusing mischief in the child is soon regarded as wayward stupidity in the adolescent boy, and as poor Guglielmo grew into a youth the world – contemporaries, adults, and especially his father – made him suffer for his non-conformity.

The curve of his reputation, within the family and outside it, had not plunged unremittingly downwards, but the occasional upturns were small, short-lived, and illusory. Soon though, the curve would begin to flatten and then slowly bend upwards to heights undreamed of at this time by anyone, except perhaps the boy himself.

In 1887, when Guglielmo was thirteen, Heinrich Hertz discovered that electrical energy could be radiated through space from one place to another, and young Guglielmo attended for the first time the Leghorn Technical Institute where he was introduced to the formal study of physics and electricity. The next seven exciting and painful years would see the boy who played with imitative scientific toys change into the young man with an invention to offer to his country.

CHAPTER 2

AN IDEA REALISED AND SPURNED

THE electrical toys which Guglielmo made in the 1880s with such boyish enthusiasm were novelties to his friends and family but they were mostly copies of apparatus which had originally been constructed many years – in some cases centuries – before by serious scientific researchers.

The Ancient Greeks had noticed that amber when rubbed with fur attracted light objects because it acquired an invisible, intangible fluid which they named after *elektron*, their word for amber. Electricity was systematically studied from Elizabethan times onwards and much was learned about the way it would pass from one charged body to another, sometimes leaping through the air as a spark which was obviously a small relation of the lightning flash. But all such effects were over in an instant, and it was not until the electric battery was invented in 1800 that it was possible to produce a continuous passage of charge around a circuit – an electric current – and so begin the series of experiments which led to the exploitation of electricity industrially and domestically as a source of heat, light and motive power.

The first step towards the invention of the battery had been taken in the University of Bologna in 1791 when Luigi Galvani noticed that a dead frog's leg twitched if touched simultaneously with a copper and a zinc wire. Another Italian scientist, Volta, in 1800 correctly interpreted Galvani's observation and pointed out that two dissimilar metals separated by any moist substance would generate a continuous electric current. The muscular spasm produced in Galvani's experiment when the current passed through the moisture between the electrodes was of great biological interest, but to the physicist it was only incidental. Volta's first practical batteries used wet paper between the metal plates. Frogs' legs were not essential: had they been, the modern battery factory would indeed be a strange place.

Electricity was a well-established college subject by 1874 when Guglielmo was born. Samuel Morse, whose dot-dash code became so important in wireless, had received formal lectures in electricity when he went to Yale in 1805 at the age of fourteen but the subject was not kept secret among the academics and researchers. By the 1830s and 1840s the general public was sufficiently interested in electricity for there to be open lectures on the subject all over Europe, and for a modestly affluent man like Giuseppe Marconi to have books about it in his library.

After the disastrous start to his formal schooling in Florence, Guglielmo was luckier the following winter when he was enrolled in the Leghorn Technical Institute. Here his studies prospered under Professor Bizzarrini, and his interest became sharply focused on physics and chemistry. He was single-minded in the study of these subjects, both for their own sake and because he could see the possibility of making out of them some sort of occupation to replace his frustrated ambition to enter the Navy. He devoted more and more time, and more of his father's grudgingly doled-out money, to experiments, and it was a constant strain for Annie to prevent an explosion in domestic relations and a total ban by Giuseppe on his son's scientific activities. The lectures at the Leghorn Technical Institute were not enough to satisfy the now eager and dedicated young student, so he persuaded his mother to arrange extra private lessons for him from a Professor Rosa, and in the years to come he was always grateful for the sound practical grounding which Rosa gave him in the fundamentals of electricity.

Although Giuseppe had started by disliking Guglielmo's scientific interest and had gone on to oppose it, and eventually to thwart it cruelly, he had never actually invoked the veto which he would undoubtedly have regarded as his right as head of the family. Great achievements in science and engineering were making news, and making money, all over the world in the second half of the nineteenth century, and perhaps

15

Giuseppe might have come to accept the idea of his son training to be a scientist if only the boy could have been seen to be following some sort of recognised scholastic path like the degree course at the University. But once more Guglielmo failed in his father's eyes; he could not pass the matriculation examination of the University of Bologna and was refused admission.

Now, as was often to happen, Annie used her influence, her charms, and her persuasive power outside the circle of her immediate family to further the career of her favourite son. Professor Righi was one of the more dashing dons at the University of Bologna. He was a fine experimental physicist and a brilliant lecturer, with a reputation throughout Europe which filled his classes with students from many countries. He also lived close to the Villa Grifone estate, so Annie arranged to meet her neighbour and tell him about Guglielmo's interests, talents, and difficulties.

The distinguished professor, with so many activities to make demands upon his thoughts and time, could hardly have been set aflame with enthusaism at the prospect of becoming involved with an amateur boy scientist who had not succeeded in being admitted as a student member of the University. But so well did Annie play her cards that for her sake Righi offered to allow her son to use certain University facilities which were within his control, although no doubt the arrangement was quite unofficial. Guglielmo was able to set up experiments in Righi's laboratory, and possibly to borrow material for further practical work at home, and he also made use of the University library where he read everything he could find about electricity and its commercial applications.

A few years later those who wished to belittle Marconi's achievements were suggesting that he had only taken advantage of other men's discoveries. Such detractors made much of the fact that Guglielmo's neighbour, Righi, was one of the most eminent workers in the field of Hertz waves. There is thus a significance both in the putting of a particular question and in the answer given by Marconi at an interview on 4 July 1897.[1]

'Did you study physics at Bologna under Professor Righi?'

'I studied under the renowned Professor Vincenzo Rosa at the Livorno Lyceum and would be most happy that it be known that he was my only physics master.'

Many of the great engineering enterprises which Guglielmo could read about in the University library were triumphant technical solutions to the problems set by an explosive demand for better communications in the nineteenth century. Railways, canals, steamships, all turned fundamental scientific principles to handsome profit by carrying goods and people between great and growing centres of population. There was, too, a need for the transport of something less tangible – information.

New York wanted to know the price of cotton in Liverpool. Mincing Lane wanted news of a vessel passing the Lizard on her way up-Channel with a cargo from the East. The increasingly powerful centralised administrative machines of European governments wanted political and military intelligence from the ends of their realms and beyond. Richer private citizens were even prepared to pay well for the swift transmission of social messages.

To satisfy many such demands for up-to-date information, strings of lonely telegraph stations had stretched out across the hills of Europe by the beginning of the nineteenth century. At each one, tall posts held the pair of thin semaphore arms silhouetted against the sky so that the operator at the next station several miles away could read the signals clearly through his telescope. Torches on the arms made it possible to work by night and messages were passed at very considerable speeds: just over four minutes to Paris from Calais and less than a quarter of an hour from Toulon.

By about 1860 this great semaphore system had been almost completely replaced by the electric telegraph. The telegraph wires were laid underground or carried in the air on posts, and thousands of operators were trained to send and receive messages, at first using magnetic pointer instruments but later the almost universal Morse key and buzzer. As soon as it had been demonstrated that electricity flowing along a wire could be made to cause practically instantaneous action at a distance, attempts were made to use it for signalling and the first

17

working system available to the public had been opened between Paddington and Slough alongside Brunel's Great Western Railway. It was under Royal patronage and news from Windsor Castle was 'wired' quickly to the London newspapers, but public interest was not strongly aroused for several years until in 1845 the system was used to catch a criminal. The candid message sent to Paddington by the telegraph clerk at Slough station contrasts quaintly with the modern temporising style of 'helping the police with their enquiries'.[2]

> A murder has just been committed at Salt Hill and the suspected murderer was seen to take a first-class ticket for London by the train which left Slough at 7.42 p.m. He is in the garb of a Quaker, with a brown coat on, which reaches nearly to his feet; he is in the last compartment of the second first-class carriage.

The railway police sergeant at Paddington followed and arrested the suspect so clearly identified. Apparently a respectable married man, he was tried for the murder of his mistress at her cottage near Slough, and publicly hanged in Aylesbury in March 1845.

The public was enthralled by this story of an evil-doer struck down as if by a shaft from a supernatural being just at the moment when escape seemed accomplished. A later public was similarly fascinated in 1910 when Marconi's wireless was used to penetrate the disguise of Dr Crippen and his companion Miss Le Neve aboard the transatlantic liner in which they were escaping to America after the murder of Mrs Crippen in London.

Money flowed into the telegraph companies after the publicity from the Slough murder, and made possible the methodical extension of the wires across Europe and America. By a combination of financial daring, painstaking technology, and tough seamanship, the two great continental telegraph networks were joined through the successful Atlantic cable laid in 1866 by Brunel's revolutionary and enormous ship, the *Great Eastern*, which had failed financially as a passenger vessel and had been bought cheaply and converted to carry the huge length of cable required.

Accounts in the University library of the world-wide establishment of the electric telegraph were stirring enough to excite any aspiring young scientist, and they may very well have strongly affected Guglielmo who already had a special curiosity about electricity. It is always difficult to isolate the influence which pushes a man's interest and ambition – sometimes indeed his whole life – in a particular direction, and perhaps in this case one should look for this decisive impulse further back, to the biography of Benjamin Franklin which the boy found years before in his father's library at Villa Grifone. Here was the story of a scientist – an electrician, to use the terminology of the time – who had uncovered great secrets of nature and made a name for himself in the field of research, but who had also achieved more generally recognised fame as a philosopher, a statesman and an international diplomat.

Franklin, whose life spanned nine decades of perhaps the most crucial century in the history of his country, performed many of the basic experiments which led to a sound understanding of the properties of electricity. The public was most aware of his scientific work in connection with electricity in the atmosphere and the development of the lightning conductor for churches and other tall buildings. He was specially known for the famous experiment in Philadelphia in 1752 when, helped by his son, he flew a kite up into the thunderclouds and proved that they were electrified by drawing the charge down the string to the earth. But Franklin had an active scientific career of comet-like brilliance lasting less than ten years, and most of his life was spent in politics and diplomacy. He signed the treaty of alliance between America and France and shone for a time in the salons of Paris, with English spies lurking in the background; he helped draft the Declaration of Independence; and he was his country's representative in England for many years.

The extent to which Franklin's many-sided fame, and his fortune, influenced the young boy reading the biography must be in some doubt, but he would surely have felt that it refuted his father's conviction that a man of science could hardly

19

be a man of substance. Guglielmo, uncertain and withdrawn in his father's library, could not know that there were to be many parallels in his own life with the events he was reading about: Franklin's kite drawing electricity out of the clouds, and Marconi's kite in Newfoundland 150 years later supporting the aerial wire which drew out of the sky the first radio signal to cross the Atlantic; Franklin sent on a delicate political mission to the Red Indians of Ohio, and Marconi sent on a delicate political mission to Fiume where the soldier-poet, D'Annunzio, had declared an independent state; Franklin signing the peace treaty after the War of Independence, and Marconi signing for Italy at Versailles after the Great War. Such parallels would owe more to coincidence than influence and the proper assessment will lie somewhere between the obvious conscious imitation of the boy repeating Franklin's scientific experiments, occasionally with success but always with pleasure, and the other extreme of entirely independent enterprise leading the adult Marconi into repeating Franklin's indiscreet attachments to women other than his wife.

Perhaps, though, it was not the written word which decisively affected the boy, but the spoken words of a nearly blind old man recalling a lifetime spent as an electric telegraph operator. Guglielmo met him by chance in Leghorn and sometimes sat with him and read aloud and in return the old man taught him to tap out the Morse code.

For whatever reason, the fertile ground in Guglielmo's mind was distinctly receptive to the moment in 1894 when he first read of Hertz's experiments with electromagnetic waves and decided that this example of electrical action at a distance could be adapted to provide telegraphy without the need for wires connecting the stations.

Hertz was a German who had set out to prove a theoretical prediction made by the Scottish physicist Maxwell that there was a new sort of wave which he called an electromagnetic wave. Such waves would have frequency and wavelength-like water waves or sound waves, but they would travel at the enormous velocity of light, 186,000 miles per second, and would pass with varying difficulty through solids, liquids and gases, but most surprising of all and unlike any other sort of wave they would travel easily through a vacuum. It was eight years after Maxwell died that his electromagnetic waves were shown to exist in an experiment devised by Hertz in 1887.

In the experiment Hertz connected the two ends of a coil of wire to the opposite sides of a gap across which a crackling spark several inches long would jump when he pressed a key connected to a source of high voltage. This was the transmitter, and a similar coil of wire some yards away attached to a very much smaller spark gap acted as the receiver. When the big spark jumped across the transmitter gap a tiny spark a fraction of a millimetre long jumped across the receiver gap, indicating that some of the large amount of energy supplied to the transmitter had been radiated in the form of electromagnetic waves and that a minute amount of this radiated energy had reached the receiver.

Hertz died in January 1894, seven years after first successfully demonstrating electromagnetic waves. That summer Guglielmo was on holiday at Biellese in the Italian Alps when he read an obituary describing Hertz's work and he subsequently said that as a result of this article the idea of wireless telegraphy using Hertzian waves suddenly came to him. In later life he said:

> The idea obsessed me more and more, and in those mountains of Biellese I worked it out in imagination. I did not attempt any experiments until we returned to the Villa Grifone in the autumn, but then two large rooms at the top of the house were set aside for me by my mother. And there I began experiments in earnest.[3]

The earnest experiments were not taken very seriously by anyone except his mother and Guglielmo himself. As soon as he returned from holiday he had gone to tell his neighbour Professor Righi about his idea for wireless telegraphy. Righi pointed out that it was the wildest flight of fanciful optimism for Guglielmo to believe that he could make important advances in science when his grasp of the fundamentals of the subject was still so shaky. He went on to suggest, perhaps a little primly, that Guglielmo was unlikely to be the one to make a great breakthrough in the application of electromagnetic waves when experimental scientists had been studying them since Hertz's first demonstration. He, Righi, had himself been working with Hertzian waves for several years and had in fact written the obituary which had so inspired Guglielmo.

Righi's advice was well-meaning and wise, but in the event he was wrong. Guglielmo went home to his attics and set out to prove that his vision was more substantial than commonsense and informed opinion would suggest.

During the winter of 1894 Guglielmo made these two attic rooms his own mysterious kingdom. He worked there through the dark, chilly days, and often far into the nights, with batteries and coils and wires and spark gaps laid out among the silkworm trays. Annie's contribution to the great project was to give up for once her regular winter trip to warmer weather so that she might watch over her son and see that nothing interrupted his concentration. When he did not spare the time to come downstairs for a meal Annie would carry up a tray and leave it outside the locked door. When he worked too late Annie would get out of bed in the middle of the night and go up to tap on the door and coax him away with the advice that overtiredness would not further his efforts. There was perhaps just a touch of martyrdom mixed with the dedication on both sides.

Old Giuseppe still loomed disapprovingly in the background and, as always, Annie had to keep him away from Guglielmo's activities. He groused about his son always being locked away at the top of the house, he complained that the servants were not able to get in to clean the attics, he grudged any money spent on apparatus, and he showed no sympathy or under-standing for what his son was trying to do. But to himself he admitted that at twenty the boy was at last working harder than any taskmaster could demand, and he noted that his son had marked out, and ruled absolutely, his own territory in the house, and showed signs of quietly doing the same thing with his life.

The first thing that Guglielmo set out to do was simply to repeat Hertz's experiments of seven years ago and so observe, under the control of his own hand, the radiation and reception of electromagnetic waves which he believed to promise such important future commercial application. He was already several years behind eminent scientists like Oliver Lodge in England, Bose in India, and Righi at Bologna University. But such men were primarily interested in the fundamental nature of the waves radiated by an electric spark, and their experiments tended to be directed towards demonstrating that Hertzian waves and light waves had in common such properties as reflection and refraction, and were truly all part of one family of electromagnetic waves. Marconi cared almost nothing for fundamental theory, indeed he knew very little of it. His interest in Hertzian waves was entirely in making them carry messages through space without the need for wires between transmitter and receiver. He did not allow wider intellectual implications, which may distract the pure scientist from practical applications, to divert him from the well-defined target of increasing the distance travelled by the waves. Nevertheless, all through the first years of earnest experimenting he was driven by the fear that he had started too late, and that someone would forestall him in producing and patenting a wireless telegraph system.

> My chief trouble [he said] was that the idea was so elementary, so simple in logic, that it seemed difficult for me to believe that no one else had thought of putting it into practice. Surely, I argued, there must be much more mature scientists than myself who had followed the same line of thought and arrived at an almost similar conclusion.[4]

The apparatus he so painstakingly set up in the attics was copied from that originally used by Hertz and later improved by the other scientists. Most of it was home-made, following descriptions given in published scientific papers, but occasionally he got a little help from Righi with the loan of some small piece of equipment.

The transmitter was still essentially a coil and spark gap as used by Hertz, although the design of the spark gap had been slightly modified by Righi, and a curved metal reflector was placed behind it to direct the waves towards the receiver.

At the receiving end the improvements made since Hertz's time were more fundamental. The small spark gap connected to the receiving coil had been replaced by a much more sensitive detector called a Branly coherer. This was a small glass tube containing an electrical contact at each end, with the space between the two contacts filled by fine metal dust. When the electromagnetic radiation picked up by the receiving coil was applied to the coherer, the dust particles cohered more closely and the electrical resistance between the two contacts was therefore reduced.

If the coherer was suitably connected to a battery and an electric buzzer, or an electric Morse printing machine, then the fall in resistance when radiation was received caused a large enough increase in current in the battery circuit for the buzzer to sound, or for the Morse machine to print a mark. The essence of the improvement was that the minute amount of electromagnetic energy reaching the receiver was no longer required to do the work of providing the audible or visible signal. By using the coherer, this small amount of received energy could be made to *control* the very much larger amount of energy available from the battery which was powerful enough to drive the buzzer or the Morse printer.

The battery circuit was also used to work a small mechanical tapper which gently struck the glass side of the coherer when one pulse of electromagnetic radiation had been received, so that the 'cohered' dust particles were shaken apart again and the apparatus was ready to receive the next pulse of radiation.

By the end of 1894 the lonely winter months in the attics had brought success enough for Guglielmo to risk a demonstration of his progress – but only to his mother, an audience whose appreciation could be guaranteed. To see a key pressed at one end of the attic and to hear a buzzer sound thirty feet away across the room could not really have been particularly impressive for Annie, but she would have sensed her son's excitement and pride, and would have found suitable words of wonder and congratulation. His next audience was a tougher one, and an uninvited one. The Prescott girls were staying at Grifone and one day they burst into the attics and demanded to be shown what he was doing up there. Reluctantly he led them around, setting up small impromptu experiments and explaining this and that in a performance that lay somewhere between nursery conjuring tricks and a serious scientific exposition.

Even the most experienced scientist hates having to fling together bits of apparatus to provide a show for unexpected visitors, and Guglielmo had suffered so much criticism in the past that he wanted to be absolutely sure of success whenever he revealed anything of his great dream to outsiders. The girls were not ones to be overawed by their cousin and they would not have been nearly as careful as his mother of hurting his feelings. But by the time they all went downstairs they were chattering about his 'wireless' with enthusiastic interest and Guglielmo was left with the pleasant thought that this un-welcomed test which he had just passed was much more realistic than that which he had prepared to show his mother.

All through the spring and early summer of 1895 the experiments went on. But the character of the work was not now the same as it had been during the previous winter when Guglielmo's immediate object had been to put together apparatus in his own laboratory so that, like other more experienced scientists, he too could reproduce and study the phenomenon of the transmission of electromagnetic energy through space by Hertz waves. The groundwork had been finished when he was able regularly to send signals from the transmitter spark gap to the receiving coherer across the attic. Now, with the principle established and demonstrable at will, Guglielmo slogged away at the unspectacular task of tidying up, modifying, and developing his equipment in order that he might be able to receive signals at increasingly greater distances from the transmitter.

He was particularly good at this consolidation and im-provement phase of scientific innovation, his patience and determination making him try every conceivable circuit re-arrangement and alternative material in his apparatus, even when there was little or no scientific basis for thinking that the modification would give improved performance.

It was enough that the modification could be made and

tested, even though with his rudimentary workshop resources the task might be extremely tedious and difficult. If it were successful then, no doubt, a scientific explanation would eventually be produced, but meanwhile the new idea could be incorporated into the equipment and the range of signalling increased.

In addition to the patience and determination to try out countless modifications, Guglielmo had the luck, or the intuition, to pick out the right things to try. He also had a high degree of manual skill and sensitivity which he exploited fully in making and improving the delicate instruments used during the early days of wireless.

The coherer was such an instrument, and young Marconi spent many hours carefully trying different metals and various methods of reducing them to fragments or dust in an effort to improve the coherence of the particles when electromagnetic energy reached them at the receiver. Eventually he decided to use for the dust a mixture of nickel with a small percentage of silver; he altered the shape of the metal contacts inside each end of the coherer, and he evacuated the air from the tube and sealed it.

With this improved coherer the receiver was more sensitive than before and was able to detect signals at slightly greater ranges. A further improvement in range was obtained when the size of the spark-gap terminals was increased by connecting metal plates to them. This was thought to increase the wavelength of the radiation from the transmitter and, so that the receiver would also respond to the longer wave radiation, similar plates were connected to the terminals of the coherer.

Such was the work being carried out at Villa Grifone during the spring and summer of 1895, and as the modest improvements in range were painstakingly achieved the receiver was gradually taken further from the transmitter: to the extreme end of the double attic, down to each in turn of the main floors of the house, and finally outside on to the terrace.

Once taken out of the remote security of the attics the experiments could be watched by family and visitors, and by the assistants who had to be recruited to stand by the receiver and report the signals transmitted from the attic by Guglielmo.

But inspection of his work no longer bothered him unduly now that confidence had grown with the successful completion of the earlier experiments. By the time the apparatus was first taken outside the house its range and reliability were probably of the same order as had been achieved by other experimenters, although many of these were probably more interested in the general properties of the waves rather than the range at which they could be detected.

But now one of Guglielmo's almost casual modifications, carried out during an experiment in the open, was to justify his personal faith that Hertz waves could be the basis of a practical signalling system. In the apparatus he was using there was a large metal plate attached to each side of the spark gap – and a similar one to each side of the coherer – in order to increase the wavelength and, hopefully, the range of the radiation.

Long afterwards he told his friend Solari how the vital discovery was made:

> By chance I held one of the metal slabs at a considerable height above the ground and set the other on the earth. With this arrangement the signals became so strong that they permitted me to increase the sending distance to a kilometre.

From this moment the pace of progress accelerated sharply. The elevated plate – the aerial – was raised to greater heights, and the other plate – the earth – was buried in the ground. With his older brother, Alfonso, and one or two of his father's employees as assistants, Guglielmo now began to stride forward towards practical wireless telegraphy. The aerial plate was replaced by copper wires and a similar arrangement was developed at the receiver which was now carried out into the fields to greater and greater distances from the house. The signals were acknowledged by the recipient waving a flag which could be seen by Guglielmo at the transmitter.

An account of the work in the grounds and fields of Villa Grifone has been left by one of those who assisted at the experiments. Antonio Marchi, a gardener on the estate, died in 1948 at the age of 105. The old man had never been able to read or write but he had several times told his son stories of the days when he had helped the now famous Guglielmo Marconi. The son passed on the story to the Mayor of the Commune of Calderara di Reno, who in turn placed with the Marconi Society of Rome a deposition which told how Antonio Marchi first went with his wife to Villa Grifone to take up work as custodian-gardener to Giuseppe Marconi's family in 1889, when Guglielmo was fourteen years old.

One of Marchi's responsibilities, he said, was to 'accompany every day the young gentleman to take his lessons from Professor Augusto Righi' and to lead the donkey on which Guglielmo rode.

The deposition goes on to state that during the summer of 1895 when the experiments were first taken out of the house Marchi was required to help with the heavier work. On one occasion 'he was ordered to dig a ditch 2 metres wide and 30 centimetres deep in the garden on the east side of the Villa Grifone. A copper plate a few millimetres thick was placed horizontally in the ditch and connected by a copper wire to the apparatus in the attic. The ditch was then covered with earth and abundantly watered.' Later he was required to deepen the ditch so that the plate might be placed in a vertical position, and this plate was sometimes connected with two other plates, of copper and zinc, also placed vertically within the same ditch.

Marchi's son also remembered how his father had told of the receiver being taken further and further from the house, and how the experiments took place 'during the absence of the young gentleman's father and without his knowledge because he desired that his son should attend more earnestly to his studies'. For one of these experiments a wooden pole was put up, and hung from it were several copper wires 'kept straight by empty petrol cans filled with stones' – presumably an early wire aerial.

The memory of leading young Marconi's donkey on frequent journeys was a personal, sensual image probably firmly imprinted and vividly recalled. Even allowing for the hazards to which truth was exposed by the remarkable way in which these recollections were eventually recorded, the donkey can, happily, be accepted – there is, anyhow, a bill for his stabling among Marconi's accounts. But the precise purpose of these journeys was quite possibly never confided to the gardener, and the frequency, destination, and object of the donkey trips might easily have become distorted in the telling and the remembering and the re-telling. Whatever the reason, the idea of daily 'lessons' from Righi is most likely wrong.

The suggestion that Righi was Marconi's teacher has been noted earlier. Possibly it arose in association with attempts to belittle the young man's contribution to wireless telegraphy. Marconi's own contradictory statement of 1897 was quoted to the effect that Professor Rosa had been his only physics master, and in 1903 Righi himself said that 'the idea of wireless telegraphy was spontaneously born in the mind of the young man from Bologna and not as had been suggested by the knowledge of similar proposals of others'. As late as 1923 an article intended for a book was submitted for vetting to the Marconi Company who returned it corrected by Marconi himself stating that 'he was placed under the tutelage of a professor, but it was not Professor Righi the eminent Bolognese scientist. Professor Righi was a friend of the family and his action was confined mostly to the encouragement of the then young Marconi in his electrical experiments.'

It seems clear that young Guglielmo's famous neighbour was his occasional patron, adviser, and encourager – important, and perhaps vital, roles – but the fact that Righi neither taught Marconi nor provided him with the idea of wireless telegraphy was affirmed several times by both men.

Perhaps the most interesting part of the Marchi deposition is the story of the ditches. A man ordered to dig a large hole in the ground during the Italian summer can be expected to remember it. He may not recall precisely the measurements of the hole or the particular material of the metal plate, but he will surely never forget that he was required to exhume a plate which he had but recently buried, and then at once re-bury it in an even larger hole so that it could stand vertically instead of lying flat.

Here again was an example of the way in which Marconi

worked. He had found by chance that the range of transmission was increased when the apparatus was connected to a
metal plate set on the ground. Now, he worried away at this
discovery to see whether some slight change in the arrangement would give a further improvement. He did not sit down
and work out logically that the horizontal earth plate would be
better replaced by a vertical one, or by several plates, or even
(if the report is correct) by copper and zinc plates which would
have made a buried electric battery. On the contrary, these
trials were prompted more by an insatiable appetite for
active experiment than by cold logic. With materials and
assistants available, nothing could stop Marconi from trying
something new every day.

When he spoke of making a discovery 'by chance' he was
usually speaking as a man who had taken many tickets in a
lottery so that chance should lack no opportunity of treating
him well. But the gambling analogy is an unreasonable one
when describing Marconi's professional style. Perhaps his
original decision to stake so much on making Hertz waves into
a commercial system might be called by some an act of faith,
and by others a gamble, but the series of 'chances' which
subsequently came Marconi's way, and which he exploited so
well, were not like a long-priced accumulator bet coming up
for one lucky punter in a million but rather, to use Horace
Walpole's word, well-organised serendipity.

The experiments in the fields around Villa Grifone prospered
rapidly during the summer of 1895. As far as possible the
work was carried out during the early morning and late evening
so that it would neither inconvenience nor be inconvenienced
by the family and servants going about their daily business.
Misty light, and dew, and the smell of wet earth long recalled
to Marconi the thrill of those successful experiments when the
range was pushed out to over a kilometre.

By this time old Giuseppe was no longer actively opposing
his son's work, and he was indeed sufficiently impressed by
what he had seen of Guglielmo's experiments to put up several
hundred pounds for materials and equipment – a considerable
sum from one so close with money. Much is made of the way
in which Giuseppe tried to divert his son from pursuing the

dream of wireless telegraphy, and there is little doubt that Marconi neither forgot nor forgave his father's harshness in those early years. In 1923 when he was famous he still took the trouble to correct a remark about his father having provided him with a workshop in the garden, and it was with some bitterness that he stated that such facilities as were available to him, however scrappy and incomplete, had been entirely the result of his own efforts. Nevertheless the old man must be credited with some share in the foundation of his son's success: he had built up the library where Guglielmo found inspiration as a child, he had insisted to his wife that the boy should receive proper schooling, and he had – albeit grudgingly – continued to maintain him at home when everyone but the boy and Annie thought he was wasting his time on silly experiments.

Towards the end of that summer of progress came another of Marconi's chance discoveries:

I was sending waves through the air and getting signals at a distance of a mile, or thereabouts, when I discovered that the wave which went to my receiver through the air was affecting another receiver which I had set up on the other side of the hill. In other words, the waves were going through or over the hill. It is my belief that they went through, but I do not wish to state it as a fact.[5]

He was wrong about the waves going through the hill – they are now known to go along the surface of the earth and over the hill – but he made no error about the importance of the discovery. As was his way, Marconi at once investigated and confirmed the effect, and in September 1895 he could say that he had a wireless telegraph system with a potentially useful range, unaffected by natural obstacles.

This was as far as he could go on his own. Now he needed financial support on a large scale to develop his wireless telegraphy from the pilot model to a practical system, and he also needed the active collaboration of an influential organisation which would have an interest in testing and using the system under working conditions. Above all he felt that he needed to stake his own claim before something similar was patented by another inventor. But to a rather immature boy of twenty-one the task of canvassing support from financiers and even governments was very daunting compared with solving alone problems which involved nothing but his own skill and patience.

Financial support and business contacts were, however, things which Giuseppe and Annie understood far better than the technology which their son was trying to promote, and in their different ways they each set out to help. Giuseppe consulted friends in the district and found that Dr Gardini, the family physician, knew the Italian Ambassador in London and was prepared to ask him to approach the Italian Government on Guglielmo's behalf. Annie wrote letters to her relations in England and received promising replies about the interest there in wireless telegraphy. In particular, her sister's son, Henry Jameson-Davis, who was an engineer with a London office in the City, had contacts in both scientific and financial circles, and other relatives were prepared to help with accommodation for Annie and Guglielmo if they came to London.

Annie was naturally attracted to the idea of taking her favourite son to England where so many of her friends lived and where she felt she could arrange introductions to people who could help him. But to Giuseppe and Guglielmo there were practical and emotional advantages in having the invention taken up by the Government of their native land. So Dr Gardini wrote to his friend General Ferrero, the Italian Ambassador in London, explaining the situation and saying that, before deciding to leave Italy for England, Guglielmo wanted to offer his invention to the Italian Government.

General Ferrero consulted the Ministry of Posts and Telegraphs in Rome who replied that, while Guglielmo should safeguard the interests of Italy when he patented his invention, the Italian Government had no wish to take up his offer.

CHAPTER 3

GPO PROTÉGÉ TO COMPANY DIRECTOR

AFTER the hard work and steadily accumulated successes of the previous summer it was a bitter disappointment to Guglielmo when the news from the Italian Government, so hopefully awaited, came that the Ministry of Posts and Telegraphs had brusquely turned down his invention without examination or further enquiry.

In retrospect, those Italians who were sensitive about one of their famous men having to go abroad for recognition wondered how the Ministry of Posts and Telegraphs could possibly have reached its decision. In its defence it was pointed out that the Ministry was responsible for national and international communications and that to meet this commitment there was a well-established and efficient system of overland line telegraphy supplemented by submarine cables. Should there be an increase in traffic beyond the capacity of this system, or should a need arise for its extension to other areas, then the extra facilities could be provided swiftly and easily by using ordinary methods. There was no need to become involved with the fragile and temperamental apparatus of wireless telegraphy – an almost untried system giving as yet ranges of only a mile or so – when all foreseeable requirements could be met by reliable techniques which were fully understood and tested.

Such criteria were reasonable enough for a Ministry concerned only with civil commitments in time of peace, but it is rather surprising that no consideration appeared to be given to the probability of submarine cables being cut in time of war. The Italian Navy were certainly concerned about this problem, along with their own special communication difficulties, and the matter had been discussed publicly in a naval journal where the writer had referred favourably to work on 'wireless communication' being done by the British Post Office. But the Italian counterpart of the British Post Office had not even seemed to think it worth referring Marconi's offer to their colleagues in the Ministry of Marine.

The 'wireless communication' being investigated by the British Post Office was not the wireless we know today; it did not use Hertz waves as did Marconi's system. The British system relied upon electromagnetic induction and had been developed by Preece, one of the very first telegraph engineers, who was sixty years old in 1896. A dozen years before, when involved with the installation of the London telephone system, he had noticed that fluctuations in the current in one circuit caused corresponding fluctuations in current in another nearby circuit, although there was no direct electrical connection between them. This was the phenomenon of electromagnetic induction and, although it did not have the potential of Hertz waves for long-range work, Preece had so developed it that by 1892 experimental messages could be sent over three miles across the Bristol Channel between Penarth and Flatholm Island, and in 1895 the system was used in Scotland to maintain communication between Oban and the island of Mull when a break occurred in the submarine cable.

There was irony in the reference to Preece's work in the Italian naval journal[1] because, by the time the article appeared in July 1896, Marconi, disappointed at the decision of the Ministry of Posts and Telegraphs, had quit Italy for England where he was welcomed and sponsored by Preece and the British Post Office.

Marconi's mother had been at once ready to bring out again her plans for the trip to England. Final details and dates were given to the relatives in London and, with the blessing of Giuseppe (who was now over seventy), Annie and Guglielmo left Villa Grifone. In February 1896 they arrived in London where they were met by Henry Jameson-Davis.

Henry was just the friend they needed. He took them to stay with relatives while he found them furnished rooms, with service, in a solid house behind the Bayswater Road, fairly near Kensington Gardens. As soon as they were installed in a place of their own, Guglielmo began to set up the equipment which he had brought from Italy, and Henry helped him to find replacements for items which had been damaged on the journey so that there should be no delay in preparing demonstrations of wireless telegraphy for any person of influence who might be persuaded to consider taking up the invention. But before making public demonstrations Guglielmo had to establish his legal right to ownership of the system, so Henry put him in touch with a good patent agent who gave advice on the task of setting out an account of the invention suitable for a patent application as soon as possible.

The two jobs, of preparing the patent application and of making the demonstrations work again, occupied Guglielmo almost incessantly for the next few months, with Annie doing anything that she thought would help, even making fair copies of some of his rough notes for him. During this time Henry Jameson-Davis's kind concern for the well-being of relatives who were strangers in a big city was reinforced by a growing interest in the project itself, and he brought scientific friends, in confidence, to see some of Guglielmo's experiments. By the end of May the work of preparing the preliminary papers for the patent was completed. On 2 June 1896 a provisional specification was filed at the Patent Office, and now that the legal claim to priority of invention was staked, it was time to seek publicity, financial backing, and facilities for large-scale experiments.

One of Henry's friends who had seen something of the private demonstrations in the Bayswater rooms was a research scientist, Campbell Swinton, who knew William Preece. Thus Guglielmo was provided with a letter written in authoritative scientific terms recommending him to Preece, the man who had a keen and long-standing interest in wireless communication and who, as Chief Engineer to the Post Office, had within his gift every sort of facility which might be needed to develop Guglielmo's apparatus into a practical communication system.

Swinton's introduction served its purpose and Guglielmo was summoned for interview to the office of the Engineer-in-Chief of the General Post Office. With him he took as much of his apparatus as he could conveniently carry, selecting the pieces which would make the best impression with the show-man's skill which he would display again and again on future occasions in front of some extremely grand audiences. But, in a way, none of these much publicised events in the future was nearly as crucial as this first modest demonstration in the room near St Paul's.

Preece was an elderly Victorian gentleman, soon to receive his knighthood from the Queen. He received young Marconi kindly on that spring morning, listened to his exposition, examined the apparatus with great interest, and then sent for a boy assistant to take his young visitor out and buy him lunch. In the afternoon Marconi returned to the office and ran through the repertoire of simple demonstrations which he could carry out with the equipment he had assembled there. Everything went well, Preece was impressed with what he had seen and heard that day, and he now arranged, with the prudence of a man of responsibility, that Guglielmo should return again and carry out a series of more penetrating tests over a period of many days in the Chief Engineer's laboratory.

Eventually Preece was satisfied that the system was poten-tially useful, particularly for communicating to ships and lighthouses. Such a navigational aid could greatly reduce the loss of life and material from shipwreck around the coast of Britain. He undertook to propose to his department that Marconi be granted such facilities and assistance as he needed to set up a formal demonstration of his wireless telegraphy in the open air before a representative audience of officials and engineers. While waiting anxiously for confirmation from Preece, Marconi was able to complete his provisional patent application which was conveniently lodged in June, and the date of the first public demonstration in London was fixed for July.

Preece gathered his inspecting party of senior officials and engineers on 27 July 1896 at the General Post Office building in St Martin's-le-Grand where they were introduced to Marconi and then led up to the roof on which the apparatus had been assembled. The purpose of certain parts of the equipment which were unfamiliar to some of the audience was explained, and it was announced that the intention was to communicate with a station manned by Preece's staff on the roof of another Post Office building in Queen Victoria Street, rather less than a mile away down beyond St Paul's towards the Thames. This first formal demonstration in England went off without any sort of hitch, and messages were instantly and clearly received on the Morse printing machine. The audience was particularly impressed by the fact that the transmission had been unaffected by the large number of buildings between the two stations, and at the end of the proceedings Preece was able to turn to Marconi and say: 'Young man, you have done something truly exceptional, I congratulate you on it.'

These words of congratulation were not a conventional vote of thanks from chairman to visiting speaker, but more a declaration to his immediate colleagues, and indeed to himself, that Marconi had satisfactorily proved his system worthy of further investigation and development, and that it was a project with which the highly professional Post Office might properly be associated. Preece now felt able to approach other Government departments with an account of results already achieved and a request for facilities to carry out more elaborate experiments and tests in front of an expert audience drawn from all parts of the public service likely to be interested.

Support for further work was obtained without difficulty, and the first of these bigger demonstrations was soon arranged to take place on Salisbury Plain on 2 September 1896. There followed an exciting and fruitful period reminiscent of those months in Italy when Guglielmo had first taken his experiments out into the grounds of Villa Grifone and had so rapidly increased the distance over which signals could be sent. Now in England he had the advantage of influential support and valuable assistance from the Post Office and the War Office. Progress was swift; in the first tests on Salisbury Plain a range of one and three-quarter miles was recorded, a second series of tests in the same place in March 1897 achieved ranges up to four and a half miles, and a record distance of nearly nine miles was reached between the mainland and the island of Flatholm in the Bristol Channel in May.

The Salisbury Plain tests had been used to gather information about the efficiency of various aerials and their ability to concentrate the radiated energy in a particular direction. Wires and metal cylinders on tall poles, very long wires supported by kites, metal plates used as reflectors: all these had been investigated before Preece decided to take Marconi and his equipment down to the West Country for the important tests over the waters of the Bristol Channel. This was the place where Preece had carried out his own experiments in electromagnetic induction signalling in 1892 and he knew how convincing would be the successful receipt on the coast of messages from one of the islands dimly visible in the mist. The earlier experiments on Salisbury Plain had attracted considerable attention at home and abroad, and the Press and public were now very interested in what was going on in the Bristol Channel. Among those invited by Preece to witness what he was sure would be an impressive demonstration was Professor Slaby, a German scientist who had experimented with Hertz waves and who had been sent by his government to assess the work going on in England. Slaby was to play a big part later in setting up the Telefunken company which was strongly supported by the Kaiser and the German Government in a bid for world domination in wireless communication and consequently became the bitter rival of Marconi's own company in the years before the Great War.

The Bristol Channel tests were a triumph for Marconi and a vindication of Preece's judgement in backing him. There was drama enough for the most unscientific newspaper reader, with indifferent results and hurried modifications on the first two days, success on the third day, and the record-breaking range of 8·7 miles on the fourth day. Most people might think that this was a time when the young inventor might have enjoyed a few days reflecting on his success and perhaps dreaming of a rosy future. But although it was only two years since he had first brought his experiments down from his attic laboratory, Marconi had already left behind the time when he could be single-minded about his science, completing one experiment and thinking of nothing but the next. Even this great public test had been planned and carried out by a mind simultaneously concerned with the problems of the man of affairs.

Marconi with father,
mother, and brother
Alfonso

Beatrice O'Brien

Villa Grifone

Marconi and Solari demonstrate wireless to the Italian Navy, 1897

Two problems unconnected with science worried Marconi during the spring of 1897. The first concerned his Italian citizenship, which meant that he was liable for military service in his homeland. The second problem was the business of considering, and rejecting, an assortment of financial propositions from various sources, and of negotiating favourable terms in the City for setting up his own company in London.

Marconi's public experiments had been reported almost all over the world, and in particular in Italy. Some officers of the Regia Marina had privately and publicly expressed the hope that the benefits of Marconi's work would not be lost to his own country, and the Italian Ministry of Marine had arranged to receive from their naval mission at the London Embassy regular reports of the work of wireless telegraphy in England. But, mixed with the acclaim and publicity in his own country, there began to appear comments about military service, some people saying that he should, like any other young Italian, give up his work and, however inconvenient, come home to join up. He had already been granted deferment of service, so the matter had now become pressing and his English relatives were very keen for him to adopt the easy solution of giving up his Italian nationality and becoming a British citizen.

This was a critical time when Marconi was needed in England both to press forward the scientific development and to be a focal point in the business of assembling investors for the Company which his cousin Henry Jameson-Davis was about to float. The idea of renouncing his Italian citizenship did not attract him – unless it was the only solution – and so he sought the help and advice of the Italian Ambassador in London. His Excellency was in touch with the progress Marconi was making under the sponsorship of the British Government, and he was also aware through his naval mission at the Embassy that the results of the experiments were of interest to the Regia Marina. Accordingly he wrote privately to Benedetto Brin, the Minister of Marine in Rome, and put the problem to him in all its aspects. The result was swift and satisfactory. Guglielmo Marconi was enrolled as a cadet in the Italian Navy and seconded as an additional assistant naval attaché to the Embassy in London. This was to be an entirely nominal post leaving him free to continue his own work, and Marconi, recognising the implications of this arrangement, had his naval pay transferred monthly to the Italian Hospital in London.

But however nominal the duties in this appointment of convenience, Marconi was legally and morally a member of the Italian forces and when he was invited, through the senior naval attaché in London, to return to Italy and demonstrate his invention to the Ministry of Marine he was in no position to decline the invitation, even if he had wished to do so. He returned to Italy towards the end of June 1897 leaving Henry Jameson-Davis to dissuade business associates from withdrawing their money because they feared that the departure of Marconi to his native land meant that the proposed new English company would thus be deprived of its principal, if not only, asset. Such fears were groundless because Marconi was as reluctant to be out of England at this time as were his backers to see him go. He got through his stint of official demonstrations and tests as quickly as he possibly could, but without neglecting any opportunity to gather new data or to impress more people of influence. He took only a few days off to visit his parents at Villa Grifone, and he was back in London in August.

The first of the demonstrations in Italy was a modest one on 6 July 1897 at the offices of his sponsors, the Ministry of Marine, in Rome. It consisted of nothing more than a simple transmission from one floor of the building to another, but it impressed the various dignitaries present, who included the Minister of Posts and Telegraphs whose department's lack of interest had so recently driven the inventor to take his work to England. Marconi must have been amused to see him there, and the message the young man chose to be transmitted and printed out by the Morse receiver was '*Viva l'Italia*'.

The Ministry of Marine had organised with great skill the presentation to Rome of the Navy's most famous recruit. In the evening of the successful demonstration to the distinguished audience at the Ministry a dinner was arranged in Marconi's honour, and the following day he was taken to the

Quirinal and introduced to both the King and the Queen, who each congratulated him on his achievements. The patriotic interest of the Italian people was naturally stirred by the excitement surrounding his return home and the Press was at hand to report all the events in the greatest detail.

Once the light-hearted celebrations in Rome were over, a naval party accompanied Marconi to the San Bartolommeo dockyard at Spezia for the more serious and prolonged work which was a series of tests designed to investigate the possibility of wireless telegraphy between ship and shore. The trials lasted several weeks and, in spite of a number of difficulties due to interference from electrical storms, messages were exchanged between the shore and the warship *San Martino*. Apart from establishing what was at the time believed to be the record for the first ship-to-shore wireless link, other results of scarcely less importance were obtained during the tests: the effect upon signal strength when the ship, and hence its aerial, changed aspect relative to the shore station; the effect when a land mass such as an island intervened between transmitter and receiver; and, most important of all for future maritime development, the fact that communication was maintained when the vessel was below the horizon. The end of the tests coincided with a public holiday in Spezia and the Navy was able to stage-manage scenes of great enthusiasm by announcing the imminent arrival of the famous young inventor and then putting him ashore from a naval pinnace in front of crowds of holidaymakers.

In Italy there was criticism of Government postal officials for not having interested themselves in Marconi's work until he had been recognised abroad. Meanwhile, in England there was complementary criticism of Preece, the British postal official, for the alacrity with which he had taken up the young Italian when he arrived from abroad with a 'magic box' which only repeated what British scientists had been doing with Hertz waves for some time.

In his autobiography[2] published in 1931 Oliver Lodge gave an idea of the feeling among some British scientists about Marconi's first year in England. Referring to the meeting of the British Association held in Liverpool in 1896, Lodge said:

41

Preece came there, knowing nothing of Hertz, but interested in space methods of telegraphy and told us in Section A of a remarkable discovery which had just been brought over from Italy. It was stale news to me and Fitzgerald, and to Lord Kelvin and to a few others; but, whereas we had been satisfied with the knowledge that it could be done, Mr Marconi went on enthusiastically and persistently, at first with the help of Preece and the resources of the British P.O. Department, till he made it a practical success.

In 1914 Lodge was less inhibited when writing to a friend about the history of wireless telegraphy.[3] He wrote of giving a lecture at the Royal Institution in the spring of 1894 at which

... my friend Alexander Muirhead conceived the telegraphic application which ultimately led to the foundation of the Lodge-Muirhead Syndicate, now bought up by the Marconi Co.... Two years later [in 1896] Marconi came over with the same thing in a secret box, with aristocratic introductions to Preece of the Government Telegraphs, and was taken up and assisted by him – who was far more ignorant than he ought to have been of what had already been done.

So with great spirit and enthusiasm and persevering energy, and assisted by Government officials, Marconi overcame many practical difficulties and really began to establish on a practical commercial basis his system of Wireless Telegraphy by Hertzian waves.

Lodge's criticism was directed at Preece and he gave unstinting credit to Marconi for realising a practical wireless telegraphy system. Nevertheless, Lodge still took the trouble to point out that he had been working in the field before Marconi. Similarly, Rutherford, a recent arrival in England who later founded nuclear physics, claimed to have worked with Hertz waves in 1894 in his native New Zealand. Nineteenth-century scientists felt keenly about priority of discovery: the man who was first in the field received public as well as professional acclaim. Science was fashionable, Albemarle Street was jammed with carriages for the Friday evening discourses at the Royal Institution, and if the Prime Minister was in the audience it was because he wanted to hear the lecture. Faraday, the resident professor, was famous for the brilliance of his experiments and for his fundamental discoveries in electricity and magnetism, but even he went to the length of depositing a sealed envelope with the Royal Society in 1832, and when it was opened in 1937 it was found to contain some very tentative ideas, which Faraday wanted to claim as his own, about electromagnetic waves. He was not prepared to publish these ideas because he had no time to test and prove them experimentally, but he was still keen to establish precedence.

The renewed arguments some years later about priority of invention in wireless telegraphy were no longer just prompted by professional pride, or vanity, but were often legal actions over patents where the litigation was against the Marconi Company rather than Marconi, although in the eyes of many, including often the court, there was no distinction. Lodge certainly, and to some extent Rutherford, became involved in such actions and indeed in 1914, at the time he wrote to his friend about Preece, Lodge was receiving from the Marconi Company a thousand pounds per year for the use of one of his patents.

But no bickering about priority soured young Marconi's triumphant Italian progress when the Ministry of Marine brought him back from England, and the laudatory newspaper reports made old Giuseppe glow with family pride. Many times in the past Guglielmo had come back to Villa Grifone – from England, from Florence, from Leghorn. He had usually returned reluctantly; apprehensive, and uncertain of how to avoid too many of the rows which punctuated any stay in his father's house. This time he returned as a famous man. The Villa Grifone routine was subservient to the needs of the honoured visitor who was sparing a few days away from the exalted society which had adopted him, and his father now gave him advice instead of instructions. Giuseppe was worried that his son's business associates might take advantage of him when framing the terms for the formation of the Company and he was most anxious that the name Marconi should be included in its title. He considered, too, that the money paid to his son when the Company was formed would give Guglielmo a wonderful opportunity to buy land adjoining the Villa Grifone so that the Marconi estates would be greatly enlarged and he could be a country gentleman like his father. But Guglielmo's material ambitions did not lie at his own back door, he was confident that his English company would give him a wider, richer future and he trusted his mother's cousin, Henry, and the other business associates who were completing the financial negotiations in London.

These negotiations were completed and the Company formally incorporated on 20 July 1897 while Marconi was still away in Italy. The registered name was The Wireless Telegraph and Signal Co. Ltd, but this was changed just over two years later to Marconi's Wireless Telegraph Co. Ltd. The Company had an authorised capital of £100,000 in one-pound shares, and sixty thousand of these were given to Marconi in return for the exclusive rights to all his patents, except in so far as he had given permission to the Italian Government to use any of his work. In addition to his majority shareholding he also received a cash payment of fifteen thousand pounds less certain expenses. This sum was provided from the general sale of the remaining forty thousand shares, leaving twenty-five thousand pounds of working capital to get the Company running. Henry Jameson-Davis was the managing director and Marconi, who was one of the five original directors, also had the right to appoint personally one additional member to the Board.

So young Marconi came to be a man of substance and influence: a controlling shareholder and company director with capital in the bank and a seat on the Board within his gift. He returned to London in August 1897, and his mother came too.

44

CHAPTER 4

REGATTAS AND NAVAL MANŒUVRES

WHILE Marconi was away demonstrating his wireless telegraphy in Italy for the Ministry of Marine his name was kept constantly before the British public. The successful experiments in Rome and Spezia were reported in the English newspapers, but the principal publicist of wireless telegraphy, and incidentally of Marconi, was William Preece. He was an excellent speaker who enjoyed addressing the large and enthusiastic audiences at the lecture-demonstrations which were arranged to satisfy public interest aroused by the experiments on Salisbury Plain. Preece had started to give these lectures before Marconi left for Italy – there is a record of the young Italian assisting with the demonstrations at a meeting in Toynbee Hall[1] – but after Marconi's departure he continued with his popular expositions at meetings ranging from one in aid of Wesleyan funds in Islington[2] to a Friday Evening Discourse at the Royal Institution.

Preece's Royal Institution lecture was given to a crowded audience on 3 June 1897 and accounts of it appeared in many newspapers and scientific journals. On 17 June Professor Oliver Lodge wrote from University College, Liverpool to the Editor of the *Times*:

It appears that many persons suppose that the method of signalling across space by means of Hertz waves received by a Branly tube of filings is a new discovery made by Signor Marconi, who has recently been engaged in improving some of the details.

It is well known to physicists, and perhaps the public may be willing to share the information, that I myself showed what was essentially the same plan of signalling in

1894. My apparatus acted very vigorously across the college quadrangle, a distance of 60 yards, and I estimated that there would be some response up to a limit of half a mile. Some of the hearers of Mr Preece's recent lecture at the Royal Institution seem to have understood his reference to these previous trials to signify that I had asserted or prophesied that more powerful apparatus would always be limited to some such distance.

Lodge went on to deny making such a prophecy and said that his early apparatus was substantially the same as Marconi's, but less powerful, and therefore capable of shorter range. He continued:

Moreover, instructed primarily by Professor Righi, and aided in his trials by the British Post Office, he has worked hard to develop the method into a commercial success. For all this the full credit is due – I do not suppose that Signor Marconi himself claims any more – but much of the language indulged in during the last few months by writers of popular articles on the subject about 'Marconi waves', 'important discoveries', and 'brilliant novelties' has been more than usually absurd. The only 'important discovery' about the matter was made in 1888 by Hertz; and on that is based the emitter of the waves; the receiver depends on cohesion under electrical influence which was noticed long ago by Lord Rayleigh and has been re-observed in other forms by other experimenters, including the writer in 1890.

Frequently during the next few years this theme would be taken up again, in public and in private, by Lodge and others. Litigation would decide relatively well-defined issues about patents, but right and wrong were not easily defined in sensitive matters of professional prestige and *amour propre*, and the arguments both of supporters and opposers of Marconi were not notable for charity, scientific detachment, or humility. Typically sharp was the letter written in 1897 to the Editor of the *Electrician* by Captain J. N. C. Kennedy of the Royal Engineers who had been lent by the War Office to assist Preece and Marconi in wireless telegraphy trials.

Adverse criticism has gone so far as to doubt Mr Preece's statement that signals were sent and received, although an intervening hill obscured the two stations. The fact that the impulses can be imparted to a receiver placed in a sealed iron case is almost universally denied. Mr Marconi will, at an early date, show that this is possible. It will be interesting then to note how many of the sceptics following their present tactics will lay claim to having done the very same thing long ago.[3]

Marconi had others like Kennedy to support his case in the correspondence columns of the journals and he did not apparently think it worthwhile – or perhaps he thought it impolitic or unseemly – to write long letters himself to the Press, although even this early in his business career he was aware of the importance of encouraging good publicity. Writing soon after his return to England from Italy in August 1897[4] he gave his father various details about his newly formed company and ended the letter by saying that an article on his work was about to be published in England and that he would translate it and have it published in the Italian newspapers as 'I am acquainted with all the correspondents.'

In this same letter he assured his father that Preece had said that the contract Marconi had signed was a personal matter only and had promised continued assistance with the development of wireless telegraphy as long as the attitude of the new Company remained friendly. He had for some months been worried that assigning all his patents to a commercial organisation would spoil the excellent relationship he had established with Preece, and through him with British government departments. As long ago as April, before the Bristol Channel experiments, he had written to Preece[5] explaining that he found himself in difficulty because the backers of the proposed new company were pressing him to complete a contract with them. On that occasion he had said that he could not consider such a step until the Post Office

experiments were completed, but when he left England for
Italy the pressure exerted on him by Henry Jameson-Davis
and his colleagues could no longer be resisted and in July he
wrote to Preece from Grifone to say that the contract was
signed. He explained that the terms were very favourable to
him – he owned half the shares of the Company in return for
his patents – but he had been persuaded to sign by many other
motives, in particular by the expense involved in developing
his prototype apparatus into a system for production in
quantity to meet the demands for demonstrations which had
now been received from most European governments. There
was, too, the cost and uncertainty of maintaining patents
throughout the world in the face of vigorous opposition by
Lodge in England, Tesla in America, and others elsewhere.
He concluded his letter:

> Hoping that you will continue in your benevolence towards
> me, I beg to state that all your great kindness shall never
> be forgotten by me in all my life. I shall also do my best to
> keep the company on amicable terms with the British
> Government.[6]

Preece's reply was sent to Marconi on 6 August 1897 at his
father's house in Italy and it was terse enough to cause some
misgiving there.

> I am very sorry to get your letter. You have taken a step
> that I fear is very inimical to your personal interests. I
> regret to say that I must stop all experiments and all action
> until I learn the conditions that are to determine the
> relations between your company and the Government
> Departments who have encouraged and helped you so
> much.[7]

Giuseppe must have been glad to receive the reassurances
about Preece's attitude in his son's letter written as soon as he
had returned to London. But, whether Guglielmo knew it or
not at the time of writing his letter, relations with the Post
Office were not to be as happy as he suggested. In particular,

48

Preece was about to undertake experiments at Fort Burgoyne, near Dover Castle, from which Marconi was to be excluded. A letter on 7 September 1897 from the GPO to the Admiralty, inviting them to send a representative, makes the position quite clear:

> I am to add that, as Signor Marconi has now disposed of his rights in the invention to a private company [The Wireless Telegraph & Signal Co.] it is thought advisable that, for the present, the results of these further experiments should not be made public.[8]

The experiments began in early September and the newspapers carried accounts of the operations in the Dover area and confirmed that the trials were being conducted under conditions of some secrecy.[9] Marconi soon realised that he was being excluded and he complained to Preece in a private letter, saying that he would be obliged to work abroad if the Post Office was not to be as friendly as he and Preece had believed it would be. He enquired, too, whether he might still expect to retain the services of the Post Office and War Office staff who were assisting him with trials at Salisbury.[10] He was allowed to keep the staff, either as a gesture of goodwill or, taking the most cynical view, because this would give the Post Office access to Marconi's results while keeping their own to themselves. If such was the uncharitable intention it was most fittingly frustrated. By the end of September both Preece and Jackson, the Admiralty's wireless expert, had decided that the results being obtained at Dover did not equal those obtained earlier by Marconi, and he was invited to come to Dover on 6 October and assist with any instrument or advice he might have to offer.[11]

After the Dover incident there was certainly further collaboration between Marconi and government officials, but during 1898 and 1899 when the Company was trying to build up interest, confidence and income, the connection was more properly liaison than active assistance. This period, when Marconi's commercial wireless system was being set up and expanded, was immediately before Preece reached the age for retirement from government service, and he was happy in his last months at the Post Office to encourage the comradely pioneering spirit in which the early technical advances were planned and achieved. But by the end of 1899 when Preece had gone and there were prices and royalty claims to be settled, the relations between the Government and the Company were anything but cordial and straightforward.

The first task for the new Company was to recruit staff and set up permanent wireless stations as bases for continuous trials and public demonstrations. The first station was at the Needles Hotel, Alum Bay in the Isle of Wight where accommodation was rented in November 1897. A second station, fourteen miles away on the mainland, was set up in February 1898 at the Madeira Hotel, Bournemouth, but after some disagreement with the management it was moved to the Haven Hotel, Poole, where it remained until 1926 as a much used centre for experimental work.

The stations were all similar, with the converted hotel rooms containing the transmitting and receiving apparatus, a few laboratory instruments for experimental work, and very simple workshop facilities. The features which most excited the interest of the lay public were the masts in the grounds carrying the aerial wire over a hundred feet high, and the loud crash and crackle of the sparks during transmission. Marconi himself often helped his scientists and mechanics to make pieces of equipment needed for the experiments, and much of the work was more a matter of improvisation than invention. Coils were wound and spark gaps adjusted with scientific exactitude, but the immediate problem might well be to drive a hole through a window pane for the admission of an aerial wire, or to file a pile of metal dust for a coherer, or to heat up a smelly can of wax or varnish for insulation.

When the time came for new trials Marconi was an enthusiastic leader and the most active participant, who seemed to revel in arduous, unpleasant and even dangerous work, when his senior position would have made it easy to officiate from afar. Kemp, an ex-sailor who had joined Marconi from the Post Office and became his devoted personal assistant and technician for over thirty years, told of trials carried out between the Alum Bay station and a small vessel in the Solent. He said that Signor Marconi was a most constant hard worker. 'I remember him having to make three attempts to get out past the Needles in a gale before he succeeded. He does not care for storm or rain but keeps pegging away in the most persistent manner.'

Marconi himself, in an interview about the same trials, was refuting a suggestion that his instruments were fragile, but in so doing he gives an idea of the conditions he was prepared to tolerate when chasing technological success, and the demands he made on his employees who might have been expected to be rather less dedicated than he was himself:

The best results we have obtained were on the small tug-boat I alluded to in very tempestuous weather in the month of November around the Isle of Wight where we had at times about two feet of water in the cabin, and ourselves and all the instruments were practically drenched with sea water. Many of the sailors and engineers of the tug seemed very anxious about their personal safety on that particular occasion. Although it seemed to have a very great influence on the crew it had no bad influence on the instruments which continued to perform their duty and to remain in correspondence with the Island which was eighteen miles away.[12]

With extra staff, and the two new permanent stations to add to the more modest facilities available with the semi-mobile field equipment and that at the Company offices in London, there was a large increase in wireless telegraphy activity between the end of 1897 and the end of 1899. The long series of tests from Salisbury Plain to various parts of the West Country culminated in the achievement of a range of over thirty miles to Bath in the autumn. Post Office, War Office and Admiralty representatives were all concerned with Marconi in this work, and there was similar collaboration in experiments between the South Foreland lighthouse, on the mainland near Dover, and the East Goodwins lightship about twelve miles away at sea. The success of these experiments, undertaken for Trinity House, gave great satisfaction to Preece who had always hoped that some form of wireless telegraphy – originally his own induction method, but now Marconi's radiation system – would provide a means of saving life and property from the sea, and it was particularly gratifying that even the experimental link should do just this, during its protracted trial of over a year, by summoning the Ramsgate lifeboat to two separate shipping accidents: a vessel aground on the Goodwin Sands, and a collision between a steamer and the lightship itself.

There were other important early steps for commercial wireless telegraphy during 1898, like the first ship-reporting service supplied for Lloyd's of London. But two events particularly caught the public interest. These were the minute by minute reports of the Kingstown yacht races for the Dublin *Daily Express,* and the strange interlude at Osborne concerning Queen Victoria, Marconi and the Prince of Wales's knee.

The summer regattas round the coast of Britain were extraordinarily popular sporting events at the turn of the century. The favourites of the general public were the biggest yachts, up to a dozen of which competed with each other throughout July and August, moving round the coast like a travelling circus from one seaside town to the next. The intense interest was all the more remarkable because the races were so difficult to follow, much of the course often being out of sight from the land, and even when they were visible the huge sails of the ocean racers were not easy to recognise as they manœuvred almost on the horizon where they were clear of the smaller craft racing closer inshore. But the names of the most successful yachts were known throughout the country and newspapers carried long accounts of each day's events and equally interesting details of the social affairs of the owners – British and foreign royalty and sporting business-men such as Sir Thomas Lipton – who attended the more fashionable regattas in their large steam cruising yachts.

The Dublin *Daily Express* decided upon a publicity scheme which gave the world the first of those innumerable wireless sports reports which would have so surprised – even shocked – those who saw the new invention as an instrument for serious military, lifesaving, and business messages. The *Express*'s idea was to make much of this first journalistic use of wireless and to publish a special commemorative supplement in connection with the centenary celebrations of its companion paper, the *Evening Mail*, which coincided with the regatta of the Royal St George Yacht Club of Kingstown. Marconi was commissioned to set up apparatus to communicate between the *Flying Huntress*, a tug hired to follow the races, and a station on the shore at Kingstown from which messages could be telephoned to the Yacht Club and the newspaper offices in Dublin.

The sailing correspondent of the *Express* observed the race from the bridge of the tug and passed his reports on slips of paper down to the cabin below where Marconi was working the transmitter. As always, the main interest was in the big yachts, racing on this occasion for the Queen's Cup. Club members, and the public who gathered round the messages posted up outside the Dublin office, were excited to read a brisk account of the twists of tactics and fortune as they occurred:

Queens 1. Rainbow having crossed the line before gun fired was recalled thereby losing 3½ minutes.
Queens 2. Times round Rossbeg mark:
  Ailsa   10.54
  Bona   10.54.33
  Isolde   10.58
  Rainbow 10.59.10
  Astrild 10.59.42
Queens 20. Bona still leading by 20 minutes. Wind dying down. *Rainbow* dropping astern fast.[13]

During the two days' racing, conditions at sea were exactly those needed for the best demonstration of the capabilities of Marconi's apparatus. At times the weather was so thick that the yachts were lost to view from the shore and the wireless reports from *Flying Huntress* were the only means of following the race. Furthermore, the seas were on occasions heavy enough to break over the tug and drench with spray the wireless equipment which was only installed in a makeshift fashion in the cabin, but which nevertheless was kept in operation under these very difficult circumstances.[14]

The *Times* reported that the great interest taken always in the Kingstown regatta was increased 'as it was used as a test of the commercial value of the Marconi system'. The test was a brilliant and well-publicised success with whole pages of the two Irish papers devoted to accounts of the proceedings and to interviews with Marconi, Kemp, his assistant, and distinguished observers. All this, with added material from other papers which had taken up the story, was reprinted in the forty-eight-page supplement issued with the *Evening Mail*.[15] Marconi was clearly pleased with this supplement and it was translated into Italian, improved by high quality paper and better pictures, and published in his home town, Bologna.[16]

Soon after the Kingstown regatta Marconi was asked to carry out a strange but exalting commission on behalf of Queen Victoria, now nearly eighty, who was in residence at Osborne House in the Isle of Wight. Her son, Edward Prince of Wales, had recently injured his knee in a fall in Paris and had chosen not to spend his period of partial personal immobility at his mother's house, but rather to pass the time aboard the Royal Yacht which was moored in Cowes Bay, about two miles away, out of sight of Osborne House. Here the fifty-seven-year-old Prince could lead an independent social life, being visited by friends from London or from the yachts and warships gathered nearby for Cowes Week. Marconi was asked to provide a wireless system so that the Queen could exchange messages with the Royal Yacht in Cowes Bay, or even when it had slipped its moorings for a brief trip.

A hundred-foot pole supported the vertical wire aerial at Ladywood Cottage in the grounds of Osborne House, and a similar aerial, not quite so high, was attached to one of the masts of the Royal Yacht. There were no great technical problems, indeed the only difficulty recorded was one of personality. One day young Marconi was walking through the grounds on the way to inspect the apparatus at Ladywood

H.M.S. *Diana* (c. 1900)
Aerial on after mast which also carries semaphore at top

Shamrock and other ocean racers

Marconi factory (c. 1900)

Cottage when he was stopped by a gardener and told to go round a longer way because the Queen was taking the air and would strongly resent any intrusion upon her privacy. The proud young man refused to be diverted and the matter was reported to Her Majesty whose comment was appropriately regal: 'Get another electrician.'

It was explained that this was not practicable and the affair was smoothed over, the Queen later granting Marconi an audience at which she wished him well for the future and congratulated him on the success of the link between her house and the Royal Yacht.[17]

Over a hundred and fifty messages were passed over this link during the sixteen days it was in use, and many of them were enquiries from the Queen about the Prince of Wales's knee. Thus on 9 August 1898 from Osborne House to the Yacht:

The Queen wishes to know how the Prince slept; how he is this morning; and if he had any news about the Queen [of Denmark].

The Queen of Denmark was the mother of the Princess of Wales, who had gone to stay with her during a serious illness. The reply sent swiftly back to Osborne House from Mr Fripp, the Prince's doctor on the Yacht, read:

HRH the Prince of Wales received last night from the Princess of Wales an account of the Queen of Denmark which on the whole is fairly favourable. The Prince slept very well indeed last night and is feeling very well today.

Many of the messages were of this type between the Queen and the Prince of Wales, others concerned routine arrangements for meeting the Prince's guests and visitors. But other members of the Royal entourages in the Yacht or at Osborne House seized the chance to use the marvellous toy for their own simple domestic purposes, like Edward's daughter Victoria's homely query from the Yacht to the Duchess of Connaught at Osborne House: 'Papa anxious to know if you and children are coming today, 12.30, for trip round the

55

Island.' Or, perhaps the least urgent of all the messages, from one lady member of the Royal Household to another on board the Yacht: 'Can you come to tea with us some day?'[18]

Marconi joined the Prince's party several times and used the opportunity to make transmissions to Osborne House while the Yacht was under way off the Island, but no significant scientific results were expected or obtained. The Cowes interlude was useful more for the favourable publicity it brought and perhaps too for an extension of Marconi's contacts with people of influence. At the end of the three weeks the *Electrical Review* reported:

> The Prince of Wales and other Royalties gave expression to Mr Marconi of their high appreciation of his system and their astonishment at the perfection to which it had been brought. The Prince presented Mr Marconi with a souvenir in the shape of a handsome scarf pin and wished him every success in this very interesting adventure.[19]

Publicity was important to the growing Marconi Company and plenty of it was generated between 1897 and 1899. There was a steady flow of influential visitors to the Company's London offices and to the stations in the Isle of Wight and on the South Coast at Bournemouth, or later Poole. In 1898 one particularly famous visitor, Lord Kelvin, sent telegrams from Alum Bay to friends, and insisted on paying a shilling for each message. The publication of this fact was regarded as a piece of coat-trailing by the Marconi Company in the face of the Post Office monopoly in inland communication, but the challenge was not, at that stage, accepted. A little later Kelvin was asked to become scientific adviser to the Company and he wrote accepting, on condition that the public should not in the near future be invited to subscribe additional capital to the Company, which he regarded as already sufficiently financed for likely future development. Evidently this condition was not acceptable because nothing further is heard of Kelvin as scientific adviser, and more capital was raised by a share issue announced at a general meeting in October 1898. Other famous, but non-scientific, persons to send messages included Lord Tennyson, who telegraphed to his nephew at Eton, and the Italian Ambassador who addressed a loyal greeting to the King of Italy. Such visits were usually reported in the national press, as was the demonstration arranged by the Company at the House of Commons for the enlightenment of the Members.

Public demonstrations and lectures were not confined to the London area and the headquarters of the learned societies. Such was the interest throughout the country that wireless telegraphy was the subject of talks and exhibitions at many local centres, and the accounts of these popular events in the provincial papers increased still further the general familiarity with the subject, and with the name of Marconi. Captain Kennedy, one of the Royal Engineers on secondment to Marconi, wrote to him from Exeter at the end of November 1897:

> My lecture went off with the greatest success. The apparatus played up capitally, nothing broke down, and the coherer could not be put out of order. I have taken off another shunt, namely the one across the spark on the tapper. The hall was crowded and hundreds were turned away at the door. I went one better than Mr Preece by sending an actual telegram through six walls as described in the papers. I have been asked to lecture all over the West of England but have struck against it. The crowd were very attentive and good. I was surprised to find how easy it is to lecture when you have got a good subject. You should have heard the applause when I said that you were half an Englishman.

This lecture was probably given as a result of an earlier Exeter demonstration which he had described in another letter to Marconi:

> I am giving a little show here with the kites this afternoon. The Commanding Officer of the place with several local big-wigs as well as the editor of the local paper will be present. As usual there is not the faintest breath of wind up to now, but I hope for the best.[20]

The more formal discourses followed closely upon each other before the learned societies. Fleming addressed the British Association where (according to Kemp who was very sensitive to any slight to Marconi) Lodge would not second the vote of thanks and 'had the impertinence to doubt the results of the Marconi system'.[21] Lodge himself spoke at the Physical Society where he cleverly identified the reasons for the difficulty in making a wireless system work at one particular frequency so that it would be received only by a receiver tuned to the chosen frequency. Then, turning from scientific analysis to commercial forecasting, he emphasised the necessity for confidential communication links by saying, 'No one wants to pay for shouting to the world.'[22] Sylvanus P. Thompson gave a talk to the Royal Society of Arts; Lodge and Muirhead to the Royal Society; Lodge again to the Royal Institution. Then, in March 1899, Marconi delivered his first paper in English, to the Institution of Electrical Engineers.

The interest in this paper was phenomenal. The chairman announced that, as so many were turned away from the door, Marconi had consented to give his paper again at a date to be arranged. A much bigger hall was booked for the following week but so many applications were received that an even bigger one had to be taken, and still only a fraction of those wishing to attend were able to do so.

In his paper Marconi described the progress of his work from the early experiments at his home in Italy to the more ambitious long-range demonstrations which had attracted so much attention recently. He mentioned particularly the way in which he came to appreciate the great importance of the addition to his apparatus of a vertical aerial wire and an earth. Acknowledgement was made to his assistants for, 'any success I have met with in the practical application of wireless telegraphy' and he referred to using Righi's oscillator in his transmitter and to the fact that 'one of the principal parts of my receiver is the sensitive tube or coherer or radio conductor which was discovered, I think I am right in saying, by Professor Calzecchi Onesti, of Fermo, and was improved by Branly. and modified by Professor Lodge and others'. He ended, characteristically, by revealing that he had that day received word of the successful conclusion of negotiations with the French Government concerning a site for a wireless station, and that he proposed to attempt to exchange messages across the Channel before the month of March was out. The printed version of the paper in the *Journal of the Institution of Electrical Engineers* has an added note that France and England were connected by wireless telegraphy on 27 March 1899.[23]

Among all the widely reported events and achievements in wireless telegraphy during this hectic period the linking of England and France, and the almost unnoticed setting up of a factory at Chelmsford at about the same time, were most significant in pointing the way in which Marconi's Company would develop into an international operating and manufacturing organisation.

The site chosen for the French end of the cross-Channel link was Wimereux, a small village on the coast very near Boulogne where, in a way, the Marconi story had started with the runaway marriage of Annie and Giuseppe. Equipment, waiting only on the French Government's approval, was quickly ferried across from England and set up without delay. The other end of the link was already available at the South Foreland lighthouse where, as Marconi had expected, Trinity House allowed the use of their accommodation and the facilities erected by the Company for the Goodwins Lightship experiments. The first exchange of wireless messages between England and France was an administrative success rather than a technical one. The earlier transmissions from Salisbury to Bath had left little doubt that results at least as good would be obtained between South Foreland and Wimereux where range was similar but the path much more favourable to electromagnetic wave propagation because most of it was over the sea. There had been difficulties with French officials[24] but these were resolved and then forgotten as congratulatory messages flashed to and fro across the Channel, many of them seemingly intended more for publication than for conveying information or sentiment from sender to recipient. Of such messages Marconi sent his share:

Marconi sends M. Branly his respectful compliments across the Channel this fine achievement being partly due to the remarkable researches of M. Branly.[25]

This gracious acknowledgement of debt to the French professor who had developed the coherer added sweetness to the newly harmonious Anglo-French relations over wireless telegraphy, while another message, to University College London for Professor Fleming, who was soon to be a very active scientific consultant to Marconi's Company, was a pleasant one, with just a hint of a dig at the Post Office monopoly:

Glad to send you greetings conveyed by electric waves through the ether from Boulogne to South Foreland and thence by postal telegram.[26]

During the weeks after 27 March 1899 visitors of all sorts came to the stations and carried away souvenir copies of the messages they sent or received across the Channel. There were journalists and businessmen, officials and politicians, scientific colleagues and personal friends: the President of the Board of Trade, Elders of Trinity House with Lord Rayleigh their scientific adviser, Post Office administrators with Mr J. Hookey the successor to Preece as Chief Engineer, delegations from Australia, Brazil and China, French naval tepresentatives, Major Baden-Powell, a Royal Engineer who had assisted at Salisbury and who was related to that other soldier shortly to become so famous in the South African War.

For Marconi personally there were bundles of congratulatory telegrams and letters from friends and strangers who were impressed by the technical achievement of wireless messages between England and France, enthusiastic about the future of the invention, and excited by the man himself whose name was now established as a scientific adventurer. Agnes Baden-Powell wrote one such letter, black-edged because the lady's father had recently died, showing something of the feeling created by Marconi and his work:

Will you allow me to congratulate you warmly on the grand success you have achieved in actually bridging the Channel? It is a splendid triumph notwithstanding the presence of the groups of French sceptics.

My mother and I will be here for a fortnight and we hope very much that you will allow us the pleasure of seeing you if you should come to Bournemouth when we can tell you how much we appreciate what you have accomplished for the progress of science as well as for the comfort of humanity.

We are looking forward eagerly to making the acquaintance of the coherer in person and only await your arrival to start on our pilgrimage towards Poole. When may that delightful excursion take place?[27]

Whatever his inclinations in that direction, Marconi could have had little time for social engagements during the spring and early summer of 1899 even when the invitation was as charmingly worded as this one. He felt obliged to be present at many of the demonstrations arranged for parties visiting his stations, he was very busy with work for the French Government on naval communications, and he had the bad luck to be put more or less completely out of action for several weeks with an injured knee as the result of a road accident when his carriage overturned after the horse had bolted.[28]

The trials for the French Navy were particularly onerous. They were concerned with transmissions between the shore and a warship in motion, and Marconi spent many days at sea in a French vessel in the sort of unpleasant weather which is common in the Channel in the spring. But, as usual during any trial for a potential customer, Marconi was not content only to demonstrate the proven capabilities of his apparatus but used the opportunity to press forward with new ideas and solutions to problems. In the Dover–Boulogne area he was usually within range of several stations, and the *Times* was able to report on 24 April 1899 that there had been exchanges of messages between Marconi, on board the French ship *Ibis*, and the stations at Wimereux, South Foreland

61

lighthouse, and the East Goodwins lightship, without any mutual interference, because it was now possible for a receiver to cut out an unwanted second transmitter. He was beginning to get to grips with the technique of tuning which was crucial to the successful operation of wireless telegraphy on any practical scale. A second bonus from these trials was that the British Admiralty was prompted into brisker action by the possibility of being forestalled by the French, and on 1 July 1899 the Secretary of the Admiralty[29] instructed Captain Jackson, the naval wireless expert, that wireless telegraphy trials would be carried out in the ship under his command during the forthcoming naval manœuvres, and that he was meanwhile to liaise with Marconi about the fitting of the equipment.

The immediate purpose of the 1899 Naval Manœuvres was to exercise and test the arrangements for swiftly mobilising reservists on threat of war. These men – coastguards, fishermen, and other naval pensioners – had to be brought from their homes all over the country to the big naval manning depots such as Devonport and Portsmouth where they were issued with kit and sent to man ships newly commissioned after long periods laid up in the Reserve Fleet. Some reservists spent their brief call-up in first-line ships, replacing regular sailors who were drafted to stiffen the crews in ships coming out of reserve. Once mobilisation was completed the emphasis moved to training so that the men and ships of the reserve could be brought once more up to fighting efficiency, and British naval strength could be impressively demonstrated, especially to foreign powers, by assembling a dauntingly large and competent force for these manœuvres in home waters, without having to make any call on the Fleets discharging British commitments in the Mediterranean, the Far East and other distant places. Finally, in the mock war phase, it was hoped that light would be thrown on technical problems of naval warfare like the interaction of fast torpedo boats and torpedo-boat destroyers and the way in which tactics needed modification to take account of these relatively new vessels. At the same time the hard-driving, warlike conditions would soon expose any flaws in newly designed equipment – a novel type of boiler was under scrutiny – or any inadequacies in the general maintenance of hulls and machinery.

The general public was sufficiently interested for newspapers to publish long reports, almost every day for three weeks or so, on the mobilisation, the events at sea, and the conclusions drawn from them. The ships taking part were all listed with the names of their senior officers, and an outline was given of the general scheme for the manœuvres.

There were to be two opposing Fleets, A and B, each complete in itself with battleships, first- and second-class cruisers, torpedo boats, and destroyers. It was to be the task of Fleet B to pick up a convoy at a known rendezvous and to escort it safely into port. Fleet A, not knowing the rendezvous, was to try to find the convoy and destroy it. The two sides had been so arranged that Fleet A was the faster, but Fleet B was the more powerful. Consequently, if the convoy was to be destroyed, this had to be done before it came under the protection of the battleships of B Fleet.

The *Times'* correspondent in H.M.S. *Alexandra*, the flagship of B Fleet, set the scene on 17 July:

The 90 ships of the B Fleet are now all assembled and they make a brave show in the glorious weather with which we are at present favoured. The destroyers will join us later on. The manœuvres of this fleet will be additionally interesting from the fact that experiments are to be made with the Marconi wireless telegraphy. The cruiser *Juno* is fitted up with the necessary apparatus and instruments and Signor Marconi will be on board of her himself. A similar installation has been made on board the flagship *Alexandra* which carries 2 of Signor Marconi's assistants. Messages are freely exchanged between the two vessels as they lie not far apart in Torbay.[30]

Alexandra's logbook for 10 and 11 July had earlier recorded the arrival on board of the Admiral and his staff together with Messrs Bullock, Bradfield, and Lockyer, Assistant Telegraph Operators, Mr Marconi, Telegraph expert, and four senior naval ratings 'in connection with wireless telegraphy'.[31]

63

The A Fleet had meanwhile gathered in Portsmouth, and after a few days of preliminary exercises both Fleets put to sea for independent 'shakedown' cruises before going to their 'war' stations to await the signal from the Admiralty to commence hostilities.

The correspondent with B Fleet describes a summer afternoon interlude on 18 July when the Fleet stopped a dozen miles off the Devon coast to pick up mail sent out from Plymouth:

> The Admiral, taking advantage of the delay, gave a general permission to bathe, and immediately there was stir enough. From every ship the swimmers were to be seen diving from the decks and ladders and all available footholds, and rollicking in the blue water. They scrambled up chains and booms and other gear from the water's edge, and took headers again and again, fine athletic fellows gleaming white in the sun against the black sides of the vessels, while all the time a boat lay ready alongside each ship in case of accident. We were looking on at the fun, or trying to make out the Eddystone a few miles off, when the A Fleet was seen approaching from the east, organised in splendid precision – a noble spectacle. We then steamed on to get out of Sir Harry Rawson's way.[32]

The journalists could expect little hard news until hostilities commenced and their despatches were mostly reports of small incidents and comment upon them as Fleet A made for Bangor Bay and Fleet B for Milford Haven where they would await the starting signal from the Admiralty. Sir Thomas Lipton's steam yacht *Erin* was sighted towing *Shamrock* out from Bangor, but unfortunately they were out of sight before the *Shamrock* hoisted sail, and the Fleet was disappointed at missing the chance to scrutinise critically the performance of Britain's challenger for the America's Cup. Another day a pigeon alighted by chance on one of the vessels: 'Not a naval pigeon' said the report. The Navy, in fact, maintained lofts and kept pigeons for communication work and there were reports of the Germans using large numbers of the birds in the manœuvres they also were holding during the summer of 1899.[33] The A Fleet ran into fog and lost formation because the only method of signalling available was by gun and steam siren. A correspondent aboard *Majestic*, the flagship, reported: 'The need is only too apparent of some more rapid and surer method of communicating such as is foreshadowed, if not as yet effectively developed, in Signor Marconi's system of wireless telegraphy.'[34] Meanwhile, on board *Alexandra*, where wireless was fitted, the very first days of this new aspect of naval life just overlapped the end of an old way. She still used hand power to assist in lowering cutters and launches, a double row of sailors on a stout rope running it forward with a rapid tramp in time with the lively air played by the ship's violinist.

Occasionally the despatches contained some more technical naval material: doubts about the efficiency of the new boilers, a report of a cruiser unable to maintain a sufficiently high speed and criticism that the bottom fouling which caused this had not been removed during the vessel's period in dock, detailed comparative accounts of the number of tons per hour each vessel took on board during the filthy, noisy process of 'coaling ship'. There were some grumbles from the journalists about censorship, although it seemed to vary in its effect upon different reporters. One paper was unable to say – or felt obliged not to do so – which ships had wireless, and whether it was available to both Fleets,[35] whereas the *Times*, which had been the subject of a Parliamentary question for publishing the programme of the manœuvres prematurely due to a misunderstanding,[36] was able to state that the equipment was installed only in *Juno*, *Alexandra*, and *Europa*, all of B Fleet, to give details of *Juno*'s frequent detachment for special experiments, and to mention that on 28 July Marconi had inspected *Alexandra*'s equipment in preparation for hostilities.

The Admiralty ordered that hostilities were to commence at 1000 hours on 29 July. At 0630 on 30 July B Fleet, with the Admiral in the battleship *Alexandra*, sailed to rendezvous with the convoy which A Fleet was trying to seek out and destroy. On 31 July *Alexandra* entered in her log: '1100. Sighted convoy and cruisers.'[37]

It was all over. B Fleet had won the game, swiftly, efficiently, and almost without major incident. This smooth success was generally and enthusiastically attributed primarily to the fact that they had the advantage of wireless communication, while the A Fleet felt doubly the lack of this facility because they were troubled by fog.

The essence of the tactics was simple: the cruisers of B Fleet ranged ahead of the battleships, looking for the convoy and for any sign of the enemy. Such was standard practice, but on this occasion the cruiser squadron included *Europa*, and stationed between the cruiser squadron and the battleships, as they all steamed towards the convoy, was the *Juno*. It was thus possible for the Admiral, back with the battleships, to communicate with his 'eyes' pushed far and wide ahead in the cruiser squadron. When the first report of sighting the convoy was sent by the cruiser squadron from *Europa* to *Juno* and from her to *Alexandra* it was estimated that the flagship was 30 miles from *Juno*, 55 miles from *Europa*, and 86 miles from the convoy. Furthermore it was pointed out that at this time neither ship knew the whereabouts of the others.[38]

Such communication facilities meant that, although the tactics employed were standard, the courses, areas of search, and dispositions available to the Admiral were very much more favourable than previously, when reporting was limited to visual signals between ships less than twenty miles apart.

The reporters were all agreed on the success of the wireless installations even though they were only temporary ones. A section of the account in the *Times* is typical:

> Our movements have been directed with an ease and certainty and carried out with a confidence which, without this wonderful extension of the range of signalling, would have been wholly unattainable. It is a veritable triumph for Signor Marconi.[39]

Perhaps even more significant was the report made to the Admiral Commanding B Fleet by Captain Jackson of *Juno* who had been chosen to liaise with Marconi and to supervise the trials because he himself had for some years been experimenting with wireless. Jackson reported that the trials were very satisfactory and recommended that wireless should now be fitted in the Fleet and a programme of training arranged. In forwarding this report to Whitehall Admiral Domvile concurred with Jackson and said that the system had been 'absolutely invaluable'.[40]

In its issue of 17 August 1899 the *Naval and Military Record* noted that at the conclusion of the manœuvres Signor Marconi was congratulated by the First Lord of the Admiralty, Mr Goschen, M.P., on having brought his invention to its present state of perfection.

With this success behind him Marconi was now ready to go to America, a course which Henry Jameson-Davis and his fellow directors had been urging for some time because they were anxious to establish an American company to exploit the growing interest there. But Marconi had been determined first to bring off the England–France link. A New York paper had seen his success at the Kingstown Regatta and had recently asked him to provide similar reports of the America's Cup races which were to be held in the United States in October 1899. Now, after the reports of the British naval manœuvres, the U.S. Navy was most anxious that he should give demonstrations for them. The fingers all pointed or beckoned to America and Marconi sailed for New York on 11 September 1899.

CHAPTER 5

SWEET AMERICAN WELCOME
AND SOUR GOODBYE

THE circumstances of Marconi's departure for America in
September 1899 were quite different from those in which he had
left Italy for England three years before. In 1896 his objectives
had been few and well defined: he had to find a sponsor for his
invention, increase its range of signalling, and found a
company to exploit it commercially.

He had done all three of these things but each had led to
difficulties and disappointments. The Post Office and the
Admiralty who had supported the invention through its
infancy were expecting specially considerate treatment now
that it was growing up; the increase in signalling range had
uncovered serious problems of interference which were as yet
unsolved by the first steps being taken towards tuning the
transmitter and receiver to the same frequency; the Company
had very successfully publicised wireless telegraphy but the
expensive demonstrations had not produced any significant
source of income.

As he set out to face the reporters, the scientists and the
financiers in New York he was now troubled by a certain
amount of confusion and inhibition about how to demonstrate
his latest technical advances without giving valuable information to rivals. Competitors in the field of wireless telegraphy
no longer limited their attacks to spiteful comment in academic
papers. Some of them were offering practical wireless systems
to potential Marconi customers whose goodwill and cash were
badly needed by the Company.

On 20 August 1897 the Secretary of Lloyd's, H. M. Hozier,
had written to Marconi expressing considerable interest in the
possibilities of wireless telegraphy and asking him to call and
discuss the matter further.[1] This meeting led to equipment

68

being installed on Rathlin Island, on the shipping route off the north coast of Ireland, for reporting to the mainland during July and August 1898 on the passage of vessels which would otherwise have been missed in bad visibility. But on 29 July 1899, a year after these tests, Hozier (who later became the father-in-law of another First Lord – Winston Churchill) wrote a private letter to Mr Goschen, the First Lord of the Admiralty.[2] He wrote from Strasbourg where he had been sent to investigate Professor Braun's wireless system because Lloyd's were not quite satisfied with the tests made by Marconi. He referred to the reports of the use of wireless in the British naval manœuvres and suggested that when Braun carried out tests for Lloyd's the Admiralty should send representatives, and that they should wait until then before deciding on the relative merits of the Marconi and Braun systems.

The letter was passed within the Admiralty to the Director of Naval Ordnance who recommended that a naval officer be deputed to call on Hozier and arrange to attend the trials because '. . . in view of the prohibitive price asked by Marconi it would be very desirable that we should have an alternative. . . .'[3]

Very soon after Hozier's letter had arrived the Admiralty's attention was again drawn to Braun's experiments, this time by the Foreign Office. The British Consul General in Hamburg had reported to the Foreign Office on 15 July 1899 that Braun was working on a wireless system which was said to be different in many respects from Marconi's and, according to certain Germans, better. In general the experiments under Braun's control had been quite private and no information was available about them. But the British Embassy in Berlin had been seeking news of wireless telegraphy from its consulates throughout Germany and on 1 September 1899 was able to send a report to the Foreign Office that trials had been held at Cuxhaven. This information was passed by the Foreign Office to the Admiralty, the Board of Trade, and the Post Office.

The Admiralty decided not to send a naval officer with Hozier to the trials in Germany which Braun had invited him to attend at the end of November 1899. They did however take the trouble to establish from the Chief Clerk of the Patent

69

Office that no wireless patents had been completed by Braun in Britain, and they asked Hozier to let them have a detailed report of the trials on his return, noting particularly the distances at which transmission was successful.

Hozier notified the Secretary of the Admiralty of his return to London on 4 December 1899 and two days later he forwarded to the Admiralty his six-page report on the trials with many technical details. In his summing up he wrote:

> As far as I could judge it appeared to me that if Professor Braun had the same facilities for elaborating his system as other inventors seem to possess, his system would possibly secure equally good results as those that may be secured by any other system I have seen, at a considerably less cost. It also appeared to me that those who are interested with Professor Braun in his system are open and straightforward and not biassed by a mere desire to utilise the invention for Stock Exchange purposes. . . .
>
> At present, as far as I can perceive, there seems to be a disposition on the part of those interested in certain invented systems of wireless telegraphy to play off the Admiralty and Lloyd's against one another.

Hozier concluded his report by recommending strongly that Lloyd's and the Admiralty should adopt the same system of wireless telegraphy.

The report was at once sent from the Admiralty to H.M.S. *Vernon,* the shore establishment in Portsmouth which among other things was responsible for electricity in the Royal Navy. Serving in *Vernon* as an additional captain was Henry Jackson, the naval wireless expert, whose comments were invited. He said that it could be made possible for signals to be exchanged between stations using Braun and Marconi equipment, but that he considered it improbable that Professor Braun could use his apparatus in England without payment of royalties. He thought that the advice of Law Officers of the Crown should be taken in case the Admiralty should in some way become involved in a lawsuit with Marconi's Company over this matter.

The Secretary of the Admiralty wrote to Hozier on 28 December 1899 thanking him for the trouble he had taken and saying that no further steps would be taken by the Navy in investigating the Braun system.[4]

Captain Henry Jackson RN, to whom the Admiralty sent Hozier's report, was not one of those experts who have done no more than learn up sufficient of a subject to be able to offer ready comment on other men's work. In wireless telegraphy Jackson was himself a pioneer, an original thinker and an experimental scientist. In the early 1890s, when the tactical threat of the torpedo boat showed the need for better naval signals which would work in low visibility, he had thought about the possibilities of Hertz's electromagnetic radiation, prompted perhaps in this direction by contact with his father-in-law who had published work on electromagnetic wave theory and who was a Fellow of the Royal Society. But Jackson was not able to pursue this idea experimentally until he was appointed Captain of the naval torpedo school which was accommodated in H.M.S. *Defiance,* an old wooden warship moored at Devonport. He started to try to make a wireless signalling system at the end of 1895, basing his work on a recent paper describing experiments in India by Bose, who had himself drawn upon previous work published by Lodge. He succeeded in transmitting signals over distances of up to fifty yards in *Defiance* in August 1896 at which time he had neither met nor heard of Marconi.[5]

But within days of Jackson's first transmission a letter dated 21 August 1896 was addressed to the Commander-in-Chief Devonport from the Admiralty.[6] It said that, 'My Lords Commissioners of the Admiralty have had under consideration particulars of an inventon submitted to the War Department by Mr G. Marconi, living at 71, Hereford Rd., Bayswater, in which the inventor claims to be able to transmit electrical signals without wires.' The letter went on to direct that Jackson should attend a meeting in London with Army representatives to consider trials of the invention. On 16 September 1896 Jackson reported to his Commander-in-Chief that he had witnessed trials of Marconi's equipment arranged by the Post Office in London and near Salisbury. He said that

71

he himself had been experimenting along the same lines for six months but that his results were not so good as those of Marconi who would not disclose details of his receiver until the patent was completed.[7]

Jackson was present at various of the tests conducted by Marconi during the spring of 1897 in collaboration with the Post Office and the War Office. He was also pursuing his own work on specifically naval applications and in a report on 22 May 1897[8] he described wireless signalling trials between the gunboat *Scourge* and *Defiance* at her moorings up the Hamoaze at Devonport. *Scourge*, steaming up the harbour at seven knots from a seaward direction, first made contact with *Defiance* at about three miles range and maintained it while she approached and then passed beyond to a distance of two miles up the River Lynher where the depth of water became insufficient for the gunboat to continue.

This success by Jackson at Devonport thus preceded by some weeks similar and more impressive experiments by Marconi, at Spezia for the Italian Navy, which are commonly quoted as the first example of a mobile naval wireless signalling system. The point is made here as one of interest rather than historical importance because the order in which the Devonport and Spezia experiments took place was not scientifically significant. The two men had met and exchanged ideas freely and both were ready to undertake sea trials, the precise dates of which were dictated largely by the convenience with which they could be arranged.

Jackson will reappear as an important character in the Marconi story just as he did in the story of the Royal Navy. In 1915 he became First Sea Lord and he held that office during the Battle of Jutland in which – though the results were said to be indecisive – the German Fleet was only brought to action at all because of a very subtle use of wireless telegraphy. Not only did Jackson reach the very top of his own naval profession but as a scientist he was elected a Fellow of the Royal Society and eventually he became the first chairman of the Radio Research Board. It was not therefore surprising that during his naval career, wherever he was serving, the Admiralty was likely to send him papers on wireless for expert comment.

His reports were sound scientifically and also filled with shrewd observations of a more general kind, so that there is nothing fulsome about the quoted opinion of him as 'quiet, unassuming, the perfection of unobtrusive, intrinsic courtesy and very, very wise'.[9]

As Marconi crossed the Atlantic in September 1899 in the *Aurania* the knowledge that he was leaving a confused situation behind him spoiled the peace of the sea trip and made him anxious to complete his work and return to England as soon as possible. His reception when the ship arrived in New York was wild, and he was obliged to answer hundreds of questions from the reporters who crowded the quayside to meet him and who waited for him at his hotel. He later gave this account of the occasion:

I arrived in New York on 21 September and had to run the gauntlet as soon as I descended the gangway of numerous reporters and photographers who awaited me. The following day full and detailed reports of my arrival, my appearance etc. came out in dozens of newspapers together with more or less accurate accounts of what I had accomplished as regards wireless telegraphy until then. For some reason or other it seemed to come as a shock to the newspapers that I spoke English fluently, in fact 'with quite a London accent' as one paper phrased it, and also that I appeared to be very young and did not in the slightest resemble the popular type associated with an inventor in those days in America, that is to say a rather wild haired and eccentricly costumed person.[10]

Marconi mentioned that he had been met in New York by a personal friend, an officer in the US Signal Corps called Squier. This name occurs again in a letter addressed to Marconi as soon as he arrived in America by an ambitious young scientist called Lee de Forest. In this letter he said that he was a graduate of Yale and had studied Hertz waves, the coherer, etc. during post-graduate work on his doctor's thesis. He continued:

73

I have been exceedingly fascinated by the subject and hope for this opportunity of following work on that line. Knowing that you are about to conduct experiments for the US Government in the wireless telegraphy I write you begging to be allowed to work at that under you. It may be that some assistants well versed in the theory of Hertz waves will be desired in that work, if so may I not be given the chance? I am sure the recommendation on your part to Gen. Greeley would be sufficient to arrange for my employment. In fact I have written to Col. Geo. O. Squier, a friend of mine asking that he speak to the General on the matter. At present I am working for the Western Electric Company of this City [Chicago] in telephone work. As a young man you will I know fully appreciate the desire I feel in just starting out, to get a start in the lines of that fascinating field, so vast in extent, in which you have done so much. It has been my greatest ambition since first working with electric waves to make a life work of that study. If you can, signor, aid me in fulfilling this desire, you will win the lasting indebtedness, as you have already the admiration of Your obedient servant.[11]

The coincidence, if indeed it was that, of de Forest quoting a friend of Marconi as a referee did not secure the job for him, but it is doubtful whether Marconi felt any need to add to the staff already available for the work to be done during his brief stay in America. Possibly he was so busy that he never even saw the letter or had a chance to consider it seriously. But for whatever reason, the chance was missed of securing for the Company the man who was to invent the amplifying valve, which was perhaps the most significant technical step forward in wireless since Hertz's original experiments, and upon which now also depends that large electronics market which is unconnected with wireless. Not only was de Forest's talent lost to Marconi's Company but he formed a company of his own which became a very serious commercial rival and a persistent opponent in some particularly costly litigation.

Events went against Marconi in several annoying ways from the moment of his arrival in America. The attentions of the

New York reporters stretched his nerves and when he discovered that part of his luggage was missing, and with it some vital apparatus, he lost his temper and threatened to return at once to England. It was fortunately discovered quickly that the missing pieces of baggage had been consigned to the wrong steamer and were in Boston, whence they were safely recovered. Later his recollection of the emotion of the time was more tranquil. He spoke of being 'aware on arrival of a slight mishap' which 'little contretemps was remedied just in time'. Almost as soon as his party arrived at the Hoffman House there was an explosion in the hotel's heating system and, inevitably, this was blamed by some guests upon the mysterious wireless apparatus which was now under their roof. More disturbing was a threat by the representatives of the American Wireless Telegraph and Telephone Company, who owned patents taken out by Professor Dolbear, to stop the wireless reporting of the yacht races and the proposed trials for the US Government. Marconi observed that the inventor was claiming 'what amounted practically to a monopoly of the ether, nothing less' and supported his complaint by referring to a statement made by the inventor's son on 6 October 1899 that 'Our patent issued on 5 October 1885 covers the entire grounds. It is for the art of wireless telegraphy. It does not matter what instruments or methods are used. Just as soon as anybody gets into the field of wireless telegraphy or telephony they are poaching on our preserves.' Eventually the legal objection to reporting the yacht races was withdrawn 'because of the great public interest' and Marconi decided, anyhow, to go ahead with the trials for the US authorities.[12]

The directors of the *New York Herald* naturally hoped that commissioning Marconi's services would generate great public excitement. Certainly there was much general interest in the America's Cup, with the international rivalry sharpened by the memory of the protests which had accompanied the last challenge in 1895 by Lord Dunraven. This time, interest had been further stimulated by the fact that the challenger, *Shamrock*, was owned by Sir Thomas Lipton, who was well known and lived in America, and who, typically, had allowed a certain mystery to grow up about the design and performance of his yacht. With scientific interest in wireless, and curiosity about Marconi to add to the sporting enthusiasm, the *Herald* could reasonably hope for first-class publicity. But now there was a danger that Marconi and the America's Cup would be up-staged by the triumphant return home from the Philippines of Admiral Dewey, the victor of Manila, who was to be given a hero's welcome by New York after his successes in the war against Spain. The yacht races were postponed so that they should not interfere with the patriotic demonstrations, and the *Herald* made an attempt to get Marconi into the Dewey limelight. It was arranged that he should put to sea in a tug hurriedly fitted with wireless so that he could send back the first news of the arrival off New York of the Admiral's flagship, *Olympia*. Again the *Herald* was unlucky: Admiral Dewey arrived two days earlier than expected and Marconi's tug never even set out. However, there was later to be a big parade of vessels of all types to salute the Admiral, so now it was arranged that Marconi should take part in this and report it by wireless, using the facilities he had made ready for the yacht races.

The *Herald* had provided stations for Marconi's apparatus in the Navesink Highlands on the New Jersey coast, on top of a tall building on 34th Street, New York, and on the cable ship *Mackay Bennett* moored over the New York cable which it had picked up so as to be in immediate communication with London and Paris. The seagoing stations were on a new 3000-ton steamship, the *Ponce*, which was undergoing sea trials for the Puerto Rico Line, and on another steamer, the *Grande Duchesse*, which had been chartered by the newspaper for as long as the races should last. The *Ponce* steamed past Dewey's flagship with the rest of the great floating parade and the *Herald* spread itself with accounts of the celebrations and especially with details of the interest in the wireless reporting of 'their man' Marconi. Under the headline 'Goodwill for Marconi' they described the scene:

> While the *Ponce* was on the way upriver a greeting of goodwill was hurled at Signor Marconi from nearly every

ship. As the *Ponce* and the *Mackay Bennett* drew into position side by side a young lady standing on the upper deck of the latter ship caught up a megaphone and shouted, 'Three cheers for Marconi.' They were given with a will by all on board both vessels. Then came cries for the distinguished foreigner to appear, but the Captain of the *Ponce* was compelled to announce by megaphone that Signor Marconi was busy and could not show himself on deck. This incident was repeated more than once during the afternoon.

Aboard the *Ponce* a crowd constantly darkened the door of the chartroom within which the tests were being made. Signor Marconi, who was all impatience before communication with Navesink was established, became affability personified as soon as that was accomplished. He was greatly hampered in his work but never complained. Questions were always answered, and few of the women passengers went ashore without first having had the system of wireless telegraphy explained to them in all its intricacy by its inventor. Many of them were more interested in the man than in his work. They met a young man with an erect athletic figure which was filled with English mannerisms. His voice was low, well modulated, and filled with earnestness. Before half a dozen sentences had been uttered the listener was compelled to take an interest and to understand what was being told.[13]

At the request of the US Bureau of Equipment a naval observer, Lt. J. B. Blish USN, was on board the *Ponce* watching Marconi make his transmissions on the afternoon of the parade. He considered the experiments to be completely successful and his wireless message reporting this to his superiors in Washington was reproduced across two columns of the *Herald* who also printed his most enthusiastic comments to the effect that Marconi had passed the stage of uncertainty, that wireless was sure to be adopted for use at sea, and that its value could not be too highly estimated. Marconi himself was more restrained and simply allowed it to be announced that everything was in working order and that 'by the time the *Columbia* and the *Shamrock* square away for the first race we will be ready to flash the news to the *Herald* without a delay of a second'.[14]

In fact when the postponed races eventually started on 3 October they provided something of an anticlimax after the excitement of Dewey's reception. The wind was light and fickle day after day, and thirteen races – some called them drifting matches – were needed before *Columbia* was able to get the required 'three out of five decisions' and so retain the Cup. Nevertheless the *Herald* did its best to keep interest going in its wireless reporting and it was helped by one or two newsworthy incidents, as well as by one or two stunts.

One of the small steamers following the race one day was driven by the current across the bows of *Ponce*, which smashed into her. Marconi seized his chance: 'Almost before the *Ponce* had been able to back her nose from the hole she had made in the hull of the *Cambridge* I had flashed the news to New York.' On another occasion a rumour circulating in New York, that a large excursion steamer had sunk with many hundreds on board, was killed by the *Herald* sending a wireless enquiry to Marconi, who was able to report that the supposedly sunken vessel was quite safe.[15] The advantages of shore-to-ship communication were also brought to the notice of the privileged New Yorkers who were having a day at sea on the *Ponce* to follow the yacht races. The *Herald* sent them by wireless the more important items of world news and the latest prices quoted on Wall Street for the leading shares in the market.[16]

As soon as the America's Cup races were over Marconi's apparatus was transferred to the battleship *Massachusetts* and the cruiser *New York* for tests commissioned by the US Government. Many Americans, who had read so much about Marconi in their newspapers, must have believed that no one had transmitted a wireless signal in the United States until the young Italian arrived in September 1899. This was certainly not true, but the commercial rivals whom Marconi feared in America were more likely to threaten victory with patent actions in the law courts than with wireless equipment in working trials. Back in December 1897 W. J. Clark had been asked to give a demonstration of wireless to the American

Institute of Electrical Engineers and had shown what he believed was the first portable equipment built in America.[17] It was extremely simple, with no facility for Morse signalling and of limited range, whereas at this time in England Marconi was sending messages a dozen miles or more. Also at the end of 1897, Tesla was reported to have signalled successfully over short distances but to be far from a practical system. But the US military authorities, like their British counterparts, had been alive to the possibilities of wireless signalling and had made good progress in tests over a period of two years before Marconi reached America. In June 1899 the Chief Signal Officer of the US Army was able to report to Washington that the Signal Corps had achieved ranges of twelve miles.[18] Had the Army and Navy not needed every skilled man for the war in Cuba, Puerto Rico, and the Philippines, they might have developed apparatus comparable in performance with Marconi's. Even so, they knew exactly what they wanted of a signalling system and were able to ask some searching, indeed embarrassing, questions when Marconi carried out the trials for the US Navy.

In November 1899 Professor Fessenden opened a discussion on wireless telegraphy before the American Institute of Electrical Engineers in New York. He revealed that it was he who had suggested to one of the editors of the *New York Herald* that they report the international yacht races by wireless. When the suggestion was adopted Fessenden himself was invited, in December 1898, to undertake the work but he declined and put the newspaper in touch with Marconi. More specific evidence of the state of wireless telegraphy in America was given at the same discussion by Clark who, two years before, had shown the Institute the first portable equipment made in the United States and had since then been constructing and selling wireless apparatus, and demonstrating its capabilities at exhibitions in New York and elsewhere, including Boston where he referred to 'blowing up a boat every day, four times a day, by wireless telegraphy from across the hall'. Clark had also been able to examine Marconi's apparatus closely and judge its capabilities because he had been aboard the *Grande Duchesse* assisting with the wireless reporting of the yacht races. He was thus particularly well qualified to assess the progress which had been made with wireless telegraphy in America, and he told his professional colleagues at the Institute, with modesty rare in this field, 'I must accord to Mr Marconi the credit for having by far the best apparatus, better than any I have seen in America, including my own.'[19]

A somewhat sourer note was sounded at the Institute's corresponding discussion in Chicago which was opened by A. V. Abbott, the Chief Engineer of the Chicago Telephone Company. He said that it had been expected that Marconi would give an account of his work in wireless telegraphy to the Institute in New York. 'Mr Marconi had to leave this country sooner than was expected, and was unable to present his paper. We are therefore about to discuss a subject we have never listened to.'[20]

There is little doubt that Marconi did leave for England sooner than had been planned, and he would have been sorry not to have repeated in front of the American Institute the extraordinary success he had achieved with his paper given to the Institution of Electrical Engineers in London. He left, too, before the American Marconi Company had been formed, before a patent suit against him for infringing Dolbear's rights was due for hearing in the US courts, and before any sort of agreement was concluded with the US Navy as a result of the trials he had made for them.

However dissatisfied he felt about leaving so much of importance unresolved, he was anxious to get back to England where he knew that the negotiations with the British Admiralty had almost broken down, and where he considered that the attitude of his fellow directors needed stiffening in spite of the letters he had been writing from New York urging firmer action. The wish to be back in England was only exceeded by the desire to be away from America where his dealings with the US Navy had reached an impasse, and the fact that his apparatus had not satisfied the authorities was becoming generally known only too soon after the ballyhoo about Marconi and his wireless during the yacht races and the welcome home for Admiral Dewey.

The naval tests had started well enough with satisfactory communication between the battleship, the cruiser, and the shore station. There had even been a newsworthy incident of the type that so often occurred during Marconi trials. The *Massachusetts* and the *New York* were under way for the wireless trials when a man was lost overboard from the battleship which was steaming some distance ahead of the *New York*. An emergency wireless message sent from the battleship reached the cruiser – ten minutes before the same message was received by visual semaphore – and she was able to launch a cutter and rescue the man.[21]

But although the preliminary trials of range and reliability were satisfactory, the US Navy knew, and Marconi knew, that the key problem in a wireless signalling system was interference, especially when the system was intended to provide communication between the relatively large number of ships in a typical naval operational force.

There was no difficulty when only two wireless stations were in communication, but if a third station then started to transmit, its signals would be superimposed on those passing between the first two stations thus making all messages unintelligible. The solution to the problem is tuning, the ability to make a receiver accept signals at one chosen frequency and ignore all others. Thus two ships in a fleet with their transmitters and receivers tuned to the same frequency could exchange messages freely, unaffected by transmissions at different frequencies between other ships in company.

But although he had made some good progress in this direction the equipment in America had none of these improvements because Marconi was not yet satisfied that he had completely found the best practical system of tuning. Consequently when the US Navy insisted on trials of two simultaneous transmissions there was considerable interference and the messages were largely unintelligible. Before beginning the trials Marconi had written to the supervising commission saying that he had an instrument which would render interference practically impossible.[22] Now he was asked to justify this claim and thus was posed the dilemma which was largely responsible for the disappointingly limited success of the trip to the United States.

He did not want to show his improved apparatus because it was not yet fully protected by patent and he was afraid that competitors would poach his ideas. But he did not want to take out patents prematurely without being sure that he had identified the best of the possible modifications and so tied them up in his specification that there was little danger of someone finding a way to adopt tuning for a rival system.

In his last letter to the US naval authorities Marconi said that he did not regard the trials as a true guide to the services his Company could offer because the equipment used was obsolescent and the improved apparatus was not yet protected by patent. He continued: 'Having consulted with my partners, I regret to be unable to give a demonstration of the devices I use for preventing interference, and of the means I use for tuning, or syntonising, the instruments.'

The Electrician, published in England, said that in spite of the persistence of the American interviewer, Mr Marconi had returned without giving any clue to the method of preventing interference. Informed American opinion after Marconi had left is probably well represented by the comment in the *Electrical World* published in New York:

> If the visit of Marconi has resulted in no additions to our knowledge of wireless telegraphy, on the other hand, his managers have shown that they have nothing to learn from Yankeedom as to the art of commercial exploitation of an inventor and his inventions.[23]

It was a frosty farewell to the young man who had been welcomed to the United States with such wild enthusiasm a few weeks before.

Marconi sailed from New York with his equipment and his technical assistants on 9 November 1899 in the steamship *St Paul.* After the hectic pace and the strain of the previous weeks in America the voyage across the Atlantic was a sweet and tranquil interlude before the scientific, commercial and legal battles which he knew were waiting for him in England.

He relaxed in the ship's lazy routine, only playing at work by supervising the unpacking of enough apparatus to set up a makeshift wireless station on board, and enjoying the therapy of unhurriedly performing the familiar tasks such as organising a temporary telegraph office and arranging for a suitable aerial to be slung from the ship's mast. There was nothing particularly important about this work, but never before had wireless been fitted in a transatlantic liner, and Marconi, as always, had an eye for a first occasion. He had cabled his London office from New York saying that he would communicate with the Needles station in the Isle of Wight as the *St Paul* approached Southampton, and an operator was kept standing by there night and day, ready to pick up the first signal from the liner whenever she came within range.

The first messages were exchanged between the *St Paul* and the Needles station at a range of about seventy miles and the passengers were provided with a selection of news, received on board by wireless and put together in a duplicated souvenir sheet grandly entitled *Transatlantic Times: Volume I, Issue Number I*.

There were several hundred passengers on board the *St Paul* and many of them were thrilled to meet the young inventor who, rarely for him, was in a relaxed mood with time to spare for social diversions. To one of these passengers he paid particular attention, enjoying the traditional shipboard pastime of romantic dalliance. The attractive young woman was Josephine Holman who came from a rich Indianapolis family. This was one of the less transient of such affairs and in due time their engagement was announced and Marconi's mother, almost concealing her reservations about her idolised son's proposed marriage, let it be known that she intended to travel to America for the wedding. But the engagement was destined to languish, as other activities almost completely absorbed Marconi during the next two years, and it was broken off early in 1902.[24]

When the *St Paul* docked in the middle of November 1899 Marconi was returning to an England which was now involved in war with South Africa, and to a year in which his Company's unhappy relations with his old patrons, the Post Office, the War Office and the Admiralty, revealed some very unpleasant features. But in 1900 the foundation was laid for the most famous of Marconi's triumphs – the sending of signals across the Atlantic.

CHAPTER 6

IMPOSSIBLE DREAM OF THE
COMPANY MAN

By the end of 1899 when Marconi returned to England from America his Company was well known throughout the world. The weekly reports to the Board of Directors referred to negotiations for the supply of wireless equipment to places as far apart as Brazil, Egypt, India and Hawaii. Marconi agents travelled thousands of miles seeking new customers all over the world and giving the demonstrations of working equipment which were often a legal requirement for the establishment and maintenance of a patent in foreign countries.

But the financial strength of the Company did not grow in pace with its fame. Indeed there was almost no tangible return from all these very expensive activities. Again and again successful demonstrations, congratulatory speeches and acclamatory newspaper reports were followed by protracted and often acrimonious negotiations which broke down without a contract being won. Marconi's highest hopes had from the first been centred on a contract with the British Government and this matter gave him his biggest worries and disappointments.

It is difficult to be sure why the negotiations between Whitehall officials and the Marconi Board dragged on so long. Perhaps both sides were inexperienced in the arts of financial compromise and concession, or perhaps they could not grasp the dynamic nature of the commercial solutions required in a rapidly developing technology where a disagreement about the price of simple equipment could be still unresolved when it was replaced as the sticking point in the negotiations by a new argument about the need for more elaborate, tuned apparatus. The civil servants and naval and army officers may have adopted a hard line because they considered the terms asked by the Marconi Company to be exorbitant. This was certainly the Admiralty view when they accepted the offer of Hozier of Lloyd's to do a little discreet commercial intelligence work for them in connection with experimental wireless systems in Germany. Possibly the official negotiators shared Hozier's suspicion, hinted at in his report, that the Marconi Board were unscrupulous financially. Whatever the reason the British Government supplemented the efforts of its representatives at the conference table with activities in a buccaneering spirit which, if uncovered, would nowadays provoke excitement in Parliament and the financial press.

In December 1899 the Admiralty wrote to Marconi's Company[1] sounding the first sour note in the relationship. They thanked the Company for the loan of wireless apparatus during the 1899 Naval Manœuvres but declared that they thought it would not be right to accept the offer of more equipment on loan in view of the failure of the negotiations between the Company and the Treasury. Thus far the letter was both reasonable and friendly but the chilly nature of future discussions was determined by a concluding section which warned that the Admiralty might themselves make the equipment under the authority of an 1883 Act which allowed the Crown the use of any patent on whatever terms the Treasury decided.

The Board's view of the situation was put by the Managing Director to a shareholders' meeting in February 1900[2] when he said that they had been told by the Admiralty that the matter must be settled with the Treasury, which, however, refused to come to terms with the Company. He thought it rather unfortunate that the Crown determined originally to leave to the Post Office the negotiations as to the amount that was to be paid, for that department had been a little spoilt by the arrangements that were made in connection with the telephone from which an enormous revenue was now derived. The Post Office had not entertained at all seriously the proposals made by the Company for the purchase or use of the latter's patents. He did not, however, believe that it was possible for the Treasury to commit an act of injustice for which there was no remedy, and the directors would do their utmost to secure justice when they went before the Treasury.

This picture of the directors in good faith struggling against injustice was not universally accepted even within the Company. A few months earlier the Company Secretary had concluded a lengthy report about the selling of patents with a frank criticism of the directors' methods:

Moreover I feel that as long as the Board are undecided as to the price they put on their patents or the royalties to be charged for the use of the instruments then no business can be conducted with satisfaction to anyone working in this office be he Managing Director, Secretary, or otherwise engaged. Moreover it appears to me that as soon as the directors find that their offers are acceptable and people come forward to close the bargains they have invariably imposed fresh conditions and tried to raise the price – and this does us harm.[3]

The negotiations for the supply of apparatus to Trinity House for lighthouses and lightships were similarly bogged down and all the dismal details of the various stalemates were sent regularly to Marconi in America, where he was having difficulties enough of his own. He cabled tersely that the Admiralty should be supplied with no more apparatus until terms were agreed, and he must have been relieved to hear from England that his old associate, Captain Jackson, had called in at the Company's offices and said that he would try to persuade the Admiralty to act independently of other Government departments. Marconi had an ally in one of the keenest seamen in the Royal Navy even though Whitehall was antagonistic. In his letter[4] reporting Jackson's visit the Company Secretary remarked, 'We have a good friend in this gentleman.' That this was a remarkably perceptive observation was to be shown almost immediately.

In 1900 Whitehall laid plans for a determined attack on Marconi's Company by either having its patents declared invalid or by getting around them with the use of similar, but legally different, apparatus. The Post Office secretly commissioned Professors Oliver Lodge and Silvanus P. Thompson to examine these two possibilities, their reports and all related correspondence[5] being treated as strictly confidential. Each man produced over thirty pages of detailed analysis and recommendation. Thompson suggested a form of apparatus which it was hoped and expected would be as effective as Marconi's and not infringe his patents. Lodge concerned himself more with the validity of the existing patents, particularly stressing the priority of his own work in the field:

> . . . the most notable and conspicuous demonstration of the method of signalling was made by the present writer in 1894 at the Royal Institution on June 1st and at the British Association in Oxford in August of the same year. This demonstration . . . drew general attention to the subject and started the work of Righi in Italy, of Popoff in Russia, of Captain Jackson in England, and of Bose in India. . . . But the writer himself did not pursue the matter into telegraphic applications because he was unaware that there would be any demand for this, kind of telegraphy.

Later in his report, referring to one of Marconi's published patents, Lodge wrote of

> . . . a tendency of Marconi to attempt a claim at everything, whether he had invented it or not. In line 30 he virtually claims Hertz's cylindrical reflector. In lines 35 and 36 he mentions the wavelength given by a sphere, and other things which he probably obtained from my writings.

The two reports were passed to the Admiralty with remarks from other departments, including the suggestion from the Post Office that Thompson's proposed apparatus should be given trials. The Admiralty at once forwarded the papers for comment to Captain Jackson who was now in command of the cruiser *Vulcan* in the Mediterranean. Jackson's comments were lengthy, and of such notable fairness and good sense that it is refreshing to remember that his talents were eventually to take him to the top post in the Navy. He wrote, through his Commander-in-Chief 'Jacky' Fisher, in November 1900:

I have the honour to submit the following remarks:
1. With reference to the historical data, and detailed claims of the Marconi patents, so minutely analysed and summed up by Professors Lodge and Thompson, there is, I imagine, except in a few unimportant details, no doubt as to their general accuracy, or the conclusions drawn by them regarding the prior publication, in a legal sense, of the uses of most of the various instruments and methods described in the Marconi Patents, and a case contested solely on these grounds would probably invalidate many of the claims; but (a) suppose that Mr Marconi could prove that his instruments and methods were gradually developed by himself, personally [commencing at a date anterior to May 1894] from the lecture room forms, in which some similar types of instrument were abandoned as useless for practical purposes by their original discoverers – and also (b) considering the extraordinary and unforeseen development of these instruments, from a form suitable for lecture-room experiments, to a practical and useful telegraph, almost solely through the ingenuity and perseverance of the Patentee, and against the weight of opinion of many of the prominent professional electrical experts of the age; is it not most probable if the validity of these patents are [sic] contested in a Court of Law, or House of Lords, that they will be upheld in the form now adopted by the Patentee. . . .
2. Now as regards (a), I would state that in September 1896, at a time when the Patentee's name was quite unknown in connection with wireless telegraphy, when his system was undeveloped, and any thoughts of a patent action at Law on the subject were entirely absent from his mind, Mr Marconi informed me he had been working at his system for at least two years, mostly at his house in Italy, where possibly Dr Lodge's work and name were less well known than he thinks possible; and therefore it seems probable the latter's statements, that his experiments gave Mr Marconi the idea of the system, are as erroneous as the same statement relative to me, which statement is not qualified in any way, but accuses me directly of having knowingly copied his ideas. I beg therefore to state that at the time I first

commenced my experiments in 1895, I had not heard of his experiments, and I had not read any of his works, nor any of those mentioned by him, and though I have since studied some of them, and have learnt therefrom much of the theory of the phenomena connected with wireless telegraphy (as far as they are yet known), I certainly have not learnt anything of any practical use from any of them. As, in his extremely egotistical and biased report, he also accuses Mr Marconi of the same attitude, it seems probable he is mistaken in that also, as Mr Marconi is from my own personal acquaintance of him, of an extremely inventive, ingenious and enthusiastic disposition, and like myself, saw a practical future use for this system of wireless telegraphy, for Naval, Military and other purposes, which Dr Lodge owns, in the next paragraph, he himself did not foresee. I should like to state that my idea of utilising Hertzian waves for signalling from Torpedo Craft originated in about 1891, and I should have started experimenting in this direction sooner than I did (in 1895), had I heard of the Coherer principle sooner, the first time I learnt of it being through reading some of Dr Bose's experiments in 1895. This important detail was all that was required in my mind to obtain signals by Hertzian waves from a distant vessel under way. Is there any reason whatever why Mr Marconi should not have thought the same with his inventive scientific nature and love of the sea, instead of waiting for Dr Lodge to publish his ideas? In fact, judging from the latter's actions, the case seems to be the other way, as is manifest, when Mr Marconi's success was assured, that Dr Lodge at once patented every device he could conceive of for improving and, at the same time, obstructing the Marconi system of wireless telegraphy, although three years before, he had not considered that there was any practical use in the system he had demonstrated, but apparently not invented nor discovered, any more than the Patentee, or myself, in fact there is now no doubt that Professor Hughes was the original discoverer of the system, at least fifteen years previous to Dr Lodge's publication, but the invention was not published in a legal sense, though well known to several English Scientists, possibly including Dr Lodge, and the original discoverer, in a more generous spirit than Dr Lodge, gave Mr Marconi full credit for the practical realisation of these experimental demonstrations in Wireless Telegraphy; similarly Sir William Preece has also given the Patentee the credit, and it is rather odd that perhaps the greatest existing authority on practical telegraphic work should either not have known of Dr Lodge's experiments in the same direction, or that in the state they were shown, they should have made such a slight impression on him.

Jackson went on to agree that the alternative system proposed by Thompson, and favoured by the Post Office, might work, but he considered that there must be some doubt as to whether it would prove as efficient as the present Marconi system, and doubt also that it might be held to incorporate only small alterations, insufficient to evade an infringement of Marconi's patents. More specifically Jackson recommended that the Government should not contest these patents in court but should discuss frankly with the Company the weakness of some of its claims and hope thereby to secure a reduction in the 'exorbitant royalty' now demanded. Furthermore, he thought that it would be very much to the Crown's future advantage to keep on reasonably good terms with the Company in view of the new developments likely to occur, especially in tuning and the security of messages from unwanted listeners.

Jackson's comments were forwarded to London, a supporting note in the file from one senior naval officer saying that he thought 'it would be unworthy to try and evade the Marconi Company's patent'. No legal action was taken by the Government, although this may perhaps have been because such action was considered unwise rather than unworthy. An order on behalf of the Navy had already been placed with the Company in July 1900 before Lodge's and Thompson's reports reached the Admiralty. Thirty-two wireless sets were ordered, their acceptance subject to most stringent tests which were duly completed, and the financial terms, settled in November

1901, included an annual royalty of £100 per set for ten years.[6]

By chance one of the directors of Marconi's Company was also a director of Ediswan and he discovered that the Admiralty had sent one of the thirty-two Marconi sets there to be copied. The Admiralty subsequently admitted that they had had fifty such copies but refused to pay any royalty to the Marconi Company for them.[7]

As long ago as May 1898 the Marconi Company had demonstrated wireless to Lloyd's of London but the placing of a contract was delayed by discussions as protracted as those with the Admiralty and, in their own way, equally devious. The principal negotiator on behalf of Lloyd's was Col. Hozier, who had not shown himself particularly friendly towards the Marconi Company in his comments to the Admiralty about wireless in Germany, and who by 1900 had his own financial interest in wireless. In December of that year the *Times* reported[8] trials of an automatic wireless beacon in the Thames estuary:

> The system of wireless telegraphy employed was that invented by Col. Hozier and Mr Neville Maskelyne which depends on the same fundamental principles used by Marconi and other experimenters but differs in the practical details of their application.

Maskelyne was the son of the famous theatrical illusionist and on each of the several times his name appeared in the Marconi story it foreshadowed a period of disturbance or discomfiture for the Company.

Letters to Marconi from Mr Cuthbert Hall,[9] who had recently been appointed Manager of the Company, kept him in touch with the Lloyd's negotiations which seemed to turn very much on personal financial arrangements made with Hozier.

On 30 May 1901 Cuthbert Hall wrote:

> Hozier would apparently be willing to have his syndicate absorbed by us for shares in this company, a seat on the

Board, and some arrangement made with regard to Maskelyne and Brown. To the last stipulation it appears to me there would be many objections.

By 28 June Maskelyne and Brown appear to have been dropped from the arrangements and the deal with Hozier began to take more definite shape.

Hozier would take about £3000 for his syndicate and come on the Board, and make an arrangement with us with Lloyd's. This arrangement will of course have to be precedent to the purchase of his syndicate. I told him that we did not value his patents at all and that the only reason for taking them over would be with a view to making an arrangement with Lloyd's. He has to prepare a statement of what Lloyd's stations he would advise his Board to equip with wireless and on what terms.

A month later Hozier was apparently trying to obtain better terms for Lloyd's by suggesting various weaknesses in the bargaining position of the Marconi Company, such as the possibility of the Government taking over wireless at sea and the emergence of competing systems. Cuthbert Hall wrote:

Re Hozier's letter, I do not know whether he has really heard what he said in his letter or whether the statement is only put forward as a means of forcing our hand. I am inclined to take the latter view. I told him I thought there was very little risk of the Government adopting the course which he says.

He went on to say that he had told Hozier that he was daily receiving news of unsuccessful attempts to imitate the Marconi system.

I told him that quite recently I had heard from the White Star people that some system that they had been trying was quite useless and that they were sick to death of troubling with it. The system in question is Hozier's own, but I referred to it in the above terms, leaving him to infer that I did not know it was his. I think it quite possible that, while Hozier is anxious to carry through the proposed arrangement, the Lloyd's Committee may think that they can make better terms. If this be the case the stronger the position we take the better.

A few days later Cuthbert Hall complained to Marconi that Hozier had now put forward proposals which involved a complete change in the arrangements preliminarily discussed and he said that Mr Goodbody, another Marconi director, considered that Hozier's change of front was only in keeping with what he had always done before – begun negotiations on a certain basis and then changed it. This observation had an element of piquancy considering that a similar view had so recently been expressed of the method of negotiation of the Marconi directors themselves.

Eventually the bargaining came to an end and on 26 September 1901 Lloyd's awarded a contract for ten of their signalling stations to be fitted with wireless. Marconi was more pleased at the prestige gained from the award of the contract and the influence he hoped it would have on potential maritime customers than he was at any prospect of immediate financial gain. Indeed the Company had at once to raise £3000 of extra capital to pay Hozier and also to transfer to him 500 shares obtained from Marconi at £3 each. Even so there was one last kick from Hozier who had to be told firmly that he was certainly no longer entitled to make further wireless experiments and demonstrations on his own behalf.

Over in the United States the Marconi Company was getting support and publicity from its old friend, the *New York Herald*, which had contracted to have wireless installed in the Nantucket Light and on Nantucket Island to give early news of shippings arrivals, and was now arranging to provide minute-by-minute wireless reports of the big autumn sailing races as they had the previous year. Yacht-racing fever was again raging in New York. The *Times* reported[10] a scandal agitating sailing circles there, with the owner of *Rainbow* refusing to accept the Lipton Cup because his skipper had been accused of cheating by the owners of the rival boat, *Yankee,* who declared that *Rainbow*'s trim had been secretly, and illegally, altered overnight.

Whatever dark deeds may have taken place in harbour there was certainly dirty work on the high seas among the wireless operators. The Marconi Company no longer had the air to themselves. Two other companies were also reporting the races: one using the Morse code (telegraphy) and the other using the more advanced technique of transmitting speech (telephony). With all three operating simultaneously there was much confusion during early trials and the *Herald* was far from satisfied. A letter to the Marconi Company in September 1901 explained the situation:

Reports of the Yacht Races were I fear very meagre and were not acceptable to the Associated Press. . . . Your experts frankly admitted that the service was not what it should have been owing to the deliberate interference of the American Company and also to the legitimate messages sent by the de Forest Company which is exploiting wireless telephony rather than wireless telegraphy. But be that as it may, something has to be done at once to enable the Associated Press to obtain its messages promptly. We think we can dispose of the American Company and it has been consented that, as to the de Forest Company, each company, viz. the de Forest Company and the Marconi Company, shall operate for five minutes each, yielding the alternate five minutes to the other company. . . . The matter of five minutes will not make any practical difference although I hope that the period against us will not occur at any crucial point in the races. We have learned that Mr Marconi has claimed to have made a device to do away with interference but the instruments furnished for us lack any such device. The policy of the American Company is simply obstructive by sending dots, dashes, vulgar and meaningless words for which we will hold them responsible. Their representative called here today and stated that they intended to continue such policy but disclaiming any knowledge of indecent or obscene words. I shall take the responsibility of arresting its operator should this continue. I may add that threats have been made to employ similar policy to obstruct our Nantucket station.[11]

In 1900 and 1901 the reports, which reached Marconi weekly or more often, wherever he was, seemed to contain little but bad news about his company's affairs. In Britain and America in particular, his plans to provide a wireless service were opposed by official obstructiveness, individual deviousness and very often open hostility. But perhaps most serious was the threat posed by the emergence in the United States of properly founded competing companies with good scientific advisers. In July 1901 Cuthbert Hall wrote to Marconi stressing the possibility of business being lost in America. He enclosed a copy of information supplied to him by the general manager of the *New York Herald* Company about important tests of wireless being conducted for the US Government by Professor Fessenden. This well-informed newspaper man continued:

> The Government is maintaining great secrecy about the experiments but we have learned that the intention is believed to be to establish a series of stations for the Weather Bureau along the Atlantic Coast from Maine to Florida using Fessenden's invention and methods. A severe test is to be made at sea by naval officers in a few weeks. The *Herald* will have a complete story of these tests through a naval officer.[12]

This worrying period when Marconi's Company was struggling to establish itself as a recognised international business organisation was in some ways similar to that earlier period when the young Italian boy had to fight for recognition as a serious scientist even in his own home. But by 1900 he was twenty-six years old and the pattern of his personal life had changed. Something of the old style remained. In Brussels there was a reminder of the times when he appeared before distinguished audiences in the solo role of inventor, entrepreneur and showman. He received the congratulations of the King after a demonstration at the Palace where the first message, sent by Marconi himself, was: 'Long live the Queen. Long live the King. Long live the Royal Family.'[13] But now there were others in the Company's employment who were competent to demonstrate equipment to possible customers. There was, too, a board of directors to run the business, and Marconi himself had little active part in the tortuous negotiations needed to push forward the financial affairs of the Company, although he was certainly not insulated from these matters. He was kept regularly informed of them wherever he was, and often wrote or cabled his own advice on tactics to be adopted. Scientific problems were of course still present and Marconi was thinking daily about ways to attack the most pressing problem of all – the tuning of transmitter and receiver to the same frequency so that interference from other stations is avoided and secrecy of communication maintained. He was, however, no longer alone and unsupported in his researches. There were staff facilities available to test his ideas, and he had recruited first-class scientific associates who were able to put forward ideas on their own initiative. Marconi's famous Patent No. 7777, which brought together into a coherent system a number of important tuning principles, was granted in 1900 and during the following year much of the development work of the Company's scientists was concerned with demonstrating under working conditions that high-power stations in close proximity could be operated simultaneously without mutually interfering.

During the period 1900–1901 Marconi did much travelling. He inspected the new stations being put up around the coast of Britain by the Company to communicate with merchant ships which were just starting to be fitted with Marconi wireless. The few British, French, German and Belgian vessels which were so equipped were hoped by the Company to be the first of a flood of such customers. There were small flattering reminders to Marconi that he was now reckoned to be a person of importance: the Company was advised to take out an insurance policy on his life,[14] he appeared in a film about wireless,[15] and he was invited to give a Friday Evening Discourse at the Royal Institution.

Marconi used the occasion at the Royal Institution to attack the War Office[16] who had criticised the performance of the five mobile stations sent to the Boer War. It had originally been planned that these stations should provide communications between the shore and the troop transports and supply ships which were arriving in South Africa in such numbers that problems of congestion were arising at the ports of disembarkation. But this plan was changed by the Army who asked the Marconi men to volunteer for service in the field. They all did so and were soon sent, with their equipment mounted in horse-drawn waggons, to provide signalling facilities around Kimberley. The local climate produced a large amount of atmospheric electricity which made the receivers very difficult to operate, and high winds wrecked the masts, balloons and kites which were all tried as means of supporting the aerials. Marconi claimed that the poor performance of the equipment was caused by the failure of the War Office to provide suitable aerial masts. He also said[17] that his men had volunteered to take wireless apparatus into Kimberley through the Boer lines but had not been allowed to do so, and he considered that it was unfortunate that Ladysmith, Kimberley and Mafeking had not been supplied with wireless before hostilities began. Marconi assured the audience that he thought it unlikely that the Boers had wireless – certainly they could not have had any of his – but some apparatus intended for them, which had been seized at Cape Town, had come from Germany and was unworkable.

All matters relating to the Boer War were extremely sensitive topics with the whole country committed and concerned to an extent which was to be demonstrated later on Mafeking night. There was jingoism, criticism of the conduct of the campaign, and outright opposition to it, for example from Lloyd George, which at once attracted the label pro-Boer. When Sir Oliver Lodge had written to the Press suggesting an electrical method of communicating with the besieged towns he was at once publicly rebuked for not raising the matter secretly with the authorities.

Certainly Marconi's critical remarks at the Royal Institution touched a nerve in the War Office, which at once ordered that the mobile stations be withdrawn and disbanded. The Army's peremptory dismissal of wireless from the field was instantly turned to its own advantage by the Navy, who installed the sets in three of their ships which were thereby able to co-ordinate their patrols much more efficiently and even to capture blockade runners capable of higher speeds than the intercepting vessels. Once again the natural affinity between Marconi and seagoing naval officers had, to the Navy's benefit, risen above official displeasure.

A long letter from Captain Jackson to Marconi, thanking him for a corrected copy of a recent paper and exchanging technical information about the best form for ships' aerials, further illustrated this most fruitful unofficial liaison, and shows how naval tactics were already being significantly improved by the intelligent use of wireless. Jackson wrote:

> I start on a cruise in two days with four WT ships in my squadron to attack the remainder of the Fleet with destroyers as we make our way from Malta to Gibraltar and I have with perfect confidence as to the result made out my plans to make the greatest possible tactical use of the WT in our squadron and hope it will enable me to do successfully that for which I want a force three times as large without it. Should the results interest you I should be glad to let you know them but I must ask you particularly not to publish anything in this letter or any other on this subject.[18]

Much of the Marconi Company's fundamental research work was carried out at the Haven Hotel, Poole. Here in 1898 rooms had been rented for use as workshop/laboratories and for the accommodation of the scientific staff and some of their wives. Gradually by the turn of the century more space was taken over, but ordinary holidaymakers still came to the pleasant little hotel near the beach and they sat down in the dining room with the Marconi staff, and very often with Marconi himself and his mother and brother, Alfonso, who frequently accompanied him. Sometimes there would be time for a musical evening with Marconi playing the piano, Alfonso the violin, and Dr Murray, one of the scientific staff, playing the 'cello.

Annie Marconi was able to get away from Italy for long periods at this time. She visited relations in Ireland, came to the Haven Hotel when Marconi was there, and stayed in London, usually at the Grand Hotel which was then on one side of Trafalgar Square. She was thus able to meet Marconi's fiancée Josephine Holman who had come to England on the *St Paul,* and she sometimes went out with the two young people to dinner and the theatre.

During the two years the engagement lasted the couple were almost always apart and Josephine wrote long letters to Marconi from her home in New York which show something of her character and the problem, which faced each woman in Marconi's life, of hanging on to the devotion of the famous man who was often on the other side of the world and always dedicated single-mindedly to furthering his wireless enterprise. Some of these letters seem strangely formal:

My dear Mr Marconi,
It is a long time since my last letter and I have a lot of things to tell you but I fear I have not many moments left before the last post. This afternoon it was so beautiful and the air so delicious, the little children so lovely as I walked along the drive that I intended to come home and have a little chat with you. . . .

In another letter is an example of the passages she often inserted written in the dots and dashes of the Morse code – one wonders from whom the words so disguised were being hidden.

I think you cannot have received one of my letters. [In Morse.] I feel that I must tell you something I have done wrong in not telling my mother what you said to me at Craigsmore. I am sure she guessed my happiness as mothers always can. My silence hurt her deeply. Then there has been another man, and most embarrassing. [Morse ends.]

The fate of this other man is revealed to Marconi in a subsequent letter:

I heard the other day that the man of whom I once spoke to you is engaged and is to be married soon. His fiancée is rather unattractive, not especially nice, and I fancy not quite of his station in life, just a bit below. . . .[19]

The letters, usually signed 'always your own true and loving Jo', were filled with the affectionate wishes and dreams which lovers always exchange. But occasionally what can now be recognised as a warning sign appears:

You say that you have been ill but that you are well again and of that I have my doubts as I fancy that I could detect a bit of dreary tone in your letter which, not being caused by disappointment or discouragement, must have meant the presence of this illness. I hope you are not working too hard, are you?

Perhaps more ominous was the postscript, in Morse, to another letter: 'Your long silences have made me very unhappy.'

But although their love soon waned and the affair ended there is no doubt about the regard Marconi had at one time for his 'true and loving Jo' because he certainly confided to her his great secret dream. She writes:

I shall wait eagerly to hear from you the results of your experiments with the 'great thing' which I do not read about in the papers. You must have a magnificent way of managing the Press to have succeeded in keeping even a line of it from the public ear. . . .

The 'great thing' was Marconi's dream of being the first to transmit wireless signals across the Atlantic. He had the greatest of difficulty in persuading the board of directors to allocate Company resources to this nebulous and extremely costly project when they believed there was a good income to be gained from less showy activities. However, the young man who as a boy had overcome very similar opposition from his father eventually obtained the grudging backing of his fellow directors. But the problem was not one to be tackled with a few bits and pieces bought in Bologna and the gardener's boy as assistant. The obstacle the signals must surmount was not now the little hill in front of Villa Grifone but the huge mountain of the Atlantic Ocean bulging nearly 150 miles high between England and America.

Many of the most eminent scientists of the time considered that, since radio and light waves belonged to the same electromagnetic family, radio signals must travel in straight lines like a beam of light and would therefore not penetrate significantly beyond the optical horizon. But Marconi had never allowed this consideration to affect his almost blind faith in the feasibility of long-distance wireless signalling, and by 1900 the experimental evidence he had acquired of successful transmission to ships below the horizon suggested that there was more to the process than could be explained by the simple optical analogy. He was now convinced that really long-range wireless communication – and hence commercial competition with the cable companies – was a matter only of increasing the power transmitted and improving the sensitivity of the receiver.

It was this requirement for high-power transmitters which changed the commercial wireless station from being an affair of laboratory apparatus set up in huts to a properly planned industrial complex with its own generating station producing many kilowatts of electrical power. To launch the powerful signal from the transmitter as efficiently as possible an enormous aerial was needed and the design accepted by Marconi concentrated on electrical performance, with appearance, strength and cost only secondary considerations. This huge aerial also ensured that, when it was used for receiving signals, it gathered as much as possible of the minute amount of radio energy which would reach the receiving station after spreading out from a transmitter thousands of miles away. In the receiver itself an improvement in sensitivity had been achieved by replacing the old dust coherer with a magnetic detector of wireless waves based on a design of Rutherford's. Then, just before setting out on the Atlantic adventure, Marconi had been given an even more

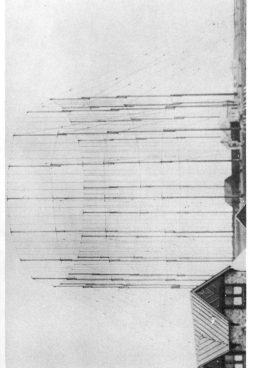

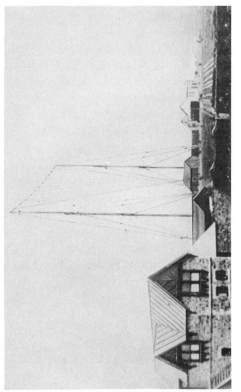

First transatlantic signals from Poldhun

(*above left*) Original aerial
(*above*) After the gale
(*left*) Makeshift aerial which transmitted the letter 'S'

Glace Bay station outside and inside

sensitive detector using a special mercury contact. This had been developed in the Italian Navy, and his old friend Solari, now a naval electrical engineer, had christened it the Regia Marina detector and while visiting Marconi at the Haven Hotel in 1900[20] had explained it to him and had put one in his baggage to use if required on the transatlantic trials.

The growth of the Marconi Company and now the special problems associated with the proposed transmission to America had required the recruitment of many extra staff. Some of these were young men like Vyvyan and Franklin who achieved their scientific fame in the service of the Company, while Fleming was already well known as Professor at University College London when he became part-time consultant to the Company to design much of the new high-power electrical equipment needed. Marconi's task was to draw what he wanted from these talented men, see that they had all the facilities they required, and organise suitable sites in England and America for the two great new stations.

In October 1900 a site was acquired at Poldhu on the coast of south-west Cornwall. This was as close as possible to America, remote from any likely source of electrical interference, and with the advantage of a large hotel nearby which could provide comfortable accommodation. Early in 1901 Marconi decided from a study of the map that Cape Cod, Massachusetts, was the best place for the American station, with nothing but water between there and Poldhu. He went across with Vyvyan who had been in charge of the site work at Poldhu and together they chose the precise locality – again there was an hotel nearby – and Marconi left Vyvyan there to build the second station.

In September 1901 the new equipment, including the immensely powerful transmitter, was installed at Poldhu and a great 200 foot diameter ring of masts 200 feet high had risen like the skeleton of a huge gasometer on the edge of the cliff. Test transmissions to other Marconi stations, in particular that at Crookhaven, Ireland, over two hundred miles away, had shown that the waves did – at least to this extent – follow the curvature of the Earth and not fly off into space. Across the Atlantic at Cape Cod the twin station was similarly

103

nearing completion and plans were made with quiet optimism for the experiment to take place in a few weeks' time.

Then on 15 September a gale struck Poldhu and the gamble which traded mechanical strength for electrical performance failed. The huge aerial structure which had loomed arrogantly over the countryside, symbolising the power of the great enterprise, now lay in a humiliating tangled heap on the ground. Marconi calmed the panic among his directors, analysed the situation, and took another gamble. He decided to go ahead using a simpler aerial at Poldhu, and he rallied and led scientists and labourers alike to such effect that in just over a week the wreckage was cleared and tests were being made with a makeshift system. Design and construction was pushed on at a tremendous rate to get the new aerial ready so that Marconi could leave for America and superintend the experiment from that end. Then in November the Cape Cod aerial collapsed.

Now Marconi's great scheme to exchange signals between two powerful stations with enormous aerials lay wholly in ruins. He must have been a desperate man rather than a cool appraiser who now decided to abandon for the time the Cape Cod station and to go across the Atlantic and try somehow to receive signals from Poldhu at a point as near as possible to Cornwall. There would now be no transmitter on the American side, the signal strength transmitted from Poldhu would necessarily be lower than with the original aerial, and whatever Marconi could set up in America as a receiving aerial would be much less sensitive to weak signals than the two hundred foot ring of masts.

At the end of November Marconi, and assistants Kemp and Paget, sailed for Newfoundland with balloons and kites to raise the aerial wire as high as possible when they found a site for their receiver after they arrived in St Johns. It was a long way from the grandiose scale on which the 'great thing' had been planned and the little party which sailed from Liverpool, with hastily gathered bits and pieces for an aerial, was a lot closer to the style of the old Villa Grifone days than Marconi and his directors would have wished after all the secret planning and the vast expense.

CHAPTER 7

THE GREAT THING ACHIEVED
AND DOUBTED

On 6 December 1901 Marconi landed at St John's, Newfoundland, with Paget, the technical assistant who was familiar with most of the wireless apparatus, and Kemp, Marconi's devoted personal factotum who on this occasion was to be specially responsible for raising the aerial by means of kites or balloons. The Newfoundland winter was bitter, and Kemp, as an old Navy man, made certain that there was plenty of cocoa – and whisky – to keep out the biting cold.

On arrival Marconi called on the Governor and the Prime Minister of the colony who received him with sympathetic interest. The real reason for the trip had been kept a close secret and it was understood that he was to undertake experiments in communicating with transatlantic liners and other shipping from land stations on the dangerous Newfoundland coast. The Press had been told of these 'routine experiments' and Marconi had provided substantiation of this cover story by asking that ships bound for America and fitted with wireless should report their positions to him.

The authorities offered the loan of any land required for the experiments, and when a site was selected on Signal Hill overlooking St John's harbour they allowed Marconi the use of some empty military buildings there, near the Signal Tower which was a memorial to John Cabot, the Italian-born explorer who settled in Bristol and crossed the Atlantic from the West of England to discover Newfoundland.

The preparations went ahead with the briskness which characterised any enterprise personally supervised by Marconi. They had landed on the Friday and on Monday were already setting out equipment in the building on Signal Hill and, with locally recruited help, digging holes for earth plates.

The weather was good enough on Tuesday for a successful kite trial, and a cablegram was sent to Poldhu arranging that signals be transmitted for a fixed three-hour period every afternoon, starting on the Wednesday.[1]

The signal chosen was the three dots of the Morse letter S because this could be transmitted continuously by a simple mechanism; a dot used less energy than a dash, thus simplifying keying, and it was considered that dots would be easier to pick out against a background of atmospheric interference either by ear or on a Morse printer. Marconi decided that a telephone receiver and the mercury detector given him by Solari might probably be more sensitive than the dust coherer and Morse printer, so both systems were included in the receiving circuit at St John's.

On Wednesday the weather deteriorated, the wind began to get up, and Kemp had difficulty in launching and controlling the fourteen-foot-diameter balloon which carried up the aerial for this first attempt to receive the signal from Poldhu. Inside the old building Marconi sat at the receiver adjusting and re-adjusting the apparatus and straining to pick out the three dots from the rushing, crackling atmospherics that rose and fell in the earphone. The wind outside added to the noise and Kemp struggled to hang on to the balloon's guideline. At three o'clock in the afternoon, when Marconi's experienced and eager ear had just managed to detect a few extremely weak S's among the general noise, the wind finally tore the balloon free from its mooring and the experiments came to an abrupt end for that day.

On Thursday 12 December the weather was even worse and it was extremely difficult to fly the kites which Marconi now decided to use to support the aerial. The first one broke away during the afternoon and was lost, but a second kite was, with difficulty, launched. In spite of the diving and tugging which constantly changed the height and angle of the aerial wire – and hence its receiving properties – Marconi managed to detect signals and he wrote in his diary: 'Sigs. at 12.30, 1.10, and 2.20.'

Friday 13th brought snow, hail and rain, driven by a wind which made it impossible to keep a kite in the air for anything but the briefest of periods. Nevertheless, during one of these, very faint signals were heard. There was little point in continuing with the kites and balloons during the wild winter weather. They had obviously been lucky to achieve even Thursday's meagre success with such unstable aerial behaviour. On the Saturday Kemp tried to obtain steadier conditions by fixing an aerial between the cliff at Signal Hill and an iceberg stuck on the shore in the harbour below, but it was not successful.

Marconi decided that this was as far as the St John's tests, in their present form, could go and so he sent off to Major Flood Page in London a message which he had been holding since Thursday 12th in the hope of better results to report. The cablegram, sent by the Anglo-American Telegraph Company, read: 'St John's Newfoundland. Saturday 14.12.01. Signals are being received. Weather makes continuous tests very difficult. One balloon carried away yesterday.'

The next day, Sunday 15th, Marconi attended the service in St John's Cathedral, told the local Press that he had received wireless signals from England, and then went to a party given for him and his assistants. On the Monday, a day of blizzard and freezing fog, Kemp went with the Minister of Lights and Fisheries to inspect a possible new site where a more permanent station might be established with an aerial properly supported by masts or towers. But the plans Marconi was considering for a second series of tests at St John's under better conditions were abandoned abruptly when he received a letter on the Monday evening from the solicitors of the Anglo-American Telegraph Company.

Marconi had hoped for stronger evidence before announcing the success of his transatlantic experiment. In view of scientific scepticism about wireless rays following the curvature of the Earth, and knowing from experience that any claim of his seemed unfailingly to provoke instant and widespread cynical criticism, he was only too clearly aware of the weaknesses in his account which could be exploited by those unkindly disposed towards him and his Company. There was no printed record of the reception of the signals which had only been heard in the telephone connected to Solari's mercury detector but had not been strong enough to activate the coherer and Morse printer. The only witnesses were Marconi and Kemp – Paget had been ill on the Thursday when the best signals were received and had never had the chance to hear them on the other days when they were only briefly detected. Many believed that an operator could be genuinely misled into thinking that he had heard a simple set of three dots when there was so much atmospheric noise present. For all these reasons Marconi was prepared for hostile comment in the papers which had all been given the news. But the immediate Press reaction was acclamatory, the *New York Times* said: 'Guglielmo Marconi announced tonight the most wonderful scientific development in modern times.'[2]

The blow which fell on Monday 16 December was a legal one. The solicitors of the Anglo-American Telegraph Company informed Marconi that their clients had a monopoly of all communications within the colony of Newfoundland and that, unless he at once stopped his experiments there, they would take legal action. There was no doubt about the AAT's monopoly, although it had only two years to run. Marconi cabled his London office to tell them that the Newfoundland experiments were over and gave the reason. Then he told the sympathetic local authorities, and the reporters who had gathered in St John's, about the action of the Anglo-American Telegraph Company and its consequences.

There was at once an outburst of indignation at the obstructive attitude of the Anglo–American Telegraph Company and, for once, if only temporarily, public and newspaper comment was unanimously pro-Marconi. The municipal council of St John's passed a resolution supporting Marconi and deploring the action of the AAT, and the Governor of Newfoundland made a point of paying an official visit to Signal Hill to see the apparatus which now lay silent by legal interdict.

This situation was not entirely unwelcome to Marconi who could accept the unfamiliar role of persecuted innocent, barred by unscrupulous commercial interests from continuing his contribution to human progress. Any obligation to demonstrate the receipt of signals from England was thus conveniently removed at a time when it would have been practically impossible to stage such a public demonstration in the highly efficient and convincing way that had become the hallmark of the Marconi style. Even if the weather and the unmanageable kites and balloons had permitted signals to be picked up at just the right moment, the lay visitor would have found it difficult to understand the enthusiasm in the Marconi camp at what would probably have seemed to him to be a meaningless cacophony in the earphone. It would be better for the public not to witness the experiments until improved apparatus, above all a stable aerial, ensured that the arrival of a signal would give an unequivocal positive indication instantly recognisable by the untrained observer.

The Anglo-American Telegraph Company felt obliged to make some reply to the obloquy so freely directed at them. The New York office said that the instructions to impose the ban had come from the English side,[3] and their solicitors in London wrote to the *Times*[4] to question the substance of the cable which Marconi sent from St John's on 17 December declaring that he must stop his experiments in Newfoundland because of the threat of legal proceedings contained in the letter received by him on the evening of the 16th. The AAT solicitors claimed that Marconi had written to them on the 16th saying: 'I may mention that, prior to the receipt of your letter, I have decided to discontinue the tests and to remove the instruments tomorrow.' Interviewed in St John's, Marconi said that the quoted extract referred 'only to a temporary measure I had taken as I wished to utilise other apparatus now on the way from England, and not a permanent withdrawal as their letter would imply'.[5] Meanwhile in London the solicitors for the Marconi Company claimed that the AAT letter to the *Times* had been deliberately written to create misapprehension.[6]

Among the messages supporting Marconi against the Anglo-American Telegraph Company were some offers of practical help which shaped the way in which the transatlantic wireless service developed. Professor Graham Bell, the inventor of the telephone, offered the use of land he owned at Cape Breton in Nova Scotia. Furthermore, enquiries Marconi had instituted as soon as he was banned from Newfoundland had produced favourable responses from the Government of Canada and the Government of the Province of Nova Scotia. On 22 December he received an invitation to visit Ottawa to discuss facilities for continuing his experiments.

The equipment at St John's was packed up and Paget was sent back to England in charge of it and with a detailed programme of experimental work which was to be carried out at once to produce a new improved receiver while Marconi remained for a time on the other side of the Atlantic. Paget left for England on Christmas Eve and on the same day Marconi and Kemp set out across Newfoundland in a private railway carriage. They spent Christmas Day on the train and that night, in a blizzard, crossed the Cabot Strait and landed at North Sydney, Nova Scotia. They were met and entertained by the Prime Minister of the Province and members of his staff and, later, taken along the coast in the neighbourhood of Glace Bay to look at possible sites for a permanent station.

On 30 December Marconi travelled to Ottawa where he met the Governor General and the Prime Minister of Canada and started negotiations on behalf of the Marconi Company. The Canadian Government was most helpful and by the time he left Ottawa on 9 January 1902 there was a draft agreement under which Marconi's Company would be given a site at Glace Bay and £16,000 of financial assistance towards the construction of a station.

Marconi went from Ottawa to Montreal to discuss the possibility of using the telegraph wires of the Canadian Pacific Railway to take messages into and out of the proposed transatlantic station at Glace Bay.[7] He had been invited to be the guest of honour at a dinner given by the American Institute of Electrical Engineers in New York, and he was also anxious to visit the Cape Cod station in Massachusetts to discuss the design for an aerial to replace the one which had collapsed. But it is possible that he had some misgivings about making these visits at this time. On 10 January he apparently received a cable from England: 'From Hall to Marconi at Montreal. *Herald* told me Holmans would serve writ on your entering United States.'[8]

Marconi's mother referring, in April 1902, to the broken

engagement between her son and Josephine Holman had said that she was glad to hear from Guglielmo that it was Miss Holman who had broken it off, and that they had remained friends.[9] Perhaps though, if these are the same Holmans, Marconi's disengagement had not been as smooth as he would have wished. Anyhow, the date of the Institute dinner was 'at forty-eight hours' notice' put forward to 13 January because the distinguished guest was 'not sure how soon he might have to leave the United States for England.'[10] In fact he attended the dinner, visited Cape Cod, and did not sail for England until 22 January.

The businessmen and scientists in New York who wished to honour Marconi did not arrange without difficulty the banquet held at the Waldorf Astoria under the auspices of the American Institute of Electrical Engineers. There was the alteration of date at short notice – always an organiser's nightmare – but a more embarrassing problem was the growth among some of those invited of uncertainty as to whether they wanted their names, some illustrious and some now unknown, to be associated with a Marconi fête.

After the acclamation which followed the announcement of the successful experiment, a number of scientists, particularly those who had most firmly believed that the rays would not follow the curvature of the Earth, suggested that Marconi might have mistaken atmospherics or interference for the very faint signals. Others thought that the announcement was premature and should have been held back until more positive results had been obtained. But after Elihu Thomson and Thomas Edison, two of the most influential electrical scientists, had both publicly expressed their faith in Marconi the guest list was soon filled with about 300 names, including some famous ones: Steinmetz, President of the AIEE; Graham Bell; Pupin; Thomson; Mrs Thomas Edison, representing her husband.

When the guests took their places at the many small tables set out in the Astor Gallery of the hotel they found that the organisers had denied them no decoration, ornament, or culinary embellishment which could possibly be expected or imagined in a banqueting hall set out to honour an Italian who had sent electric signals across an ocean in winter.

111

The menu was coloured olive green and carried a medallion in which was set Marconi's picture framed in the Italian flag. At the top of the menu was a drawing of two wireless masts separated by sea with a stream of S's passing between them. This theme was more ambitiously developed across the room itself, with a tablet at each side, one labelled Poldhu, and the other St John's, and a string of 'fairy lights' joining the two tablets blinked on and off in the dot dot dot of the Morse S. Marconi's name was spelled out in lights above the high table which was backed by the Stars and Stripes, and more lights supplemented the floral decorations on the tables where the final touch was the setting down of ices stuck with tiny frozen telegraph poles. From the gallery above the hall crowds looked down on this busy scene, listened to the flow of congratulatory speeches and messages for Marconi, and cheered his simple unassuming little reply.

When Marconi sailed for England on 22 January on the *Philadelphia* out of New York he did so with the pleasant memory of that city's acclamation. It is true that there were still some doubters in the United States, as well as in England, but Marconi had won over most of the prominent scientists in America and he had already laid plans which he was confident would confirm his results beyond all question. As part of these plans the *Philadelphia* had been supplied in New York with the latest tuned wireless system and Marconi, Kemp and Vyvyan, who were all travelling together to Southampton, carried out preliminary tests during the crossing.

When he returned to London where he was to address a meeting of the shareholders of the Company, Marconi received more acclamation, although on different lines from the banquet at the Waldorf Astoria. There was, too, that peculiarly English accolade: an article about his work had been published in *Punch* on the day he left America.

The article consisted of a number of 'marconigrams' which might appear in 'next year's *Times*'. The writer, like many others at this time, did not understand that if two receivers lay in the path of the wireless rays then *both* picked up the message – it was not intercepted by one and lost to the other. Neither, apparently, had he grasped that, if two similar signals were received simultaneously at the same station, then neither of the messages carried by those signals would be intelligible.

In the first of these 'extracts from the *Times* a year hence' a sympathetic and a hostile report of a speech on South African policy are mixed up, followed by this 'editorial note':

The account of this meeting at Birmingham was transmitted to us by wireless telegraph. Unfortunately, a portion of the report intended for the *Daily News* seems to have been tapped by our receiver, and time does not permit us to disentangle the two versions.[11]

The second 'extract' is headed 'From the Berlin Correspondent':

The importance of a pronouncement made yesterday by the German Emperor cannot be exaggerated. Indeed, the diplomats with whom I have discussed it are unanimous in the belief that it will gravely affect the course of European politics for many years to come. But without further preamble, I will give you the Emperor's exact words. Addressing the Chancellor in a voice which trembled with emotion, he said: [Editorial Note. By a vexatious accident the rest of our correspondent's message has not reached us. At the moment of its transmission a French battleship, fitted with the Marconi apparatus, was lying in the Channel and contrived to intercept the remainder of the telegram.]

A third extract is in the form of a letter to the Editor.

Sir, It is high time that steps were taken to check the scandalous misuse of our telegraphic system. This morning I despatched a wireless of great importance to a friend asking him to meet me at one o'clock. For two hours, Sir, I waited at the receiving instrument for a reply, within which time the following messages arrived:

'Send me £500 at once and buy Otaheites – Sharpem, outside broker.'

'Have you a furry tongue? Take Pepper's Perfectly Painless Pilules!'

'Jones and Robinson's sale now on. Jones and Robinson. Great bargains in all departments. Don't forget the name. Jones and Robinson.'

'Your life is in danger! Run! All is known! Only one thing can save you – reading *Noodleby's Nightcap*, the most brilliant and sensational novel of the season.' At great expense, Sir, I have had a pole 250 feet high erected on the top of my own house in order to receive telegrams expeditiously. And whenever I go to the instrument I am bombarded with these abominable advertisements.

Yours etc., INDIGNANT.

Punch had a stronger feeling then, as now perhaps, for the social future than for the scientific present.

CHAPTER 8

FRIENDLY KINGS
AND A HOSTILE EMPEROR

MARCONI arrived back in England with Vyvyan and Kemp at the end of January 1902 on the *Philadelphia*, and on 22 February he returned to America on the same ship. Vyvyan was with him again, and so too was the girl whom Vyvyan had married during the four weeks in England, and there were several others in the party including experienced engineers and operators. Marconi was determined that during this voyage the fact that he could transmit signals across thousands of miles of ocean should once more be demonstrated to the world and that the undeniable evidence, signed, sealed and certified, should be rammed down the throats of those who had raised doubts about his earlier success.

During these four weeks before he returned to America Marconi picked up the threads of the receiver development which Paget had been sent back from Signal Hill to initiate, and he decided upon the form of apparatus to be used in the forthcoming long-distance experiments to be carried out with the benefit of good fixed aerial systems replacing the kites and balloons; he told an enthusiastic shareholders' meeting of the transatlantic aspirations of their Company; he selected staff and equipment for the trials to be made on the crossing in the *Philadelphia*; he thrashed out with the Marconi Board the terms under which the new American Marconi Company would be formed; and he obtained approval for a final agreement with the Government of Canada. He must have been working at a tremendous pace during these few weeks and he found it necessary to keep his London address secret from all but his mother and Solari and a few other very close associates. Such a step taken by one so energetic as Marconi was an indication of how great was the pressure at this time.

Commenting in December 1901 on the transatlantic wireless signals a scientific journal[1] drew attention to the fact that whereas about seventy-five years elapsed between the invention of the electric telegraph and the laying of the transatlantic cable, it had only taken Marconi about five years to increase his wireless signalling range from just over two miles to over two thousand miles.

The perspicacious writer identified a fundamental feature of the next twenty-five years of wireless: an insatiable world demand for communication channels which would be fed by Marconi who had the vision, the drive and the nerve to reduce drastically the period between the laboratory demonstration of a scientific principle and its commercial exploitation, often on a very large scale. These talents did not endear Marconi to certain established scientists whose researches were directed to extending the frontiers of knowledge – into barren and fertile lands alike – and whose ambitions had been satisfied by scholarly published papers, academic honours and professional advancement, the traditional rewards of their work. Such men, having ignored commercial applications or even despised them, were astonished at the dazzling international honours, clamorous public adulation, and the money thrust upon Marconi. Their jealousy was not necessarily entirely personal but was perhaps on behalf of the whole of 'pure' science. Financial adventurers, uninterested in science but ready to exploit it, were jealous that Marconi as a commercial competitor had the advantage of influence cultivated carefully in high places through his family and scientific friends. Finally there were the cable companies whose jealousy and fear of Marconi was less complicated: their shares were being unloaded on to the Stock Markets and prices were declining sharply.

The unfriendly comments, so much resented by Marconi, about the experiments he had struggled to conduct under such arduous conditions at Signal Hill ranged from mild disapproval from those who thought Marconi's methods flashy to the direct accusation that he had used without acknowledgement someone else's invention, namely the Italian Navy mercury detector. Lodge wrote to the *Times* referring to the manner of Marconi's announcement as 'incautious and enthusiastic',[2] while when Edison was told the news he said that he did not believe it. But almost immediately Edison withdrew his statement[3] and Lodge, too, declared that his remarks had been misunderstood as unsympathetic to Marconi.[4] More lasting, and more damaging, was Silvanus P. Thompson's attack on the 'excessive claims' of Marconi and his misappropriation of Solari's detector.[5] The first step in Marconi's determined and meticulously planned destruction of all this criticism was the *Philadelphia* voyage.

The America Line who owned the *Philadelphia* were persuaded to have her masts lengthened so that the aerial height was 150 feet above the deck. Since this aerial was firmly supported it was possible to connect it to the more sensitive syntonic receiving equipment, whereas at Signal Hill the wild fluctuations in the electrical properties of the aerial when the kite soared and dived had made the delicate business of tuning impossible. In the receiver the arrival of signals was detected by a conventional metal-dust coherer which operated a Morse printer so that a permanent tape record was obtained, and any witnesses were able to observe directly the dots and dashes being marked by the machine. The evidence that signals had been received was now in no way dependent upon the reliability or the honesty of a human operator.

During the voyage messages were received regularly by night and day, and were witnessed by the Captain or the First Officer, who signed the tape and noted the ship's position. The last full message to be received from Poldhu in readable form was at a range of 1550 miles, but the single letter S which was also being transmitted was marked distinctly out to a distance of over 2000 miles. Marconi also reported[6] that the Italian Navy mercury detector was tested in the circuit from time to time but it had not been successful beyond 700 miles.

Hidden among the results was a most significant observation: that the maximum rage at which signals were received was very much greater at night than by day. But to Marconi this was of only secondary importance – nothing more than an inconvenient variability in the performance of his system. He was concerned on this voyage only with getting good signals at very long ranges, recorded on tape, signed by unexceptionable witnesses, and ready to be displayed to the world through the journalists who would meet the ship in New York. He wanted to prove to the doubters and disbelievers that he could transmit signals thousands of miles round the curvature of the Earth and the primary result of the *Philadelphia* experiments was to furnish such proof. But it was the secondary result – the day and night variation in range – which was the clue to why radio signals did not behave as the established scientists expected and shoot off into space in straight lines over the horizon. The clue was followed by Heaviside and Kennelly who suggested that the surprising behaviour of Marconi's radio signals could be explained by the existence of an ionosphere. Their initial work, and that of others in the 1920s, explained how several layers of electrically charged particles many miles up in the atmosphere bend back towards the Earth's surface the path of radio signals which might have been expected to shoot off into space.

Ultra-violet energy in the Sun's radiation converts into positive and negative charged particles, or 'ions', some of the gas molecules in the thin atmosphere at great height. These positive and negative ions tend to come together and neutralise each other and there is a dynamic equilibrium between the production of ions by the sunlight and their disappearance due to neutralisation. The interplay of these two processes with the density of the air, which decreases with height, results in the production of three or four fairly well defined layers of ions which between them bend back towards the ground radio waves of certain frequencies, and absorb strongly waves of other frequencies. Because the charged particles in the ionosphere are originally produced by solar radiation the nature of the layers changes by day and night, and so too then does the effect of the ionosphere on radio propagation. For communication between two particular points on the Earth's surface there is an optimum frequency which would be different for two other points and which will vary with the time of day or night and the season of the year. It was over twenty years after

118

Marconi and Kemp at Poldhu testing directional aerial floating on sea

"All the News That's Fit to Print."

The New York Times.

THE WEATHER.
Cloudy Friday; Saturday, fair; moderate to brisk west winds.

VOL. LXI...NO. 19,809.   * * *   NEW YORK, FRIDAY, APRIL 19, 1912.—TWENTY-FOUR PAGES   ONE CENT   TWO CENTS

745 SAW TITANIC SINK WITH 1,595, HER BAND PLAYING

HIT ICEBERG AT 21 KNOTS AND TORE HER BOTTOM OUT

'I'LL FOLLOW THE SHIP,' LAST WORDS OF CAPT. SMITH

MANY WOMEN STAYED TO PERISH WITH HUSBAND

Rescue Ship Arrives— Thousands Gather At the Pier.

FOUR BODIES BROUGHT IN

206 of the Crew and 4 Officers Are Among Those Rescued.

THREE LIFEBOATS LOST

Two Filled with Women Were Drawn Under and One Was Swamped.

SURVIVORS HURRIED AWAY

Many Among Them Ill as a Result of Long Hours Spent in Open Boats.

HOW BRUCE ISMAY ESCAPED

Several Versions of This—One Is That He Was Persuaded by Women in a Lifeboat to Go.

The Cunard liner Carpathia, not only a rescue ship, but a hospital ship as well, steamed slowly up the harbor last night and docked at her pier, at the foot of Fourteenth Street and North River at 9:35 o'clock. She brought with her the first definite, authentic news which has been received since Monday of the sinking early on that morning of the giant White Star Liner Titanic, the biggest steamship afloat.

For hours the pier to which she made fast echoed with the shrieks of women and men of men, who seemed driven temporarily insane by their experiences of the last few days. But finally these facts were learned from the rescue ship:

The sinking Titanic carried with her to death 1,595 persons.

More than this number were picked up from the Titanic's boats and from pieces of wreckage to which they clung, but four died of exposure after having been transferred to the Carpathia and were buried at sea.

Of the 745 who reached here last night 206 were members of the crew, most of them stewards and firemen. Only four officers were saved.

Two Versions of Ismay's Escape.

A great deal of interest among the crowds awaiting to greet survivors on the Titanic. Various tales of his going were told, one having it that he was a passenger in Lifeboat 1.

In this boat also were Mr Cosmo and Lady Duff Gordon, and only nine other persons, and some of the survivors spoke of it last night at "The Millionaires' Special." It was said that Mr. Ismay later had the crew of this boat photographed aboard the Carpathia and that he liberally rewarded them.

Another version, according to a statement said to have been made by T. D. M. Cardeza of Philadelphia as the lobby of the Ritz-Carlton last night, was that Mr. Ismay had been persuaded to enter one of the lifeboats by the women who already embarked in it.

The hardships of those who were rescued were extreme. Dozens of women were taken from the Carpathia last night ill and almost demand for the moment

Band Played As Titanic Sank.

Survivors said that the lifeboats in which they floated for hours were not stocked with food or water and that they added greatly to the hardship which the exposure to the midnight...

Two of the lifeboats were sucked beneath from the Titanic were swamped as she went by the sinking of the giant liner. Another, loaded, as were the other two, with passengers, nearly swamped as she tried to get away from the Titanic.

Many persons were picked up by the lifeboats after the Titanic sank. The big steamship went down with the band playing "Autumn." Every soul remaining aboard the vessel had

THRILLING STORY BY TITANIC'S SURVIVING WIRELESS MAN

Bride Tells How He and Phillips Worked and How He Finished a Stoker Who Tried to Steal Phillips's Life Belt—Ship Sank to Tune of "Autumn"

BY HAROLD BRIDE, SURVIVING WIRELESS OPERATOR OF THE TITANIC.

(This statement was dictated by Mr. Bride to a reporter for THE NEW YORK TIMES, who visited him with Mr. Marconi in the wireless cabin of the Carpathia a few minutes after the steamship touched her pier.)

(Copyright, 1912, by The New York Times Company.)

In the first place, the public should not blame anybody because more wireless messages about the disaster to the Titanic did not reach shore from the Carpathia. I positively refused to send press dispatches because the bulk of personal messages with touching words of grief was so large. The wireless operators aboard the Chester got all they asked for. And they were wretched operators.

They knew American Morse but not Continental Morse sufficiently to be worth while. They taxed our endurance to the limit.

I had to cut them out at last, they were so insufferably slow, and go ahead with our messages of grief to relatives. We sent 119 personal messages today, and 50 yesterday.

When I was dragged aboard the Carpathia I went to the hospital at first. I stayed there for ten hours. Then somebody brought word that the Carpathia's wireless operator was "getting queer" from the work.

They asked me if I could go up and help. I could not walk. Both my feet were broken or something, I don't know what. I went on crutches with somebody helping me.

I took the key and I never left the wireless cabin after that. Our meals were brought to us. We kept the wireless working all the time. The navy operators were a great nuisance. I advise them all to learn the Continental Morse and learn to speed up in it if they ever expect to be worth their salt.

The Chester's man thought he knew it, but he was so slow as Christmas coming.

Those who were rescued could not have gotten off and only nine more saved, one having it that he was a passenger in the wireless cabin. I could sit on it and rest my feet while sending sometimes.

To begin at the beginning, I joined the Titanic at Belfast. I was born at Nunhead, England, 22 years ago, and joined the Marconi forces last July. I first worked on the Haverford, and then on the Lusitania. I joined the Titanic at Belfast.

Asleep When Crash Came.

I didn't have much to do aboard the Titanic except to relieve Phillips from midnight until some time in the morning, when he needed to get through sleeping. On the night of the accident, I was not sending, but was asleep. I was due to be up and relieve Phillips earlier than usual. And that reminds me—if it hadn't been for a lucky thing, we never could have sent any call for help.

The lucky thing was that the wireless broke down early enough for us to fix it before the accident. We noticed something wrong on Sunday and Phillips and I worked seven hours to find it. We found a "secretary" or something and repaired it just a few hours before the iceberg was struck.

Phillips said to me as he took the night shift, "You turn in, boy, and get some sleep, and go up as soon as you can and give me a chance. I'm all done for with this work of making repairs."

There were three rooms in the wireless cabin. One was a sleeping room, one a dynamo room, and one an operating room. I took off my clothes and went to sleep in bed. Then I was conscious of waking up and hearing Phillips sending to Cape Race. I read what he was sending. It was traffic matter.

I remembered how tired he was and I got out of bed without my clothes on to relieve him. I didn't even feel the shock. I hardly knew it had happened after the Captain had come to us. There was no jolt whatever.

I was standing by Phillips telling him to go to bed when the Captain put his head in the cabin.

"We've struck an iceberg," the Captain said, "and I'm having an inspection made to tell what it has done for us. You better get ready to send out a call for assistance. But don't send it until I tell you."

The Captain went away and in 10 minutes, I should estimate the time, he came back. We could hear a terrible confusion outside, but there was not the least thing to indicate that there was any trouble. The wireless was working perfectly.

"Send the call for assistance," ordered the Captain, barely putting his head in the door.

"What call should I send?" Phillips asked.

"The regulation international call for help. Just that."

Then the Captain was gone. Phillips began to send "C. Q. D." He flashed away at it and we joked while he did so. All of us made light of the disaster.

Joked at Distress Call.

We joked that way while he flashed signals for about five minutes. Then the Captain came in again.

"What are you sending?" he asked.

"C. Q. D.," Phillips replied.

The humor of the situation appealed to me. I cut in with a little remark that made us all laugh, including the Captain.

"Send 'S. O. S.,'" I said. "It's the new call, and it may be your last chance to send it."

Phillips with a laugh changed the signal to "S. O. S." The Captain told us we had been struck amidships, or just back of amidships. It was ten minutes, Phillips told me, after he had noticed the iceberg, that the slight jolt that was the collision's only signal to us occurred. We thought we were a good distance away. We said lots of funny things to each other in the next few minutes. We picked up first the steamship Frankfurt. We gave her our position and said we had struck an iceberg and needed assistance. The Frankfurt operator went away to tell his Captain. He came back and we told him we were sinking by the head. By that time we could observe a distinct list forward.

The Carpathia answered our

signal. We told her our position and said we were sinking by the head. The operator went to tell the Captain, and in five minutes returned and told us that the Captain of the Carpathia was putting about and heading for us.

Great Scramble on Deck.

Our Captain had left us at this time and Phillips told me to run and tell him what the Carpathia had answered. I did so, and I went through an awful mass of people to his cabin. The decks were full of scrambling men and women. I saw no fighting, but I heard tell of it.

I came back and heard Phillips giving the Carpathia fuller directions. Phillips told me to put on my clothes. Until that moment I forgot that I was not dressed.

I went to my cabin and dressed. I brought an overcoat to Phillips. It was very cold. I slipped the overcoat upon him while he worked.

Every few minutes Phillips would send me to the Captain with little messages. They were merely telling how the Carpathia was coming our way and gave her speed.

I noticed as I came back from one trip that they were putting off women and children in lifeboats. I noticed that the forward was increasing.

Phillips told me the wireless was growing weaker. The Captain came and told us our engine rooms were taking water and that the dynamos might not last much longer. We sent that word to the Carpathia.

I went out on deck and looked around. The water was pretty close up to the boat deck. There was a great scramble aft, and how poor Phillips worked through it I don't know.

He was a brave man. I learned to love him that night and I suddenly felt for him a great reverence to see him standing there sticking to his work while everybody else was raging about. I will never live to forget the work of Phillips for the last awful fifteen minutes.

I thought it was about time to look about and see if there was anything detached that would float. I remembered that every member of the crew had a special life belt and ought to know where it was. I remembered mine was under my bunk. I went and got it. Then I thought how cold the water was.

I remembered I had some boots and I put those on, and an extra jacket and I put that on. I saw Phillips standing out there still sending away, giving the Carpathia details of just how we were doing.

We picked up the Olympic and told her we were sinking by the head and were about all down. As Phillips was sending the message I strapped his life belt to his back. I had already put on his overcoat.

Every minute was precious, so I suddenly felt a passion not to let that man die a decent sailor's death. I wondered how he ever did it. He was a brave man. I learned

Col. Astor Went Down Waving Farewells to His Bride.

SOME STORIES OF PA—

Others Say Order Was Maintained—Mrs. Straus Clung to Husband's Side.

SHOCK CALLED "SLIGHT"

Carri Playing Continued In Cabin and None Knew the End Was Near.

SOME HEARD SHOTS FI—

A False Rumor of Captain's cide and of Shooting of M—Rushing for Boats.

MEN LEAPED INTO THE

Col. Gracie Saved Another Himself—Says Titanic O—Not Blow Up.

their life belts. I felt I simply had to get away from the ship. She was a beautiful sight then.

Smoke and sparks were rushing out of her funnel. There must have been an explosion, but we had heard none. We only saw the big scream of sparks. The ship was gradually turning on her nose—just like a duck does that goes down for a dive. I had only one thing on my mind—to get away from the suction. The band was still playing. I guess all of the band went down.

They were playing "Autumn" then. I swam with all my might. I suppose I was 150 feet away when the Titanic, on her nose, with her after-quarter sticking straight up in the air, began to settle—slowly.

Pulled Into a Boat.

When at last the waves washed over her rudder there wasn't the least bit of suction I could feel. She must have kept going just so slowly as she had been.

I forgot to mention that, besides the people forward who were being wrenched. I had not known how we were. We also spoke the Baltic. I began to figure what ships would be coming toward us.

I felt, after a little while, like sinking. I was very cold. I saw a boat of some kind near me and put all my strength into an effort to swim to it. It was hard work. I was all done when a hand reached out from the boat and pulled me aboard. It was our same collapsible. The same crowd was on it.

There was just room for me to roll on the edge. I lay there not caring what happened. Somebody sat on my legs. They were wedged in between slats and were being wrenched. I had not the heart left to ask the man to move. It was a terrible sight all around—men swimming and sinking.

I lay where I was, letting the man wrench my feet out of shape. Others came near. Nobody gave them a hand. The bottom-up boat already had more men than it would hold and it was sinking.

At first the larger waves splashed over my clothing. Then they began to splash over my head and I had to breathe when I could.

As we floated around on our capsized boat and I kept straining my eyes for a ship's lights, somebody said, "Don't the rest of you think we ought to pray?" The man who made the suggestion asked what the religion of the others was. Each man called out his religion. One was a Catholic, one a Methodist, one a Presbyterian.

It was decided the most appropriate prayer for all was the Lord's Prayer. We spoke it over in chorus with the man who first suggested that we pray as the leader. Some splendid people saved us. They had a right-side-up boat, and it was full to its capacity. Yet they came to us and loaded us all into it. I saw some lights off in the distance and knew a steamship was coming to our aid.

At last those there was rail of survivors and all were taken. Half an hour later I knew I had to fight for it and I did. When I got out from under the boat I do not know. But I felt a breath of air at last.

There were men all around me—hundreds of them. The sea was dotted with them, all depending

1,595 Went to Death on the Titanic.

NUMBER ABOARD		THE SAVED	
First Class	330	First Class	210
Second Class	320	Second Class	125
Third Class	750	Third Class	200
Officers and Crew	940	Officers and Crew	210
Total	**2,340**	**Total**	**745**

Of the members of the crew saved, 4 were officers, 39 seamen, 96 stewards, and 71 firemen.

One Dead on the Raft.
One man was dead. I passed him and went to the ladder, all

Continued on Page 3.

Marconi's first transatlantic S before enough was learned about the ionosphere to allow the optimum frequency for any task to be chosen with confidence as it is today. Ironically the ionospheric conditions would have made reception of the Poldhu signals at Signal Hill, Newfoundland, very much better at night than by day when Marconi was trying so desperately to pick them up.

Possibly the two most important influences in Marconi's life were his enterprising mother and the ionosphere. Certainly if the latter had not existed Marconi's signalling range would have been limited to something less than 100 miles just as his eminent scientific elders predicted. Probably he would then have been better liked and no doubt he would have developed and exploited such a modest system into a famous and profitable enterprise, but one which lacked the international political and commercial influence eventually exercised by his Company. Without his mother he might have become an officer of the Regia Marina, without the ionosphere he might have become a Tommy Lipton.

When Marconi landed in New York in March he had irrefutable evidence of transatlantic radio reception. The implications of the voyage in the *Philadelphia* were perfectly clear: there was no need to say 'I told you so.' He went to Ottawa and agreed final terms with the Canadian Government for the transatlantic service and he installed Vyvyan at Glace Bay to supervise the erection there of a powerful station. When he returned to New York he found the officials there courteous but he was not as warmly received as in Canada. American scientists were working on wireless communication and there was no wish to commit the US Government to agreements with a foreign national. The only business success achieved in New York was on 1 April 1902 when the rights to exploit Marconi's inventions in America were transferred at an agreed price to the American Marconi Company whose shares were now opened to public subscription. By 12 April 1902 Marconi was at sea again on the way back to England in the *Majestic* where he had time to write a long letter to Solari giving him the results of the *Philadelphia* experiments and describing his plans for the future, with some ideas he had of interest to the Italian Government.

All controversy about whether he could send signals across the Atlantic was silenced by the time Marconi landed in England but the unpleasant attack upon him by Silvanus P. Thompson about priority of invention and abuse of the patent laws provoked a hostile reply from Marconi and a rejoinder from Thompson.[7] Marconi's use of the Italian Navy mercury detector caused much comment, and explanation was sought by the Press when it was revealed in the Patent Office Journal that Marconi had asked that a patent application of his in connection with the device be amended to an 'application for a patent for an invention communicated to him from abroad by the Marquis Luigi Solari of Italy'. Marconi had little time, taste or talent for public argument in the Press and he had endured a great deal of it recently in connection with the transatlantic signals and the Anglo-American Telegraph Company. His predilection was to crush paper critics with scientific demonstration and he might well have felt that he had no other chance of winning against Thompson of whom it was said,[8] 'There is no doubt that so far Professor Thompson has had the best of the arguments, but he would be likely to have that whether right or wrong.' In this particular case Marconi felt that he was close to producing a new magnetic detector which would be greatly superior to the mercury detector given him by his friend Solari. This, he thought, was the way to close the argument for all practical purposes. The new magnetic detector, an improved and reliable version of an earlier model by Rutherford, was described by Marconi in a paper before the Royal Society on 12 June 1902, and it was patented and used with great success by the Marconi Company for many years.

Before leaving for America in the *Philadelphia* Marconi had discussed future plans with Solari who was visiting England. He told his friend that he expected to prove the feasibility of long-range communication over water, but he wanted to be equally sure that the intervention of a large land mass would not prevent signals passing between two stations. Only when this second point was established could he proceed with confidence towards his goal of a wireless system covering the world. Marconi wanted a ship placed at his disposal so that he could sail from England down into the Mediterranean and test whether the Poldhu signals could still be detected after they had crossed the hills and plains of Europe. The Italian Navy possessed a small number of wireless sets with which they were well pleased, and Marconi stations were being built to communicate between Rome and Sardinia. Marconi hoped that this favourable acquaintance with his equipment, and the fame he had acquired with the transatlantic S's, would persuade the Italian Government to agree to his proposal that a warship be made available to him for trials. Solari was about to return to Italy and Marconi asked him to put the case in Rome, mentioning that the British Admiralty would probably provide a cruiser but that he would prefer to carry out such important work in a vessel from his own country. Marconi's letter to Solari from the *Majestic*[9] not only gave the results obtained in the *Philadelphia* to support the case but added that the successful outcome of the proposed trials in an Italian warship could lead to the provision of a station to communicate between the mainland of Italy and ships anywhere in the Mediterranean and, even more attractive politically, other stations to communicate with the Italian possessions in Eritrea and with South America where there were large colonies of Italian emigrants.

Solari discharged his commission well in Rome. He spoke to friends in the Ministry of Marine, to the Minister himself, and he was granted an audience with the King. Fortunately for Marconi his proposal fitted in very well with the immediate plans of the Government to send to England the *Carlo Alberto*, a new cruiser and the pride of the Regia Marina. She was to represent Italy at the Spithead Naval Review taking place in June in honour of the coronation of Edward VII. It was hoped that exhibiting this fine modern vessel to all the influential foreign visitors gathered in England for the celebrations would help to secure for the comparatively new united nation of Italy recognition as an equal partner by her European neighbours. The publicity inevitably attracted by Marconi would reinforce the impression of Italy as an up and

121

coming young country. It was arranged that Solari should join the *Carlo Alberto* to superintend the wireless equipment when she sailed from Italy for England under the flag of Admiral Mirabello. Marconi would come on board when she reached England and the experiments with Poldhu would be carried out on the return trip to Italy in July 1902.

As the *Carlo Alberto* steamed up the Channel from Italy she put in towards the great Lizard promontory and the ship's company were able to see in the distance the tall masts of Poldhu to which they would be connected by an invisible string of dots and dashes for the next six months in every sort of weather and sea condition as they sailed with Marconi through waters as widely separated as the Gulf of Finland, the Mediterranean and the Canadian North Atlantic. No one on board had any inkling that there would be such a long involvement with Poldhu, as Cornwall dropped out of sight over the port quarter and they steamed on towards Portland. But within a day or two of their arrival King Edward was operated on for appendicitis and the naval review was postponed indefinitely.

The future movements of the *Carlo Alberto* were hurriedly reconsidered and it was decided that she should now take the King of Italy on a state visit to Czar Nicholas II, leaving England on 8 July for the Russian naval base at Kronstadt near St Petersburg. There was a tremendous rush to get extra wireless equipment aboard and to fit a new aerial suitable for long-range communication with Poldhu, but all was completed by the time Marconi was picked up at Dover by the ship, which had left her anchorage at Poole the night before. With Solari's help he at once started work on setting up and tuning the apparatus and very soon they were receiving signals from Poldhu. The night and day effect was quickly evident and whatever adjustments were made on board they never received signals during the day once the range exceeded 500 miles, although by night they eventually received signals in Kronstadt, 1600 miles from Poldhu with a significant part of the path lying over land in Sweden and Denmark.

During the time he spent on the *Carlo Alberto* Marconi

formed a close friendship with Admiral Mirabello who was a bachelor with a reputation for liking the more obvious enjoyments, of the social life which his career offered him. In his company Marconi showed his cheerier nature and when the time came for them to part the Admiral presented him with the *Carlo Alberto*'s flag and said that he regarded Marconi as a son and would never forget the time they had spent together.[10]

Solari describes a very rough night when he and Marconi were working in the radio cabin, with the Admiral looking on and filling the air with the smoke from one of his particularly strong cigars. The motion of the ship had already made Solari, unlike the other two, feel and look queasy, and the smoke cloud was making him feel even more uncomfortable, although this was not a point which could profitably be made by a lieutenant to his Admiral. The situation had however not escaped Marconi who asked the Admiral if he had not heard that a German professor had discovered that a column of smoke could be a barrier to electromagnetic waves. Mirabello at once threw his cigar out of the cabin and then, seeing Marconi's grin, recognised the trick and joined in the laughter.[11]

There were many invitations and social events to divert the crew of the *Carlo Alberto* while they were in Kronstadt, and many visitors came to look over the ship and perhaps catch a glimpse of young Marconi. On 16 July at the invitation of King Victor Emmanuel the Czar came on board to inspect the ship and its wireless installation. The Czar's Royal Yacht drew alongside to the sound of saluting guns and ceremonial cheers from the Russian and Italian crews, and Marconi waited nervously because the demonstration he had prepared for the occasion had only been working intermittently. But when the moment came, everything went well and the King and the Czar actually handled some of the equipment and saw signals being transmitted and received. Marconi, Mirabello and Solari were kept in discussion by the two rulers and their retinue for some time and Solari in particular was very much impressed by the 'air of goodness' about Czar Nicholas and could not understand how he could have become a symbol of cruelty to the Russian people.[12]

The *Carlo Alberto* left Kronstadt on 21 July 1902 and set course for Kiel where a large part of the German Fleet was at anchor. Marconi recorded that 'on the whole we were treated with remarkable coldness during our stay in Kiel.'[13] This may have been due to the German sense of national supremacy, particularly strong in the Navy, being offended by the appearance from abroad of a very smart modern cruiser possibly better than their own in conventional fighting qualities and obviously overwhelmingly superior in wireless communication. There were other possible reasons more particularly connected with Marconi and his Company. The German Government had been interested in Marconi's work as soon as he started his demonstrations in Britain with the Post Office, and it was in response to a German request that Professor Slaby was invited by Preece to witness one of these demonstrations. Slaby returned to Germany and set about developing a wireless system of his own which the Marconi Company felt infringed their patents in many respects although they were unwilling to enter into litigation in which they believed they would effectively be fighting the German Government. The Slaby system was fitted in German war-ships where it was believed to be giving ranges of less than 200 kilometres, and it had also been installed in certain German liners, although others used the Marconi system. The Kaiser's brother Prince Henry had recently travelled to the United States in the Marconi-equipped *Kronprinz Wilhelm* and had been impressed with the efficient handling of a large amount of wireless traffic. But he had returned in the *Deutschland*, which had Slaby equipment, and the Prince was amazed at the almost total lack of messages handled in the vessel, which did not communicate with any of the Marconi stations off New York or in the English Channel. The Germans considered that this was a deliberate slight to their Emperor's brother, while the Marconi Company main-tained that they would certainly have communicated with the *Deutschland* if they had been asked.

When the *Carlo Alberto* dropped anchor at Kiel Admiral Mirabello at once made his formal call upon the German Admiral. He mentioned, not without pride no doubt, that his ship was in communication with England and he invited the German Admiral aboard to witness the arrival of signals. The invitation was not accepted.

On the 26 July, a few days after the Italians had arrived in Kiel, they were informed that the Imperial Yacht *Hohenzollern* was expected at midnight with the Kaiser on board and they were ordered to fire a twenty-one-gun salute. Mirabello protested that his naval regulations did not prescribe the firing of salutes after sunset, but the order was repeated. Mirabello at once ordered steam to be raised and *Carlo Alberto* put to sea an hour before the Kaiser was due. Inevitably they passed the *Hohenzollern* just outside Kiel and Solari signalled the yacht asking the operator whether he wanted news from England, news received directly from the Marconi station at Poldhu. The German operator signalled that this was presumably a joke, and then transmitted a meaningless stream of dots and dashes to make further communication between the two vessels impossible. Both Solari and Mirabello regarded this as a victory; Marconi's feelings were not recorded.[14]

On this note the *Carlo Alberto* ended her unexpected cruise in northern waters and set course for Portsmouth where she arrived on 1 August to the more convivial atmosphere of England in Coronation Week. At the rearranged Coronation Naval Review she was given the place of honour next to King Edward's Royal Yacht *Victoria and Albert*.

Towards the end of August the Italian cruiser set off down the English Channel and once again the ship's company saw the masts of Poldhu. This time perhaps the sight meant more to them, and certainly they had a closer look because the *Carlo Alberto* anchored off the little bay and some of the officers came ashore to visit the station. Then finally, weeks later than originally intended, the cruiser weighed anchor and set off down through the Bay of Biscay with Marconi on board to test the reception of signals in the Mediterranean.

Most of the teething troubles with the cruiser's long-range equipment had been discovered and cured during the unplanned shakedown cruise to Russia, and communication with Poldhu was quickly and reliably established. In the wardroom, too, the ship's officers and the 'passengers' had settled into the easy fellowship which comes with shared experience in foreign parts. They put in at Ferrol and the local Italian consul, a rich Spaniard, was invited to dine on board. In an expansive moment after a good meal he decided to venture upon a speech in a mixture of Italian and Spanish, ending with a most unsuitable and ill-worded toast. There was, Solari wrote, '*silenzio glaciale*' and after an awful pause Mirabello replied sternly that it was not possible to accept the toast. Marconi jumped to his feet with his own toast. '*Viva l'Ammiraglio!*' he shouted, and the general embarrassment was over.[15]

On 4 September the ship arrived in the Straits of Gibraltar where Marconi proposed to carry out what he regarded as the crucial test of long-distance wireless by attempting to receive Poldhu with the ship steaming well in against the Spanish coast in the 'shadow' of the high ground. German scientists had already declared that the land mass would block all signals.

It had been arranged that Poldhu should transmit on every hour throughout the period of darkness and so Mirabello had reduced speed to come into position a little before 2 a.m. Marconi tried every possible adjustment in the radio cabin without success, and at 2.30 a.m. he had to tell the Admiral that he had detected nothing, always assuming that the transmission had in fact taken place and not been prevented by some fault at Poldhu. There was nothing to be done but try again at 3 a.m. If the ship was to be in a suitable test position at this time it meant that she must be taken into Gibraltar Bay. Mirabello did not welcome this course because there was dense fog and he knew that foreign warships were not allowed to achor in the Bay without previous permission. He decided therefore to steam very slowly in circles and hope thereby to give the desperately anxious Marconi sufficient time to try everything possible to pick up the 3 a.m. transmission.

Just after the hour, V's were picked up from Poldhu. Then the Morse printer tapped out the first message just at the moment when the searchlights from the British Fleet in the Bay groped towards the *Carlo Alberto* and lit up her hazy shape. Mirabello waited long enough to confirm that Marconi was satisfied with the message, and then he ordered full speed away into the fog before he could be interrogated on his ship's strange behaviour. The text of the crucial message was 'The Empress of Russia has had a miscarriage,' which caused the Admiral to remark that it was strange that a great failure should confirm a great success.

Messages were exchanged with Poldhu as the *Carlo Alberto* made her way through the Mediterranean towards Italy, and Marconi arranged, as he always did on such occasions, for the despatch of a ceremonial message of congratulation. It was sent from Poldhu to the ship where it was recorded and printed, ready to be handed to the King when they reached Italy. Marconi left the ship at Spezia, exchanging emotional farewells with the friends he was leaving behind now that the special-duties cruise of the *Carlo Alberto* was over. He went on to have discussions with officials about wireless within Italy and the possibility of a high-power station for overseas communication, and he was also invited to an audience with King Victor Emmanuel.

The King received him most cordially and recalled incidents they had shared in Russia and England during the *Carlo Alberto*'s cruise. Marconi explained the details of the tests between Poldhu and the ship, and told the King that he was now going to England and Canada to start the new commercial wireless service across the Atlantic between Glace Bay and Poldhu. Both men felt that much prestige would have accrued to their country if the venture had been supported by the Italian Government. The King telephoned Admiral Morin in the Ministry of Marine and it was arranged that the *Carlo Alberto* should sail to Canada to show the Italian flag in Glace Bay and, like the guard ship at a regatta, preside over the inaugural experiments as long as they lasted. Marconi was jubilant at the prospect of sailing again with his friends, but more especially he was very gratified with the thought that, as well as the scientific success achieved, the recent voyage in the *Carlo Alberto* had established his position as a man of importance to his native land, and one whose advice

127

and friendship were welcomed in the most influential circles in Italy.

Before he left for England Marconi visited his birthplace, and the citizens of Bologna prepared a great welcome. Prominent in the festivities was Professor Augusto Righi his neighbour at Villa Grifone in the old days when he first began to experiment with wireless. In his speech Righi said,

> I remember with great pleasure his visits when quite a young man, for asking my advice, for explaining his experiments, made with simple apparatus ingeniously put together, and for keeping me informed of his new projects, in which his passion for applied science always stood out.[16]

In view of the subsequent controversy about Righi's exact relation with Marconi these remarks seem to confirm the view that Righi was his neighbourly patron rather than his teacher.

Back in England Marconi attended to business affairs including a highly organised demonstration of wireless put on by the Company for the Colonial Premiers who were visiting London for the Coronation, and then he joined the *Carlo Alberto* in Plymouth and sailed for Canada. He was very much aware that his directors in London were relying on him to produce a big success which would boost the Company's fortunes and justify the enormous capital expenditure on the Glace Bay station and on its counterpart at Cape Cod in the United States. Solari sailed with him but, to everyone's regret on board, Admiral Mirabello had not been released from more important duties for this second unexpected cruise of the Italian Navy's show ship. They arrived at Glace Bay on 31 October 1902 having received the Poldhu signals by night all the way across the Atlantic.

From the start it was evident that a regular commercial service between Glace Bay and Poldhu was not to be easily achieved. The first transmission was made from the Canadian station on 19 November but Poldhu received nothing until the night of 28 November, and these signals were so weak that they could not be read. Still more adjustments were made by Marconi and his assistants, some of whom were beginning to doubt whether they would ever manage to hit upon the right arrangement of circuits to make the aerial radiate enough power at the correct frequency to be picked up in England. Then, at last, on 5 December the first readable signals were sent from west to east across the Atlantic and recorded by Woodward, a skilled receiver operator whom Marconi had chosen to operate the Poldhu equipment during the trials. There was great excitement and relief at Glace Bay, and the following day everyone waited impatiently for nightfall so that the success could be repeated and perhaps a few minor adjustments made which might still further improve the strength of the signals. But excitement gave way to mystified despair when all the hours of darkness passed without anything being received in Cornwall. It so happened that the frequency they were using was particularly susceptible to the minor variations in conditions in the ionosphere which occur like changes in the weather on the Earth's surface. During the next few nights the conditions sometimes allowed signals to pass, and more often they did not. Because Marconi and his assistants did not yet understand the nature and influence of the ionosphere they were only aware that identical experimental arrangements gave results ranging from very successful to complete failure. The essence of scientific progress lies in the reproducibility of results, and without this Marconi was extremely uncertain and uneasy when his directors pestered him to give the world a tangible sign that a commercial system was established, or at least not far off. On 14 December very good signals were received in Poldhu for a two-hour period, and with considerable reluctance Marconi was persuaded to allow the transatlantic service to be opened with a message sent the next night, 15 December 1902, to the *Times* by their correspondent, Parkin, who was at Glace Bay: '*Times* London. Being present at transmission in Marconi's Canadian station have honour to send through *Times* inventor's first transatlantic message of greeting to England and Italy. Parkin.'

During the next few nights, as and when conditions permitted, four more messages were sent. Predictably they presented formal homage from the Governor General of Canada and from Marconi to King Edward and King Victor Emmanuel. Protocol demanded that no one message should appear to have precedence over the others, and so all four were held at Poldhu until each had been checked and re-checked, a lengthy business with variable ionospheric conditions and atmospherics. It was not until 21 December that the checking was complete and the four messages were released simultaneously.

On 30 December Marconi was guest of honour at a banquet given in Sydney, the nearest town, a few miles from Glace Bay. But he listened to the speeches of praise and made suitable reply without the inward glow of self-satisfaction which should be present on such an occasion. He was well aware that only a handful of messages were being sent from Canada to England and that because of the unfavourable conditions the time taken to transmit and check each message was far too long for a serious commercial telegraph system.

However hard Marconi had tried to prevent his directors' premature claim to have a working commercial service he had no doubts about the eventual success or the importance which posterity would attach to the recent experiments. On 2 January Solari received orders from the Ministry of Marine to return to Rome and report on the Marconi experiments.[17] That evening the two men sat talking together in front of the fire until nearly midnight, and when they parted Marconi declared that he would never forget how Solari had been at his side almost continually during this most important period of his life and he gave him what Solari described as 'a fine photograph of himself with a dedication so flattering and affectionate that I was deeply moved'. Marconi said that in fifty years, when the two of them were no longer there, Solari's sons and grandsons would read the dedication and know how he had helped in the first conquest of space between America and Europe.

On 14 January Marconi left Glace Bay to supervise the first trials from Cape Cod station which had just been completed. This was intended to be the United States end of the commercial service to England, and its transmitter power at this time was only about 10 kilowatts whereas that at Glace Bay was 75 kilowatts. The plan was to send American messages from Cape Cod to Glace Bay and from there across the Atlantic. Because Poldhu only had 25 kilowatts of transmitter power it was not at this time intended to operate a service from England to Canada and the United States, and in any case such a service would have infringed the British Post Office's monopoly. But in spite of the ceremonial messages, the publicity and the celebratory banquets, it was clear to Marconi before he left Canada that more work was required before a true commercial service could operate across the Atlantic. Vyvyan, the Chief Engineer at Glace Bay, recorded[18] that some messages had to be sent as many as twenty-four times before they were received in England and he had particular cause to remember the disturbing effect of atmospherics. One of the messages was a personal one from him to the *Times* to have an announcement of the birth of his daughter published. The insertion was to read: 'Jan. 3rd. Wife of R. N. Vyvyan – a daughter.' But a particularly ill-timed burst of atmospherics caused the Morse machine at Poldhu to print an extra dot – letter 'e' – and the message then read 'Jane 3rd Wife of. . . .'

At the end of January Marconi left America for England to put in hand further development work. The transatlantic service, such as it was, was suspended and the *Carlo Alberto* left Glace Bay to show the Italian flag in South America. The service was briefly resumed in its original form a few weeks later to provide a news service from America for the *Times* which had pressed the Marconi Company hard for this facility which they thought would help them in the fierce newspaper competition of the time. The news service opened on 28 March and ended in fiasco on 6 April when the Glace Bay aerial fell down due to ice forming on the wires. All three of the transatlantic stations, Poldhu, Cape Cod, and Glace Bay, had now suffered the ignominy of losing their aerials because faulty mechanical design had not allowed sufficient strength to stand up to the local weather.

This was a miserable time for Marconi, working in an atmosphere of public failure and the gleeful criticism of rivals. As always, work offered escape from an unsympathetic world, but it was frustrating work with confusing and apparently contradictory results making progress painfully slow as, with no knowledge of the ionosphere, he tried to find ways to increase the reliable range. How he must have welcomed the chance to get away to the warmth and colour of Italy when he was invited home in May 1903 to be made a Citizen of Rome!

On his way to receive this great honour from Prince Colonna, the Mayor of Rome, Marconi went to Bologna for a few days with his mother and father. Giuseppe was now nearly eighty but he made the great effort and accompanied Annie and their son to the capital on 2 May 1903. Rome was having a week of festivities: King Edward VII had left on 1 May and the Kaiser was due to arrive on 3 May.

For Marconi there was a tremendous welcome at the station and he had to fight his way through great crowds to reach the carriage of the Mayor of Rome who had come to meet him. No sooner was he in the carriage than a large group of cheering students unhitched the horses and themselves pulled him to the Grand Hotel.

On 4 May Marconi was to address the Accademia dei Lincei – equivalent to the Royal Society of London – on wireless telegraphy. But the Kaiser, who had arrived in Rome in great state the day before, was on 4 May paying the visit to Pope Leo XIII which caused so much conjecture in European political and religious circles. The streets were crowded, and the congestion was made worse by the fact that the German Emperor did not go directly to the Vatican from the Quirinal where he was staying as the King of Italy's guest. So that he should give no offence to the Italian Government, the Kaiser had gone first to the German Embassy in the Vatican and had set out from there – diplomatically his own territory – to the Papal Palace. Marconi, held up by the crowds and the soldiers lining the route, was an hour and a half late for his lecture at the Accademia. He noted in recalling the incident:

As the newspapers wittily remarked, I who had been able to overcome the boundless wastes of the ocean was unable to overcome the resistance of a cordon of troops until the 'other Guglielmo', as the press termed Kaiser Wilhelm, had concluded his visit.[19]

That same night there was a dinner in honour of the Emperor at the Quirinal, and Marconi, who was also a guest, was presented to him by King Victor Emmanuel. The Kaiser was aware of the struggle to dominate world wireless communications going on between the English Marconi Company and government-supported interests in Germany. Possibly he did not realise that Germany was losing this race, but he certainly remembered the recent 'slight' upon his brother travelling on the *Deutschland* in almost complete wireless silence, and he might also have felt that the young Italian's presence neutralised to some extent the air of German supremacy which lay over the evening. Marconi noted:

The Kaiser's conversation with me and his general attitude were strangely characteristic of the role of omniscience which he had already assumed at that time. After having congratulated me on my work and my wireless he proceeded to tell me that he considered that I was wrong in 'attempting to obstruct wireless communications from German ships'. I told William of Hohenzollern that although I thanked him for his advice I felt confident both on technical and other grounds that the course of development for wireless telegraphy which I was following was the right one. . . . At dinner whenever the King of Italy tried to direct the conversation towards wireless telegraphy and its achievements the Kaiser just as resolutely headed it towards other subjects. Needless to say, owing to our natural Italian politeness and the fact that he was the King of Italy's guest, his efforts were quite successful.

The celebrations over, Marconi left Italy, no doubt refreshed by the climate of praise and stimulated by his brush with the Kaiser. He was back in England in time for Professor Fleming's famous – or notorious – lecture on wireless telegraphy at the Royal Institution in June 1903, when the extraordinary appearance of spoof messages provoked charges of 'scientific hooliganism'.

CHAPTER 9

COMPETITION, LITIGATION,
AND MARRIAGE

MARCONI returned to England to face three major struggles, each of which he rightly feared would be a long campaign of attrition rather than an exciting battle boldly undertaken and swiftly decided. The British Government was unwilling to grant him the commercial facilities he needed in England, the German Government was set on displacing him as the principal supplier of wireless equipment throughout the world, and the unknown laws of nature continued to thwart his attempts to realise a commercial transatlantic service.

The position within the United Kingdom was clearly indicated by an editorial in the *Electrician*:

> Mr Chamberlain's statement [in Parliament] as to wireless telegraphy matters, throws much light on recent controversies, and enables the public to form a clear judgement as to the questions at issue. It is not merely a question of giving Mr Marconi or his company facilities for wireless telegraphy, the company ask for an *exclusive right* to work wireless telegraphy in this country; they ask for permanence; and they ask that the Post Office should act as receiving and forwarding agents for their transatlantic service, just as that department does for the cable companies.[1]

Certain other factors affected the political decision on the fundamental matter of a Marconi monopoly. The cable companies felt threatened by long-range wireless, particularly so because the Postmaster-General, Austen Chamberlain, had gone on to say in the House of Commons that he was awaiting events before establishing new cable routes. The Admiralty was concerned that the high-power signals needed

135

for transatlantic communication might interfere with naval wireless. There was also the complication that an agreement already existed with Lloyd's providing for the exclusive use of Marconi equipment in their many signalling stations and in the vessels of a dozen shipping lines.

The Post Office delivered its first thrust on the last day of 1902:

Sir, I am directed by the Post Master General to acquaint you for the information of the directors of the Marconi Wireless Telegraph Co. Ltd. that he has carefully considered your letter of 10 Oct. last in which you refer to an interview with Lord Londonderry in April 1901 and ask for an exclusive licence for the practice of wireless telegraphy between England and ships at sea, between England and foreign countries, and between England and the British colonies. The Post Master General has referred to the records relating to the interview in 1901 but he cannot find that his predecessor gave any such intimation as you suggest in your letter and I am to say that it is not in his power to give the licence for which you now apply.[2]

This terse note from the Post Office opened the intensive period of official and irregular negotiations leading to the Wireless Telegraphy Act of Great Britain which came into force three years later on 1 January 1905. Marconi wrote formally to the Postmaster-General setting out the conditions which he thought should exist between his Company and the Government, and explaining the need to justify the large capital sums already expended, and the additional money needed, to set up the transatlantic service.[3] Austen Chamberlain suggested discussions particularly of the situation created by the exclusive contract between Marconi and Lloyds.'[4] Questions were raised in Parliament, Henniker Heaton, M.P., a close friend of Marconi continually put the Company's case in public and private, and the matter was commented on at length in the technical and lay Press.

Marconi played his part too in the less public areas of the negotiations and regular letters to him from the Managing

Director, Cuthbert Hall, showed how carefully considered were the tactics of exerting influence. Commenting on a luncheon which Marconi had arranged with Austen Chamberlain's successor as Postmaster-General. Cuthbert Hall wrote:

It is very likely that you may get some valuable information at the proposed lunch and the chief danger is that some conclusion may be arrived at which may involve our addressing a letter to the Post Office which discloses the fact that the business has been settled apart from the permanent officials. If therefore you can so steer matters that any action which has to be taken as a result of the interview is taken by the Post Office it will be advantageous. If Lord Stanley goes to the Post Office after the interview and says, 'I met Mr Marconi at lunch the other day when we thought the following course might be adopted and I think we should write to the Company in the following terms,' the permanent officials have an opportunity of discussing the matter before the Post Office is officially committed, and at any rate of appearing to be keeping the reins in their hands.

I dare say Lord Stanley will try to persuade you (as Austen Chamberlain tried to persuade us) that it would be to our advantage to accept any licence which the Post Office will give us. But having regard to the bad faith which the Government has again and again displayed in its dealings with us in the past, it would be reprehensible for us to accept any arrangement which is not a business-like one. . . .

Even if Austen Chamberlain had not so clumsily let the cat out of the bag the intention of the Government would be very clear. They see that wireless is fraught with all sorts of possibilities and that finality has not nearly been reached. They wish therefore to remain in a position to take the whole thing over without paying compensation to us when they can work it successfully themselves, or to shut the whole thing up if it suits their convenience for naval purposes or because of the cable interests. . . .

At the present moment I consider we hold the cards in our hands because it is no mere bluff to say that if we do not

137

get security here for the fruits of our enterprise the business will be established elsewhere. . . .

I should give Lord Stanley to understand that the Board is with difficulty restrained from proceeding at once to establish in a foreign country, without saying which. If he asks I should say that this is a matter which we are not free to discuss but that a contract is already signed giving us the necessary security if we choose to establish the station – the European terminus of transatlantic telegraphy.[5]

Cuthbert Hall was a great believer that in any negotiation with a government 'the permanent official is the key to the situation' and he felt that anyone who failed to recognise this fact was foolish. He wrote to Marconi of one such man that he was 'heart and soul with us and is a most persistent person and has I think a certain weight in the House and in the country'[6] but that in seven years of seeking to influence affairs the fellow had not recognised the importance of 'securing the public official' and that he was not therefore 'the most intelligent agent'. In another matter of Company business Cuthbert Hall wrote to Marconi,

One official who will settle a certain matter has drafted for us the form of our application to himself. There is nothing corrupt in this arrangement, he sees an advantage in our apparatus being adopted and desires that the matter shall be properly handled.[7]

But no matter how helpful the pressure exerted by Marconi and his fellow directors through influential friends, the credibility of their case for a monopoly was much reduced by the fact that the transatlantic service was not working. So much of the argument concerned this service: the advantages which it would bring to the country, the necessity for it to be run by the same company which provided the ship-to-shore services so that frequencies could be properly controlled to prevent interference, and the importance of integrating the service with Post Office inland communications. Unfortunately it was obvious in 1903 and 1904 when the negotiations were in progress that the Marconi Company was quite unable to provide such a commercial transatlantic service.

By the time the arguments had dragged on to some sort of conclusion and the Parliamentary lawyers had drafted the Bill, the Marconi Company got less than they had hoped for. When the Wireless Telegraphy Act of Great Britain became law on 1 January 1905 there was no exclusive monopoly, but it was laid down that Post Office permission must be obtained before any wireless station could be operated in Great Britain, and the Marconi Company was given licences for all its shore stations for eight years. Ship-to-shore messages passing through these stations would in future be accepted by the Post Office for onward transmission over inland telegraph lines in the same way as cablegrams. But although the Company had not won all its points, Cuthbert Hall was told that certain permanent officials and members of the Government 'were going around breathing out vengeance against him'. He reported this fact to Marconi with a certain satisfaction but it was soon apparent that some of these vengeful officials had kept a rod in pickle for the Company.

In 1909 the Post Office declared that they themselves wished to operate those shore stations which handled messages for ships. They made a cash offer which the Company was constrained to accept because it was made clear that, in any case, Marconi's licences to operate the stations would certainly not be renewed when they expired in what was by then only four years' time.[8] The nine shore stations were transferred to the Post Office in September 1909 together with a licence on all existing and future Marconi patents relevant to ship-shore operation.

The path of developing official recognition, interest, and control followed for wireless telegraphy in England was repeated internationally during roughly the same period of half a dozen years at the beginning of the 1900s. Sectional interests opposed Marconi on this wider front as they had done in Britain. In this case the struggle was with Germany whose aggressive policy in support of her own wireless interests was in line with her general diplomatic attitude at this time.

German interest in Marconi dated back to the very early

trials in England, when Preece had been asked through diplomatic channels to invite Professor Slaby to attend. The German wireless system was based upon Slaby's subsequent work, and the contention between the Telefunken Company and Marconi's Company intensified between 1900 and 1914 in step with the growing antagonism between Germany and England. There had been claims and counterclaims about performance and patents, the incident between Marconi in the *Carlo Alberto* and the German Fleet in Kiel, the row about Marconi stations not accepting messages from Prince Henry of Prussia travelling in the *Deutschland*, and Marconi's personal brush with the Kaiser in Rome. The Marconi Company would not employ Germans or allow them to inspect its stations and Vyvyan recorded how he frustrated what he believed to be a deliberate attempt by the German Navy to smuggle a party into the transatlantic station at Glace Bay after they had been refused entry at the gate.[9] Captain Jackson wrote from his ship in the Mediterranean that the Germans were determined to erect a high-power station in Berlin for communicating with their Fleet, and Cuthbert Hall considered this to be good news because it would probably involve their spending a lot of money to no purpose.[10]

On 4 August 1903 in Berlin a conference was held of delegates from the Great Powers and it was there agreed, with some reservations, that governments should be recommended to make it obligatory for all coastal stations to communicate with any vessel no matter what wireless system it carried. This conference had been called by Germany with the specific object of making illegal the Marconi Company's rule that its shore stations must only communicate with ships fitted with Marconi equipment. Despite intensive lobbying by the Company the proposals of the 1903 Berlin Conference were formally ratified by the full International Wireless Conference held in Madrid in October 1906, by which time the control of the British coastal stations was in the hands of the Post Office. Any possibility of a Marconi monopoly in the supply of maritime wireless was now killed for ever.

During the protracted arguments, national and international, about the legislation and control of wireless there were many criticisms of Marconi and his Company, made by people who considered a monopoly in maritime communications to be against the public interest, or who thought Marconi's claims to be extravagant and misleading, or who welcomed any chance of handicapping a competitor who had established a handsome lead by being first in the field. Of all the attempts to undermine Marconi's standing perhaps the strangest was that which took place before a distinguished audience at the Royal Institution on the evening of 4 June 1903.

Professor Fleming of University College London had been engaged for some years now as consultant to the Marconi Company and he was to give a set of lectures on wireless telegraphy at the Royal Institution. Marconi had attended the first of these on 28 May 1903 and had then gone down to Poldhu from where it was planned that he should send messages to the Royal Institution for Fleming's second lecture on 4 June. At this lecture there were to be demonstrations of the receipt of wireless messages from University College and from the Marconi factory at Chelmsford. A telegram of greeting had been sent from the President of the Royal Society to Marconi at Poldhu and it was intended that a reply should be sent to Professor Dewar PRS by wireless. But because the temporary aerial at the Royal Institution was only about sixty feet high, the message would go from Poldhu to Chelmsford and be relayed from there to London.

The lecture started at 5 p.m. and at 5.45 the receiver began to print out a number of 'messages' containing exclamations such as 'Rats!' and derogatory remarks about Marconi.

The morning after, Fleming wrote to Marconi:

Everything went off well yesterday at the R.I. and we got through your reply to the President's telegram both before and at the lecture perfectly, and I have the tapes this morning from Chelmsford. There was however a dastardly attempt to jamb [sic] us; though where it came from I cannot say. I was told that Maskelyne's assistant was at the lecture and sat near the receiver.[11]

141

The next day Fleming wrote again to Marconi saying that he had found out a little more about the incident and that someone had deliberately tried to 'wreck the whole show' by putting strong electric currents into the earth nearby. He continued:

As it was a purely scientific experiment carried out for the benefit of the R.I. it was a ruffianly act to attempt to upset it, and quite outside the 'rules of the game'. If the enemy will try that on at the R.I. they will stick at nothing and it might be well to let them know. If we are exposed to this risk I question whether it is worthwhile to make any further show on June 19 [when he was giving another lecture on wireless at the R.I.].

It was soon revealed that Fleming was incorrect about the method of injecting the spurious messages into his apparatus, but correct about the name of the culprit. Neville Maskelyne wrote to the *Times* on 12 June 1903 to say that he had transmitted wireless signals from the roof of the Egyptian Theatre in Piccadilly, which was less than half a mile from the Royal Institution. Assisting him was a fifteen-year-old boy who, over fifty years later, confirmed Maskelyne's account.[12] Neville was the son of the famous illusionist J. N. Maskelyne who owned the Egyptian Theatre and who had used a form of wireless telegraphy in a thought-reading act. The purpose of the demonstration directed against Fleming's lecture was to disprove Marconi's exaggerated claims that his wireless communication was secret and could not be intercepted or interfered with in any way.

Much press coverage was given to the affair and it prompted letters and editorials in many different publications. The *Times, Morning Leader, Daily Express, Star, St James's Gazette, Illustrated Scientific News* and the *Electrician* were some of those printing news or comment under such headings as 'Scientific Hooliganism', 'Rats!', and 'Wireless Plot'. Details of the lecture itself – for example the authenticity of the message from Poldhu to Professor Dewar – were closely questioned in the correspondence columns and, more generally, all the arguments were again paraded for and against the Marconi style of conduct. An editorial piece in the *Electrician* was a warning to academic scientists tempted out from their university laboratories into the dusty business arena:

If it turns out that Mr Maskelyne made use of extraordinary means to upset the lecture Prof. Fleming has some grounds for his protest. But if, as we think, the means employed were fair, and such as might be encountered in practice, then the protest must be made by the public against the Professor. In his dual capacity of savant at a learned institution and expert to a commercial undertaking Professor Fleming is discovering that while the public have nothing but courtesy and respect to offer to the one, they have searching criticism and still more searching experiment to oppose, if need be, to the statements of the other. When the philosopher stoops to commerce he must accept the conditions of commerce. . . . It is ridiculous for him to appeal in his dilemma to the reverence which we all feel for the traditions of the Royal Institution. Faraday, to begin with, would never have placed himself in so anomalous a position, and moreover Faraday would have displayed more interest in what Mr Neville Maskelyne was trying to discover than in what, if we are to believe Mr Maskelyne's statement, Professor Fleming was seeking for commercial reasons to withhold from public knowledge.[13]

The stir which Maskelyne succeeded in creating was particularly unwelcome to Marconi in the middle of 1903 when things were not going well for his Company and anything to its discredit, no matter how stale or unjustified the argument, hindered the delicate negotiations being conducted with the British and foreign governments. Whether Maskelyne stood to gain personally from any discomfiture of Marconi is not certain, but he had been concerned with Hozier of Lloyd's in 1900 in a business venture with wireless, and in 1905 he was acting as an agent for de Forest's Company.[14]

The month after the Maskelyne affair it was a pleasant change for Marconi to find himself the centre of the kind of publicity which he liked and sought. It was a royal occasion, with the Prince of Wales and a distinguished party being shown over the station at Poldhu from which the historic S's had been transmitted across the Atlantic. Flags decorated the tall masts, and the local villagers stood in the sunshine at the side of the cliff-top road to watch the royal party drive past in their upright Edwardian motor cars.

Marconi gave his visitors a demonstration in the style which he had perfected during many such performances in front of distinguished and influential audiences in the past seven years. During these years the Company had grown so that it was now much more Marconi's employer than just his instrument, and there was evidence of this now in the firm indication given to Marconi by the Managing Director about the way in which the royal visit should be handled.[15] In particular, reporters, although allowed on to the site, were to be kept out of the station buildings, and the staff were given most rigid instructions not to discuss with anyone, including the royal suite, the telegram service between England, America and Canada. All such questions were to be referred to Marconi who would state that Poldhu was being reconstructed to incorporate recent important discoveries and that the present work at the station was largely experimental.

Since what Marconi had regarded as the premature announcement of a full commercial transatlantic service in December 1902 and the abrupt cessation of the limited press service when the masts fell down in April 1903 the Marconi Company had been extremely sensitive about its transatlantic telegrams. Marconi was embarrassed by the failure and wanted to push on with experimental work on aerial design and high-power transmitters so that the service could be re-established as soon as possible on a reliable basis. But the Board of Directors considered that the best interests of the Company lay elsewhere, and instead of continuing experiments in England Marconi was required to sail to New York to attend to some business connected with American patents. On the journey over and back in the *Lucania* he was to confirm the feasibility of providing a daily news service for passengers all the way across the Atlantic by wireless communication with either the long-range station at Poldhu or with Glace Bay on the other side. The Cunard Company had declared that they were interested in this project and the Marconi Board hoped and expected that it would quickly be a source of badly needed revenue.

Marconi sailed for New York on 28 August 1903 with a party which included Woodward, his receiver expert, and observers from the British and Italian Navy. The Italian was Marconi's friend Solari who was soon to become the Company's full-time representative in Italy. The reception of signals from Poldhu and Glace Bay was very satisfactory, contact being maintained with one or the other during the whole voyage and there being a long overlap in mid-Atlantic when signals were received from both sides by day as well as by night. Marconi arranged to stay in America just over a month, leaving his equipment on board the *Lucania* so that he could continue the experiments during the return trip.

Much of Marconi's time in New York was taken up with a patent case brought by the American Marconi Company against a rival company whose aggressive management and technical ability were winning for it a large share of the United States market. This was the de Forest Company which was not only taking a good share of new markets but was also making inroads into traditional Marconi areas. They had arranged with the British Post Office to demonstrate wireless transmission across the Irish Sea between Holyhead and Dublin,[16] de Forest equipment was installed in Sir Thomas Lipton's yacht *Erin* which had just escorted his racers *Shamrock II* and *III* across the Atlantic for the America's Cup series,[17] and the de Forest Company was under contract to report these races for the American Publishers Press.

Marconi's other patent business to be transacted while in the United States was with Edison whose standing as an inventor was very high in America and whose support had been so welcome to Marconi when doubts were cast on his first claim to have received the S's in Newfoundland. Edison was preoccupied with his scientific work to the point of eccentricity and cared little for appearances or material comforts, as Marconi and Solari discovered when they visited

145

him at his house outside New York to find that his wife was away, Edison had given the servants the day off, and the three men had to forage through a near-empty larder to find some sort of snack lunch when their keen discussion was halted by hunger.

Long ago in 1885 Edison had experimented with what he called a space telegraph which used a mast about a hundred feet tall with a plate at the top which induced electrical charges on a similar plate some distance away. Marconi was not interested in this system, which Edison had patented, but the elevated aerial was a key feature of his own patents and he feared that if Edison's patent fell into the hands of competitors they might somehow contrive a troublesome case in the courts. Fortunately Edison admired the way young Marconi had overcome great difficulties to achieve his dream of long-distance wireless. He had in fact already been approached by a group wanting to buy this patent but he had sensed that they intended to make trouble and had stipulated that it should be sold only to Marconi who was thus able to conclude the deal successfully in 1903.[18]

Marconi sailed back to England in October 1903 on the *Lucania,* continuing his experiments during the voyage with the equipment left on board since his outward journey less than six weeks before. The pace of his business life became even faster and more demanding during the next few months. He sailed to Gibraltar on board H.M.S. *Duncan,* commanded by Capt. Henry Jackson, and supervised tests of long-range reception from Poldhu. This followed the completion of an agreement for the supply of equipment and technical information to the Royal Navy up to the year 1914 and for the Admiralty to have the use of a long-range station for twenty minutes each day. He made several journeys to Italy and Montenegro in connection with the inauguration of a wireless service across the Adriatic to speed up telegraph communication between Italy and the Balkans. He visited Scotland to establish a land station over five hundred miles from Poldhu to make more systematic tests of long-range transmission than were possible on a passenger ship on a regular transatlantic run. He spent time at the Haven Hotel,

Poole, on fundamental experimental work, he attended business meetings in London, and he crossed the Atlantic twice more to supervise the inauguration of the regular Cunard Daily News Service.

During these busy months Marconi still managed to find time for a little self-indulgence and once again the relaxed life of a transatlantic liner and the production of a ship's newspaper combined to provide an atmosphere which he found romantically overwhelming as he had a few years before on board the *St Paul* with Josephine Holman. This time the woman who captured not only his heart but his proposal of marriage was Inez Milholland, and he became engaged to this good-looking lively American with strong views on social and political matters.[19]

With the Company under pressure in its negotiations with the British Post Office and experiencing strong commercial competition from German and American rivals the demands made upon Marconi at this time were particularly heavy. He had to travel the world to advance or protect the Company's interests in patent courts and government lobbies, and to set up commercial stations on land and at sea. But all this time his driving interest was in the long-range problem and he sought every opportunity for trial and test which would lead him towards the improvements he needed for his stations at Poldhu, Cape Cod, Glace Bay, and now the most powerful of all being built at Coltano for the Italian Government.

In the midst of this specially busy and worrying period in Marconi's life old Giuseppe, now nearly eighty, died in Bologna on 28 March 1904 but Guglielmo was not able to find time to go to Italy for his father's funeral. Indeed, that summer Marconi's mother, writing from Italy on paper with the thick black edge of early widowhood, asked a Mr Kershaw at the Company's London office if he could confirm that her son was receiving her letters and if he could give any forecast of Marconi's movements in the near future. Mr Kershaw often corresponded with Annie, forwarded her letters to her son, and made travel arrangements for her when she came to England.[20]

147

War broke out between Russia and Japan in February 1904 and Marconi's wireless equipment was engaged on both sides. As soon as war commenced the Russian Government asked the Company to provide field stations for the Army and this equipment was taken out from England and assembled and tested by Marconi staff. It worked well throughout the campaign, although the English engineers were greatly surprised by the rigours of the Russian winter and astonished when priests sprinkled holy water on the apparatus in a blessing ceremony which instantly short-circuited the high-voltage supply with a terrifying crashing spark which put the station out of action.[21] On the Japanese side Marconi equipment had been installed and working in the Navy for some time before the war. As soon as the *Carlo Alberto* had returned to Spezia in 1902 from her cruise to Russia and England with Marconi on board, an emissary of the Imperial Japanese Navy had visited the ship and arranged to be supplied with Marconi equipment and training in its use at sea. Later it was generally accepted that the crushing defeat of the Russian Fleet was to a significant extent due to the superiority of the Japanese wireless equipment over that of the Russian Navy which – unlike the Russian Army – was not using Marconi apparatus.[22]

But although the ultimate analysis of the Russo-Japanese war was satisfactory to the Marconi Company its immediate effect was to cause considerable disturbance and worry to Marconi and the rest of the Board. Again the cause of their discomfiture was Lee de Forest.

In January 1904, the month before hostilities commenced, de Forest had persuaded the war correspondent of the *Times*, who was on his way to the Far East, that by using wireless he could scoop other journalists reporting the expected naval battles in the Yellow Sea and the Gulf of Korea.[23] In a matter of days the Marconi Company had somehow got wind of this proposal and Cuthbert Hall was writing to Marconi and discussing with newspaper owner Alfred Harmsworth[24] how the *Daily Mail* might steal the *Times*'s thunder. Harmsworth said that de Forest had permission from the Government to erect a station at Weihaiwei, the British naval base leased on the mainland of China, and the plan was to transmit despatches to this station from a ship fitted with de Forest equipment and cruising within a radius of a few hundred miles wherever action seemed most likely to occur. These despatches would then be cabled to London but with a start of many hours on those sent by correspondents who had to wait for their own, or their reporter's, vessel to return to port. Harmsworth considered that if the Marconi Company could get him a wireless despatch to print in the *Daily Mail* before the *Times* had had a chance to publish one from de Forest, then the *Times* scheme would be stopped 'as it is a case of first in the field'. Cuthbert Hall believed that it might also stop the de Forest Company, and he asked for quick action from Marconi who thought that the Italian Government might be persuaded to allow such a message to be carried over the wireless link between its embassy in Peking and an Italian vessel at sea. However, in spite of much high-speed effort by Cuthbert Hall, Solari and Marconi – who was working on the experimental station in Scotland – the de Forest Company and the *Times* brought off their scoop and reported 'by wireless' the naval battles around Port Arthur.

There was trouble too for Marconi from an old adversary who once had opposed as a scientist but who now was a commercial rival. Lodge had joined with Muirhead, and their syndicate was beginning to take business from the Marconi Company. They, like de Forest, had been invited by the Post Office to demonstrate wireless communication across the Irish Sea, they supplied equipment for the British Army Manœuvres in 1903, and their apparatus was being adopted by the Government of India.

For the 1st and 2nd Army Corps Manœuvres of 1903 in England, Lodge–Muirhead equipment was attached to the 2nd Corps and Marconi's to the 1st Corps. Both systems performed much as expected by their designers and there was little to choose between them. But the British Army was not yet ready to welcome an unfamiliar communication system. The General commanding the Royal Engineers of the 2nd Corps summed up the results in September 1903 by saying that the aerial was too cumbersome in packing and that a range of fifteen miles was not of great value in the field. He considered that wireless telegraphy in its present form was scarcely suited for military purposes but he agreed that there should be further experiments.[25]

Since April 1902 the Marconi Company's agents in Calcutta had been trying to persuade the Indian Government to use wireless in the Bay of Bengal.[26] They pointed out that the British Admiralty and Lloyd's were using the Marconi system, and they offered to fit up stations at their own expense with the stipulation that the installations should only be taken over and paid for by the authorities when the success of the system had been proved. But Simpson, the Electrician to the Indian Government Telegraph Department, preferred the Lodge–Muirhead system and had used it in experiments to join the Andaman Islands to the general telegraph system of India by wireless to the mainland of Burma.[27] In June 1904 he reported:

> I also recommend that we adhere to the Lodge–Muirhead system in our experiments as I am still of the opinion it is the best available. That it is affected by atmospherics is true, but so also are admittedly the Marconi and Slaby–Arco systems. The Fessenden system claims to be unaffected by atmospheric disturbances, but the claim has yet to be substantiated.
>
> In spite of what appears for obvious reasons in Newspapers and Company Reports, there is no doubt that up to date no system has really yet evolved beyond the experimental stage.

Simpson's recommendations were adopted, but the subsequent Marconi–de Forest litigation in America raised doubts about whether the Indian Government could use equipment other than Marconi's without risk of legal proceedings. Neville Maskelyne, who was acting for the de Forest Company in London, was summoned to the India Office to give his views, and British legal opinion was consulted.[28] A minute in the India Office file recorded that a telegram was being drafted to the Government of India stating:

... no objection to their continuing to use either the Lodge–Muirhead or de Forest system of wireless telegraphy, in spite of the uncertainty existing as to the validity of the claim of the Marconi Company that they hold a master patent covering all forms of aerial telegraphy.

Finally in June 1905 the Secretary of State for India informed the Viceroy:

I am advised that it is doubtful whether the view taken by the American Courts would be upheld in English law. Pending any litigation in this country or India between the rival patentees, I see no objection to your continuing to use Lodge–Muirhead or de Forest systems. . . .

The Marconi Company privately shared the view of the India Office about the uncertain strength of its patent position vis-à-vis the Lodge–Muirhead Syndicate and, in fact, after some years of worry, particularly about Lodge's tuning patents, the Company bought out the Lodge–Muirhead Syndicate and took over its patents.

In 1904 Marconi was thirty years old, famous, rich, and single. He enjoyed sailing and the social life that went with it, and he liked driving his Mercedes up to London from wherever he happened to be working, or perhaps to a friend's country house. He was welcomed, indeed sought after, as a guest at fashionable receptions in Town and at elaborately organised Edwardian weekends in the country. Hard pressed though he was with business affairs at this time he zealously pursued a social life. When he was down working in the makeshift laboratories at the Haven Hotel he frequently lunched with his friends the Van Raaltes, who owned Brownsea Island a few miles away across Poole Harbour. One day in the summer of 1904 when Marconi came across in his boat he found that Mrs Van Raalte had sent one of her house guests down to the jetty to meet him. The guest was an attractive young girl of nineteen, Beatrice O'Brien.[29]

Her father, the thirteenth Baron Inchiquin, who sat as an

Irish peer in the House of Lords, owned an estate at Dromoland in County Clare and a house in London. Bea's home life
was warm and lively with six brothers and seven sisters, and
the house in Ireland filled with her brothers' school or university friends during the holidays. The house and estate were
kept running smoothly, indeed lavishly, by a great number of
servants and tenants but there was no large reserve of family
capital. When Bea was fifteen her father died and the estate
passed into the hands of the eldest son, leaving Bea's mother
with eight daughters on her hands and a very inadequate
income. She moved to a large rented house in London and
set about establishing places for her daughters in society, with
good marriages very much in mind. During visits to England
when their father was alive the children had frequently stayed
at the country homes of some of their very large circle of
relations and family friends. Bea played with the royal
children from Sandringham when she was staying nearby with
relations, and her friendship with one of them, Princess Ena,
brought her comfort at a difficult time later in her life. Lady
Inchiquin's difficulties were not in securing for her daughters
the entrée to the right houses and parties, but in finding the
money to fit them out and properly maintain them in such
society.

When Marconi first saw Bea she was not sophisticated or
rich like many of the women who 'for some years now had
thrown themselves (or their daughters) at his head and would
for the rest of his life go on throwing themselves at him'.[30]
Certainly she was pretty, and one of the brightest of the group
of flirting, joking young men and girls who were her usual
companions. But her appearance was anything but smart and
she was noticeably ill at ease in Marconi's presence, intimidated
by his fame and his thirty-year-old maturity. Nevertheless
Marconi was strongly attracted and he visited the Island
often during the next few days, making an opportunity to
mention that he was asking Inez Milholland to release him
from their engagement, and he returned to London as soon as
Bea did. In London the pursuit continued, and very soon he
proposed. Bea asked for a few days to consider the matter,
and then turned him down.

Marconi went off abroad about his business but he treated his rejection by Bea as he dealt with a failure in his scientific work: he quietly worked out plans for another more successful attempt. This is not to say that he was unmoved by the refusal: he apparently even told his mother all about Bea, and then worried that this was indiscreet, because he ended a letter to her from the *Arabic* on the way to America in September 1904: 'Please don't tell people what I told you about the Irish girl.'[31]

By December 1904 Mrs Van Raalte was once more taking a hand at matchmaking. She had Bea to stay again on Brownsea Island and then wrote to Marconi, who was abroad, and invited him too. This time his courtship was carefully prepared and successful. Bea accepted his proposal, subject to family approval, and they returned to London where he bought her an expensive ring and called on her mother. Lady Inchiquin disapproved, but referred the matter to her son, the head of the family, and in due course he agreed with his mother.

By the time Bea's brother had indicated his disapproval Marconi was in Rome on business and Bea was miserable and angry, and gave her family a thoroughly bad time because she was now absolutely set on the marriage. Her unhappiness was increased when her attention was meanly drawn to newspaper reports that Marconi was being much seen in the company of an Italian princess and that there were rumours of an engagement. But Marconi had also seen the reports and at once came back to London to declare again his love to Bea and to win over the family. His persuasiveness, his obvious concern for Bea, the fact that he was considered by many to be a very good match, and that, surprisingly, he was a Protestant, all combined with Bea's nagging to reverse the earlier refusal and they were married on 16 March 1905.

The wedding celebrations might almost appear to have been planned to stretch beyond endurance the nerves of a young Irish girl and an Italian man of the world who scarcely knew each other and now found themselves locked in the closest of relationships. The ceremony itself was turned into a public spectacle with crowds besieging St George's Church in Hanover

Square. It was hours before they could get away from the reception and then they had to face the overnight journey across the Irish Sea to Dromoland which Bea's brother, who was in London to give her away, had lent them for the honeymoon. It was the first time that Bea had seen her old home since the death of her father and she now found it empty and desolate in comparison with all the warmth and family fun of the old days so recently passed. Neither was Marconi charmed by the lonely place which meant nothing to him. Bea sometimes felt miserable, her husband was sometimes ill-tempered, and she wept when he went off to walk on his own leaving her in the house.

After only a week, the honeymoon came prematurely to an end because Marconi was needed for business in England. Whether or not the recall might have been ignored, there is little doubt that both were happier back in the less constricting atmosphere in London where she could gossip with her friends again, and he could get away to his work.

CHAPTER 10

BURDENS OF BUSINESS AND FAMILY

THE humiliating failure of the transatlantic wireless telegraph service on its premature début at the end of 1902 badly damaged the prestige and the finances of the Company. For three years afterwards Marconi had loyally devoted himself to lesser projects to bring in something to help the balance sheet. Now the Board was prepared to back Marconi's judgement that his new plans for the transatlantic service would bring commercial success. For the first two or three years of his marriage this task of re-establishing the Company's standing in long-distance telegraphy was for Marconi a matter of personal pride as well as business necessity and it dominated everything else he did.

When Marconi returned abruptly from his honeymoon in Ireland his wife came with him and they stayed in London for just under a month. A smart hotel was a great novelty for Bea, she was delighted by the studied luxury and found the bustle of the public rooms much to her taste after the rather gloomy week at Dromoland. She was often left alone when Marconi went out on business, but there was so much for her to do and see that she found his absences were no hardship. She was, however, astonished to discover that her husband became greatly disturbed when he found that she was going out alone. He demanded to be told exactly where she intended to go and, if she was late or departed in any way from the stated plans, she could expect to be greeted by an outburst which revealed in her husband a startling intensity of worry and anger.[1]

In May 1905 Bea and Marconi sailed to New York in the Cunard liner *Campania* on the way to Glace Bay, Canada, where a new station of much increased power had just been com-

155

pleted and was ready for Marconi to carry out final adjustments. On the boat Bea soon enjoyed being the centre of attention as the attractive wife of a famous man, but her popularity among the passengers upset her husband. His jealousy, only suggested before by the obsessive concern about her unchaperoned outings in London, now led to open accusations of flirting, and he gave her little jobs to occupy her during the voyage.

The couple had a few days of glittering parties in New York and then there came for Bea the grim contrast of life inside the wire fence at the Glace Bay station. The Marconis shared the tiny two-bedroom house in which Vyvyan, the Chief Engineer, lived with his wife and their baby daughter. Marconi and Vyvyan were out nearly all the time and the two women in such close confinement did not get on. Eventually Bea broke down and told her husband that all her efforts at friendliness were being rebuffed by Mrs Vyvyan. There was a tearful showdown and the situation in the house improved for Bea, but life generally was boring and uncomfortable. She sometimes went with Marconi and sat for hours in the background in one of the huts while the men carried out long tests. At other times she went for walks alone, occasionally rashly straying too far from the camp and returning late to a worried husband and a storm of reproof. Under all the circumstances it seems to have been an act of remarkable callousness when, after only a few weeks at Glace Bay, Marconi left his young wife behind and sailed back to England in the *Campania*.

The purpose of the return was to make tests of the strength of the Glace Bay signal received in the *Campania* during the voyage, and also at Poldhu. The results in the *Campania* were not as good as expected[2] and Marconi made considerable modifications to the station at Poldhu before good signals could eventually be received there from Glace Bay by day as well as by night. During the course of these experiments at Poldhu Marconi discovered that there was a great improvement in signal strength if a very long wire aerial was set up with its length pointing towards the transmitter: a similar aerial at the transmitter still further enhanced the signal

156

strength. This discovery of the horizontal directional aerial
was of great importance to long-range wireless and Marconi
lodged a British Patent in July 1905. Apart from this experimental work at Poldhu, and a number of meetings undertaken to try to improve the Company's financial position,
Marconi also went to Ireland and prospected for a site for a
new station to replace Poldhu as the European end of the transatlantic service. All this took time, and there were three
lonely months for Bea in Glace Bay before Marconi returned to
Canada.

The possibility of finding an alternative to the rather
restricted site at Poldhu had been under consideration
for some time and the west of Ireland was particularly
attractive because it was nearer Glace Bay, and better transatlantic signals might therefore be expected. After the
original failure there was no doubt that two new stations
would be required for the transatlantic commercial service:
one would be on a new site at Glace Bay and the other could
possibly be at Poldhu but was more likely to be elsewhere.
Wherever the European terminal was erected the Company's
finances would be severely strained, so Cuthbert Hall tried
to raise some money from the Government to help out.

Early in 1904 he had agreed with Marconi on the Poldhu
matter:

> I think everyone understands that to carry on a commercial
> service – a service which would represent serious competition
> with the cable – would necessitate the construction of an
> entirely new station. Indeed it is ridiculous to expect that a
> station which has been constructed for experimental pur-
> poses will serve commercial purposes, and it is a pleasant
> surprise to know that the old station will be utilised for any
> commercial purpose – such for example as the long-distance
> ship telegraphy.[3]

But when the attempt was made[4] to persuade the Admiralty
to meet part of the costs of a new station the response
was unhelpful.[5] Their Lordships indicated in September
1904:

Whilst they would be glad to see the long distance station removed from so exposed a position as Poldhu to one where there would not be the same risk of damage from a hostile raiding cruiser they are not prepared to defray the costs of removal and the other expenses involved.

Reporting to Marconi the failure to secure Admiralty financial help[6] Cuthbert Hall seemed doubly anxious to avoid decision making at this critical time. He wrote:

If therefore you are perfectly satisfied to go ahead with the two stations simultaneously, the European and the Cape Breton (Glace Bay) we will start at once. On hearing from you that you see no risk in spending the money on two new big stations simultaneously I shall proceed to go ahead. . . .

From a managing director operating in a highly speculative business this was surely a remarkable problem to put to a scientist. He concluded:

Tactically, keeping in mind future relations with the Government, there is as you will appreciate a tactical disadvantage in not completing at Poldhu because the Admiralty will be inclined to think that when we asked for a subsidy we were bluffing them.

But Marconi was more concerned with technical success than tactics and, after making some tests of reception in the district, he chose a site at Clifden in Galway on the west coast of Ireland.

At last Marconi returned to Glace Bay and after tests on the station's newly modified directional aerial he and Bea sailed back together to England. Soon after Marconi had left her three months before, she had discovered that she was pregnant and the ensuing sickness had made her state even more dismal while she waited for her husband to return. Immediately they arrived in England Marconi went to Poldhu for further experimental work, taking Bea with him and installing her in the Poldhu Hotel.

With Marconi away across the fields working at the station, life out of season in the isolated hotel on the Cornish cliff seemed not all that different from Glace Bay. But Lady Inchiquin took a hand and found a house in London for Bea so that she could be properly looked after while awaiting the birth of her child. Lady Inchiquin's choice of a house was governed more by a fond mother's idea of the importance of her daughter's husband than by the reality of his immediate financial position. It was a smart place in Charles Street, Berkeley Square, and Lilah, Bea's favourite sister, came to stay there to give an eye to her sister's health and be company for her because Marconi was away most of the time at Poldhu.

In February 1906 Marconi's first child was born: it was a daughter and Bea decided that she would like her to be called Lucia. But within a few weeks, before a christening had been arranged, the child died. Marconi wrote to his mother:

My own darling Mama,
Our darling little baby was taken away from us suddenly on Friday morning. (I was at Poldhu at the time and only got here when it was all over.) She had been very well all the time before and the doctor said she was a more than usually healthy baby. On Thursday night she had what was thought to be a slight attack of indigestion and at about 8 a.m. on Friday morning an attack of convulsions and all was over in a few minutes. Bea got a most awful shock and she is now very weak. . . .[7]

He did not tell his mother of the harrowing experience of trying to arrange the burial of his unbaptised child. The clergyman who had so recently married them at St George's, Hanover Square, helped them all he could and read the service at the graveside when Marconi eventually found a cemetery at Ealing which would accept the funeral.

It took Bea a long time to recover physically and mentally from the dreadful shock. It was particularly fortunate that she had the comfort of friends and relatives close to her in

London at this time because Marconi, as always, was away at Poldhu or the Haven working under pressure to realise the new transatlantic service which it was hoped would set right the Company's finances. But he himself was not in good health and suffered a series of feverish attacks which culminated in a period of nearly three months during which he was confined to the house in Charles Street. He proved to be a most difficult patient, taking a near-hypochondriacal interest in every aspect of the treatment prescribed. Even so Bea worried that once he was up and about he would not look after his health. In January 1907 she telegraphed from London to Poole:

> For goodness sake don't go near Giovanni's room if he has influenza. Let him see a doctor and you take plenty of quinine. Do please take great care. You might be so bad if you got it. Heaps of love. Thanks for letter. Bea.[8]

By early in 1907 all seemed ready for the final adjustments at the two long-distance stations Glace Bay and Clifden. Lilah, who was now back living with her mother, was surprised to receive a special message from Marconi asking her if she would accompany him on a short trip to Canada[9] to be a companion to Bea whom he proposed to take with him on this occasion. Lilah was to hold herself ready to go immediately, but technical difficulties delayed the trip and eventually they did not leave until 28 June 1907, sailing from Liverpool in the *Empress of Ireland*. It was in many ways an exacting journey: there were icebergs and thick fog on the voyage, with the Captain not leaving the bridge for three days, there was a long railway ride across Canada, a delay of several days when Marconi caught another of his fevers, but the two women enjoyed most of the adventures and when they reached Glace Bay they met Barney O'Brien, their brother, who now worked for Marconi.

The party did not stay long at Glace Bay. On 15 July messages were satisfactorily received there from Poldhu which was temporarily being used for these tests. It was then time to get back across the Atlantic to put the Clifden station into commission, and they were all in London again by the end of July. Marconi then went at once to Clifden to supervise last modifications and by September he was back again in Glace Bay ready to inaugurate the transatlantic service.

Wariness rather than uninhibited celebration characterised the opening of the commercial transatlantic service. Within the Company there was caution, outside there was scepticism. Three months before, when emphasising the urgent need to inspire investment confidence, Cuthbert Hall had told Marconi[10] that he would much prefer the success of the service to announce itself than have an organised exchange of ceremonial messages which would look very much like a repetition of what had been done three or four years ago. He warned that although financiers were ready to buy shares they must not be invited to do so if there was the smallest risk of a fiasco or of a considerable delay. In October 1907 when the service did at last start, the *Electrician* did not praise extravagantly, partly because of difficulty in finding out exactly what was happening, nevertheless the editorial said:

> We desire to heartily congratulate Mr Marconi on the advance he has made. Every credit is due to him for the indefatigable way in which he extends the possibilities of wireless telegraphy. Nevertheless, we wish that he would take into his confidence those who can claim to pass some judgement upon what he has been doing, rather than the lay reporter, and that his methods of dealing with the public were less theatrical.[11]

Most people with no financial or professional interest in wireless or cables would probably have felt that such conditional congratulations were appropriate in view of the past history of Marconi announcements. On the other hand the fact that the Company was based on scientific innovation did not relieve it of the need to advertise, to impress investors, and to confuse competitors. Such ordinary commercial requirements precluded running the Company as though it were some sort of sub-branch of a learned society, which was apparently what

many critics of its methods wished. Without the risk capital
attracted by methods which some found distasteful the great
technological leap forward of transatlantic wireless would
have been much delayed, and equally delayed would have
been the consequent advances in pure science such as the clear
understanding of electromagnetic wave properties and the
discovery of the electrical nature of the Earth's upper
atmosphere.

The early months of operating the commercial service
between Glace Bay and Clifden were on the whole very
successful. There were some complaints from journalists
that the times at which they could file their copy for transmission were more limited than they would have wished.[12]
The time taken for messages to pass between England and
America was sometimes much longer than expected but this
was put down to delays in the land lines at each end of the
wireless link. Competitors seized upon such difficulties and
decried the service[13] but there was no doubt that in general
it was a technical triumph, although a long way yet from
making the Company's fortune. With the success of the
service 'announcing itself' as Cuthbert Hall had hoped,
Marconi felt able to be more restrained in his claims. Even
his old critic the *Electrician*, which had always honoured his
technical successes while complaining of the style of publicity
given to them, now became quite conciliatory towards
Marconi the man. In an editorial in February 1908 a speech
of Marconi's to the Liverpool Chamber of Commerce was
noticed:

> Mr Marconi has evidently learned the value of reticence,
> and at Liverpool on Monday he showed a more cautious
> spirit which would have served him well had it come
> earlier. . . . Certainly no statement was made by Mr
> Marconi at Liverpool to which we can take any serious
> objection, except so far as these statements relate to what
> has already been accomplished by the wireless service.
> Mr Marconi makes lighter of the difficulties which have yet
> to be overcome before wireless telegraphy is a serious
> competitor in commercial telegraphy than we should have

done, but he has evidently, rather late in the day, adopted a less confident tone than when, in the years now passed, these difficulties were either ignored or greatly understated. If Mr Marconi and those who have engineered the Marconi Companies had adopted at the start the tone in which Mr Marconi delivered his address at Liverpool on Monday, his entrance into the general field of telegraphy would have been shorn of much of the opposition which he has had to meet from those who have been engaged in the task of perfecting the submarine telegraph system of the world during the past half century and in earning reasonable dividends upon the large capital commitments which submarine cable enterprise represents.[14]

Marconi replied with a letter to the Editor:

In a note in the *Electrician* of February 28th, you imply that indiscretion and overconfidence have characterised my statements in the past on wireless telegraphy. I am unable to understand how you arrive at this conclusion, unless, as I suspect, you have been influenced by the paragraphs which from time to time appear in the daily press. . . .

Let me cite an example of misleading paragraphs of this kind. Some time ago I read in a Montreal newspaper an interview (in dialogue form) alleged to have taken place between a reporter and myself when I was actually 3,000 miles away from the place of the supposed interview. . . .

In conclusion I may say that, in spite of all that others may say on the subject, I have myself never felt more confident or more optimistic than at the present time in regard to the practical and general application of wireless, or, as we on the Continent say, radio telegraphy.[15]

The Editor appeared ready to forgive Marconi the sins of others, commenting, '. . . those who have engineered the Marconi Companies have not been as discreet as himself', and by the end of March it was not Marconi but his audience at the Royal Institution who were obliquely chided:

Both the body and the gallery of the theatre were filled to their utmost capacity some time before the appointed hour, and evidently a number of the audience had been long and patiently waiting as if for the premiere at a well known theatre. Whether this was due to a genuine desire for knowledge for its own sake, or to the idea that something sensational would be disclosed, it is impossible to say. If any came for the latter reason, they were disappointed, for the lecture was quite uncontroversial and disputed topics were scarcely touched upon.

Although the *Electrician* had no fault to find with Marconi's pronouncements at Liverpool and the Royal Institution, these, and similar engagements undertaken by him at this time, were intended to advertise the long-range service which was now available from the Company, and in particular to bring to the public notice as often and as strongly as possible the feasibility of an Imperial Wireless Chain connecting Britain with all the major Dominions and Colonies.

Some such large contract which would provide a substantial and guaranteed income was desperately needed by the Company at this time. In the latter half of 1907 there were times when the Company had only sufficient cash resources to cover its activities for a matter of days ahead. The Managing Director spoke of trying to raise £30,000 to give them three months' breathing space, and of meanwhile being grateful for sums of £1000 which had been contributed from various sources. The directors, including Marconi, were asked whether they could not also make some such welcome gesture, if they had not already done so.[16] In 1908 Vyvyan had an article on Imperial Wireless published in the *Times*, but when he proposed to go and try to sell wireless to the South African Government he was told that only if he succeeded in getting orders could his expenses be paid. He did in fact sell two coastal stations, and when he was explaining the economic advantages of an Imperial Wireless Chain he was surprised that General Smuts replied, and Botha agreed, that '. . . what appeals to us more particularly is that it will draw more closely the bonds of Empire'. Vyvyan commented in his memoirs, 'I did not think they really meant it, and had accepted the idea of Imperial unity so wholeheartedly as the words indicated, and their future careers so amply proved.'[17] The lack of ready money to pay representatives who should have been out trying to fill the firm's order book was a bad enough business sign, but even more alarming was the dismissal of 150 people from the factory to save wages when there was plenty of work for them on current orders which would soon have brought in cash.

The financial straits of the Company did not greatly affect Marconi's family circumstances, but he was a singularly undomesticated man and, at this particular time of intense work and travel, he was little concerned with hearth and home. Economy did not come naturally to Bea and with her husband so much away she arranged a full social life which was not inexpensive. Not that Marconi's more frequent presence would have been likely to reduce the bills. Whatever he was doing he expected, and usually got, the best of accommodation and service, although when work so dictated he would endure great discomfort and hardship without complaint. They gave up the town house in Charles Street, taking instead a country mansion down in Hampshire, and when Marconi was in London Bea came up and they stayed at the Ritz. When he had to go to Italy on business he took her with him, first to stay at Villa Grifone with his mother, and then to Rome, where she greatly enjoyed the parties and the café society with his many friends. Back in London, Marconi took a town house for Bea to live in while he went to America, and on 11 September 1908, with Marconi still abroad, his daughter Degna was born.

These few years in the middle of the first decade of the twentieth century were eventful ones for Marconi, for the Marconi Company, and for radio communication generally. During this time Marconi had married, two of his children were born, and ominous strains appeared between him and Bea. But the science of wireless communication had made some enormous advances, and foundations had been laid for further advances more spectacular than anyone imagined. Although the many talented people now working in the field were in competition, their individual major successes were each

165

integrated quickly into the structure of the developing subject and their failures or second-best ideas were forgotten by all but their shareholders.

The spark gap was being replaced as the source of electromagnetic waves at the transmitter because a spark contains a wide, and largely unknown and uncontrollable, range of electromagnetic frequencies like the range of sound frequencies contained in the crash when a metal plate is struck with a hammer. Instead of the spark gap, some form of generator was used which gave an alternating electrical voltage at a single, very high frequency, bearing the same relation to the spark as the pure acoustic note of a tuning fork does to the metallic crash. If dots and dashes were obtained by switching on and off such a single frequency generator then it was possible to achieve much more precise tuning of the circuits in the transmitter and the receiver, and consequently very much improved general performance, e.g. larger ranges for the same power, and greater ability to receive one wanted transmission in the presence of unwanted signals from other stations. A further advantage of using a single frequency generator was that it could be used as the basis of a system of wireless telephony, in which messages are directly transmitted as speech instead of being encoded into dots and dashes. Once the spoken word – and music – could be transmitted, broadcast entertainment became possible.

The 1905–9 period also saw the invention of the thermionic valve which was crucial to the forthcoming great burst of achievement in wireless technology and to the later development of non-communication electronics such as computation. Back in the 1880s the Edison Electric Light Company was concerned about discoloration of their lamp bulbs due to particles of the carbon filament being given off and deposited on the glass wall of the lamp. In investigating this problem a small metal plate was placed inside the bulb and Edison discovered that if a battery was connected between the metal plate and the hot filament a current of electrons would pass from the filament across the lamp to the plate; but if the battery was reversed there was no flow of electrons in the opposite direction from plate to

Marconi's yacht *Elettra*

Melba's broadcast from
Chelmsford

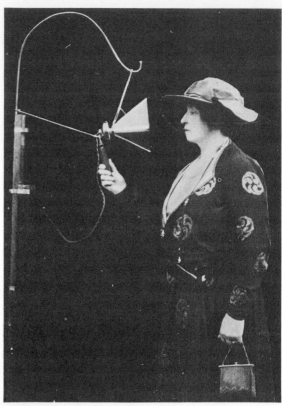

Marconi and Godfrey
Isaacs with car radio

filament. In 1904 Fleming remembered this Edison effect, on which he himself had worked twenty years before, and the fact that current flowed one way only across the lamp. He applied the very rapidly oscillating voltage from a wireless receiving aerial to such a modified Edison lamp – a diode valve – and found that the valve gave rise to an ordinary direct current which could be detected by using a simple current meter. Later de Forest inserted a third electrode, the grid, into the valve and this triode valve was not only capable of detecting signals, like the diode, but it could be made to amplify them too.

Although the best ideas of companies like Marconi, de Forest and Fessenden were pushing wireless technology forward in great bounds at this time, these companies were all in financial difficulties of one sort or another. Fessenden had made tentative approaches to the American Marconi Company about a merger,[18] and in 1906 the de Forest Company was badly in debt.[19] In the Marconi Company the financial situation precipitated a management reorganisation in the course of which the resignation of the Managing Director, Cuthbert Hall, was accepted by the Board in March 1908 and Marconi was appointed temporary Managing Director with two ex-holders of that office, Jameson-Davis and Flood-Page, to assist him. The appointment of this triumvirate probably placated the shareholders and convinced them that something was being done to retrieve the situation, but there was an air of panic about it and the papers hinted[20] that Cuthbert Hall possibly had a grievance about his sudden departure.

After these few years of mixed fortune in business and personal affairs it was a tonic for Marconi when in 1909 he received the Nobel Prize for Physics, these awards having been first given in 1901. Marconi's name had first been put forward some eight years before. Fleming wrote to him from University College London at the end of 1901:

I do not know whether you have ever heard of the Nobel Prizes of the Swedish Academy. Mr Nobel was the inventor of dynamite and he left an enormous fortune to the Swedish Academy for founding Institutes and awarding prizes to

167

inventors. These prizes are awarded once a year by a committee appointed by the King of Sweden. One of these is for physics or inventions in physics. I am one of six people in England who have been appointed to nominate someone for a prize. I believe this consists of a sum of money and a gold medal. I don't know how much money. It occurs to me that your name should be put forward as a candidate if you have no objection and I shall be very pleased to nominate you. The nomination has to be supported by documentary evidence. I should want to have printed copies of your several papers and lectures and some published articles such as that you wrote for the *North American Review*. If you care to let me have these I will send them in, in the hope that you may be successful.[21]

Some time later there was another approach, this time in a letter from Norway to Cuthbert Hall:

An idea occurred to me to raise a movement that this year or next year Marconi get the prize in Physical. For Mr Marconi himself the prize would be one of the greatest honour he could attain to and for your company a mighty advertisement. . . . It will of course be quite impossible beforehand to tell how much money I need but as larger amount as more magazines we can get to take interest in the affairs. I should think a lot could be done for a hundred pounds.[22]

Cuthbert Hall at once forwarded this strange communication to Marconi on 6 February 1904:

This is a copy of a letter which I have received this morning from a man who has been trying to do business for us in Norway. He is a lawyer of the High Court and appears to have access to well placed persons in the public services of Norway and Sweden.

I should be disposed to thank him for his offer, point out that your name has already been proposed for the prize by various scientific societies of high standing of their own initiative and that we think it better that we should not move personally in the matter. If this meets your views please let me know. Of course if there should be any advantage in a Norwegian or Swedish proposal of your name I should be glad to take up the matter as Lutken is right in saying it would be a considerable indirect advantage to the Company if the prize were awarded to you. . . .

But one way or another the matter came to a successful conclusion in 1909 – or at least to a half-successful conclusion, because the Nobel Prize in Physics for that year was awarded jointly to Marconi and Professor Braun of the Telefunken Company, Marconi's bitterest commercial rivals. There was apparently some coolness between the two men when they first met in Stockholm at the presentation, but they became more friendly after a day or two. Such little frictions have not been uncommon in the history of the Nobel Prizes and there was a controversial echo from Marconi's year three years later when it became known that it had been intended to award the prize for Physics jointly to Tesla and Edison. But they never got the prize, which was awarded to a Swede, because although Tesla needed the money he could not stomach the double 'insult' of Marconi having got the award three years before him and now of being asked to share with an 'inventor', Edison.[23]

Bea came with Marconi to Stockholm to attend the celebrations, and the trip was one of guarded reconciliation following another violent row between them a few months before. When Marconi was crossing the Atlantic to Liverpool after visiting America Bea, who had recently discovered that she was again pregnant, decided to surprise and delight her husband by going on board his boat to give him the good news that he might very well be getting the son he so much wanted. She went across from London to Ireland and out with the pilot boat from Cork to meet the liner and spend the last few hours of the voyage with her husband as the ship made its way to Liverpool. She certainly surprised her husband who had been enjoying to the full the society of a gay and congenial mixed group of travelling companions.

169

Bea was made to feel very much an uninvited and late arrival at a brilliant party. She was furiously unhappy and he was humiliated and angry. The frigid mood lasted long after the boat docked at Liverpool, but by December it had softened enough for them to travel together to Stockholm, taking Lilah with them.

CHAPTER 11

AFRICAN DESERT
AND ATLANTIC ICEBERG

IMMEDIATELY after the Nobel Prize celebrations at the end
of 1909 Marconi had to cross the Atlantic yet again and he
expected to be away some considerable time. Adding to the
Company's many difficulties, the Glace Bay station had been
almost completely destroyed by fire towards the end of 1909
and the transatlantic service once more interrupted. Marconi
was to supervise the final stages of rebuilding, and the
incorporation of a number of improvements which had already
proved successful at Clifden. The station came into full
operation again in April 1910.

Marconi was hoping that Bea's expected child would be a
boy, and he very much wanted the birth to take place in
Italy so that his son – if fate was kind – should have full
Italian nationality. Before he sailed for America he managed
to persuade Bea to take their four-year-old daughter Degna to
Villa Grifone, where with her sister Lilah again for a companion Bea would await the birth of the new baby. The old
house, closed since the death of Marconi's father six years
before, was to be decorated and generally refurbished to
receive them. Bea got on well with Annie, her mother-in-law,
who would be nearby in Bologna, and the two sisters were no
doubt attracted by the prospect of spring and summer in
Italy in a strange and exciting establishment of their own.

Marconi sailed from Liverpool for America in January 1910
and when the *Majestic* called at Queenstown he sent off a
hurried note to Solari.[1] The purpose of this note was to thank
Solari for arranging financial backing at very short notice.
Marconi had asked him most urgently to do this because the
Company's cash resources were almost exhausted and no
further help was available in England. Solari persuaded the

171

Bank of Rome to advance twenty thousand pounds to Marconi and the draft had reached him just before the *Majestic* left Liverpool. In this same letter Marconi revealed a most important step which had just been taken to re-establish in the long term the financial stability of the Company. A new Managing Director had been appointed to serve jointly with Marconi for six months and then to take over on his own: his name was Godfrey Isaacs.

Isaacs had been introduced to Marconi in the autumn of 1909 by Bea's brother Donough O'Brien.[2] Marconi was impressed by him and considered that, with his connections in the City and particularly his influence with finance houses in London and on the Continent, he would make the sort of chief executive and planner the Company needed at that difficult time. Isaacs was vigorous, agile and enterprising in business; he was appointed in January 1910 and in March he submitted to the Colonial Office a scheme for a chain of wireless stations throughout the Empire. In that same March, Godfrey's brother, Rufus Isaacs, a very successful barrister who had been a Liberal M.P. for six years, was appointed to the Government as Solicitor General.

While Marconi was away at Glace Bay, Bea and Lilah were in Italy at the Villa Grifone with Degna and her English nanny. They had some difficulty in making themselves comfortable at first, finding neither the food nor the servants satisfactory. But these problems were soon solved by having English-style food sent up regularly from Florence and by bringing out from England a married couple to run the household, to be joined later by an English nurse in readiness for the new baby.

When his son was born in May 1910 Marconi was on his way back to Europe. He hurried to Villa Grifone and the child was christened Giulio by a Waldensian Protestant minister, in which faith Marconi had been brought up and confirmed as a child, although baptised a Roman Catholic. Among the godparents were Lady Marjorie Coke and William Waldorf Astor.

The following months of the summer of 1910 were pleasant ones for Marconi and his family, enjoying the warmth and peace of the Italian countryside with a new son and heir to show off to visiting friends and relatives. Although he had to make a number of business trips Marconi was away less than usual and, now that Godfrey Isaacs had been appointed, he was much freer to concentrate on the technical side of the Company's activities. He was now much concerned with realising his ambition of a world-wide network of inter-communicating Marconi stations and in this scheme the station built for the Italian Government at Coltano, near Pisa, was very important, providing a link with Clifden, Poldhu, Glace Bay, Eritrea and, hopefully, South America. Solari was responsible for setting up this station,[3] in which the King of Italy showed a personal interest, and Marconi took advantage of his stay in Italy to pay it several visits.[4] In September 1910 Marconi sailed to Buenos Aires to test long-distance reception on the voyage and, using kites flown from the ship to support the aerial, obtained signals from Clifden at ranges of 4000 miles by day and nearly 7000 miles by night. In the winter of 1910 Marconi, Bea and their now considerable household returned from Italy and took a house just outside London.

The large house they rented was called the Old Palace, in Richmond Park, and the few months they lived there almost destroyed their marriage. Marconi, of course, often had to be away, but in the spring and summer of 1911 he made little effort to get to Richmond because he so much disliked the style of life which Bea adopted there and in which he was expected to participate when he returned from his travels. Bea had seized the opportunity of being near London to take up the active social life she loved, and which she made doubly extravagant and demanding by choosing to take a very large part in the entertaining necessitated by the 'coming out' of her two youngest sisters. Marconi himself was not averse to fashionable society and it seems probable that his anti-pathy towards the Old Palace life was really due primarily to jealousy of the attentions paid to Bea at the parties she attended in his absence, and that this jealousy was exacerbated by the uncomfortable fact that he could not easily afford to pay for her extravagant entertaining. He wrote to his bank manager in February 1911[5] that he would be 'overdrawing more than usual in the next few days' but expected to be receiving shortly a substantial payment, and in August he gave instructions[6] that no Company shares were to be bought for him even if they fell below 40 but that any amount were to be sold up to a certain limit if they went above 45 and 'the money paid directly into the bank'.

There were many bitter quarrels between Bea and Marconi and they came very close to making a formal separation of the estrangement which kept them apart that year. The family and friends, well aware of the situation, dissuaded them from such a drastic step and in August 1911 Marconi took Bea with him on a short trip to Canada, but this must have been something of a flop because the weather was frightful and Bea was plagued with sea-sickness and toothache.[7] International events overtook the domestic quarrel when Italy declared war on Turkey in August 1911 and Marconi returned immediately to his own country to volunteer his services.

The war between Turkey and Italy over Libya was part of the general scramble of the big powers over Africa. This complex political and economic struggle involved war and threats of war and did much to establish alignments for the great European war now only three years off. The rivalry between Marconi's Company and Telefunken was strangely interwoven with the greater conflicts at this time. Germany and France shared economic influence in Morocco, with France responsible for order, and when the two powers quarrelled over the country's affairs in 1911 Germany sent a warship to Agadir to 'protect the lives and property of Hamburg merchants in the area'.[8] It was suggested that the German intention was only to push France into negotiations independent of Great Britain and Russia, but in fact Lloyd George on behalf of the British Government made a speech indicating that Britain would be prepared to go to war and this bolstered France and the Triple Entente and a peaceful settlement favourable to France was reached in a few weeks. For a time the threat of war involving France, Germany, and Britain seemed very real and to turn on whether the Germans 'meant business' with their warship *Panther* sent to Agadir.

The Marconi Company and Telefunken had both provided

wireless equipment for the Spanish Government, and in July 1911 Vyvyan, Marconi's senior engineer, was in the Canary Islands to hand over an installation to Spanish inspecting officers. In his memoirs he wrote:

> One day while in Las Palmas the German warship *Panther* anchored there and certain officers came ashore. I was sitting in the window of my hotel overlooking the street and talking to Capt. X (a Spanish officer) when he drew my attention to two men accompanying certain German officers, and pointed out that they were two Telefunken engineers who had helped to build the military wireless station near Madrid.[9]

Vyvyan told X to conceal his connection with Marconi and get into conversation with the two men.

> After about an hour's absence he informed me that the *Panther* had in her hold a complete wireless telegraph station which was destined for Agadir and which these engineers were to construct. This was clear evidence that Germany did definitely intend to occupy Agadir, and as the information might be important I cabled it to England on the chance it might be useful to the Foreign Office.

Further along the coast of North Africa in the Mediterranean, Turkey and Italy were unable to settle their differences without a war which dragged on for over a year and took Marconi to the battlefront where he no doubt felt some satisfaction in observing the effect of Italian shells on Telefunken wireless installations. When he returned to Italy on the outbreak of the war he spent some time at the Coltano station which would have an important part to play in communicating with the widely dispersed Italian naval and army units along the Libyan coast. The King, who since the *Carlo Alberto* voyage had become a close friend of Marconi, visited the wireless station while he was there and soon afterwards Marconi went off to North Africa. He wrote to Godfrey Isaacs:

I left Italy so suddenly for North Africa that I hardly had time to write to you in regard to your trip. The Ministry of Marine asked me to proceed to Cyrenaica and Tripoli in order to inspect the new stations which are being erected and also to test the receivers to be used in communication with Coltano. I also decided to carry out some experiments on new lines concerning the use of masts or poles. . . .[10]

The realisation of the imminent perils of war appeared to help Bea and Marconi to put into perspective their own differences and she and the children had gone to Pisa to be near him while he was at Coltano. A little later his mother wrote to him at Tobruk:

I am so glad to hear you are well and that the climate is so beautiful. I am sure it will do you good and I hope and pray that the Lord will keep you safe, free from all peril and danger. I can't help feeling anxious about you, darling, for it is an awful dangerous country to be in at present, but I suppose you are always on the warship and I am glad they are all so kind and that you are well looked after. I was very glad to hear from dear Bea that she had accompanied you to Taranto and had seen you off, and that you were so happy going. She mentioned how charming the Admiral is, and the officers, and what a beautiful large cabin you have, and I felt so glad to hear this. . . .[11]

The warship R.N. *Pisa* with Marconi on board was operating close off-shore along the North African coast in support of Italian ground forces. He made frequent trips ashore to inspect wireless installations, often riding out into the desert on a mule to perform experiments with mobile Army wireless stations carried by camel. He described something of his life at war in a letter to Bea from Tobruk:

I visited yesterday the remains of the Telefunken station at Derna which was destroyed by this ship. It was supplied with four large towers about two hundred feet high and a building placed between the towers which contained the engines and instruments (the operators were given ten minutes' warning to get out before the buildings were shelled). . . . The most impressive sight I have seen during the war was the bombardment by our and other ships of a Turkish position during the night. I never saw anything more like what could be described as hell on earth – the accuracy of murderous guns. . . . In regard to the alleged cruelties by Italian troops I absolutely believe that the reports sent out to some English and foreign papers are entirely and absolutely false. . . . I shall be a bit more busy at Tripoli with the arrangements of the field stations. As you know, I tried the arrangement with the aerial wire on the ground and it seems to work awfully well in the desert. It is a great advantage to be able to do without the poles which are difficult to carry about and show one's position to the enemy. A few of them come occasionally and fire at our outposts at night and in the morning but there has not yet been any real battle. Yesterday a few of them appeared on horseback on a hill close to which we are anchored. We immediately fired three shots at them with the ship's guns. Before leaving they fired a few shots at us with Mauser rifles but were much too far to hurt us.

I am in the best of health and spirits. There is only one woman in the whole place, she is an old Arab. We have a splendid hospital ship here, beautifully equipped but with no nurses on board. They had to send them away, for as they had no wounded to attend and nursing to do they flirted too much with the officers.

We have six aeroplanes here and I am learning heaps about them and it would be much fun if you were here too. The officers are such good fellows and the sailors and soldiers as keen as mustard. Nothing is said of this place in the newspapers as no reporters have been allowed to come. The torpedo-boats are continually stopping shipping going in and out of Alexandria in Egypt. The Egyptians seem to be doing all they can to help the Turks. I wonder what England thinks of having Alexandria blocked. . . .

You might drop me a line to Tripoli in Africa. That address would find me. . . .[12]

177

Most of the larger armies and navies in the world now used wireless, business and social messages were sent regularly by wireless between ships and shore and across the Atlantic, and the general public was increasingly familiar with news reports 'by wireless' in the Press. Communication through the air, just as a concept, had mystified and excited the public in 1900 and Marconi's transmission of signals across the Atlantic had seemed fantastic. Now over ten years later the reality of wireless communication was accepted but popular romantic interest was still stirred by particular circumstances of its application, especially in connection with that vulnerable and isolated community on a ship at sea.

In 1909 the White Star liner *Republic* out of New York with nearly five hundred passengers was in collision with the Italian vessel *Florida* and badly damaged. Fortunately the equipment in *Republic*'s wireless cabin was not harmed, although the electric power was cut off, and the young Marconi operator Jack Binns was able to switch to the emergency batteries and send out CQD, the old call for assistance, later replaced by SOS. In a dramatic search-and-rescue operation in the fog, controlled by wireless from the shore about thirty miles away, the liner *Baltic* eventually took nearly 1700 people on board from the two vessels, and although the *Republic* sank, the only casualties were the five people killed when the collision occurred. Cheering crowds gave Jack Binns a tremendous reception in New York and later at his home port of Liverpool.

In 1910 an even greater public followed with macabre fascination the story of Crippen and the way in which ocean wireless brought about his arrest. Crippen, who was fifty, murdered his wife in London, but before the crime was discovered and Inspector Dew of Scotland Yard put in charge of the case Crippen had disappeared taking with him a young woman, Ethel Le Neve. The newspapers gave great publicity to the hunt for the missing pair and one of these papers was seen by Captain Kendall, an observant and astute man who was master of the liner *Montrose* bound for Quebec. Two of his passengers, a Mr Robinson and his son, had aroused his interest by their surprisingly affectionate behaviour and by the fact that they seemed to be disguised. As the ship crossed the Atlantic Kendall exchanged wireless messages with England in which he reported his suspicions and received instructions from Scotland Yard. The 'Robinsons' were allowed to continue unmolested on board *Montrose* but Inspector Dew took passage in the fast liner *Laurentic* which got him to Canada in time to board the *Montrose* in the St Lawrence river, disguised as a pilot, and arrest Crippen and Ethel Le Neve. Captain Kendall, describing the voyage later,[13] remembered little 'Mr Robinson' listening to the noise of the ship's wireless transmitter and remarking what a wonderful invention it was. Crippen was found guilty and hanged but Miss Le Neve was acquitted.

It was, however, when the *Titanic* sank in April 1912 that the newspapers of every country splashed before their readers page after page of reports and comment on this great and altogether astonishing tragedy. A very large proportion of this material was about wireless: the miracle of wireless as a life saver, the scandal of inefficient wireless organisation costing lives; the human story of heroic wireless operators, the accusation of false messages broadcast to rig the markets. In the thick of all this early confusion was Marconi, back from the war in Africa and recently arrived in New York, by the merest chance having cancelled a tentative arrangement to travel on the *Titanic*.

The bald facts of the tragedy were that the *Titanic*, the largest and most luxurious liner in the world, sailed on her maiden voyage amid tremendous publicity about the wonders of the 'unsinkable' vessel and her glittering passenger list. At 11.40 p.m. on Sunday 14 April 1912 she struck an iceberg and at 2.20 a.m. the following morning she went down. The *Carpathia,* which had heard the *Titanic*'s wireless SOS, arrived on the scene about two hours after she sank and picked up over 700 survivors: about 1500 passengers and crew died in the icy water of the North Atlantic.

Within hours of the sinking a confusion of wireless signals from all manner of ships and shore stations jammed the air between the wreck and the land, largely preventing reliable news from reaching America or Britain. The chaos of the sinking, the shock and grief among the survivors, and the lack of information ashore about what had happened, led to such rumour and scandal that it persisted twenty-five years later. When newspapers recalled the disaster on its anniversary in 1937 the references to the angry murmurs, the wrongful accusations, and the castigation of the Board of Trade in 1912, were tempered by the knowledge of improvements in maritime safety which had resulted directly from the *Titanic* case and had proved themselves over the last quarter of a century. The *Manchester Guardian* wrote on 14 April 1937:

Thanks to the short range of the wireless installations carried by the vessels of a quarter of a century ago the first SOS calls and the definite news of the disaster were not relayed to land for hours. A vast number of confused and misleading messages from the American continent were reaching this country on the Monday afternoon, and up to midnight of that day it was believed that the great ship though badly damaged was making her own way to port. But by the early hours of Tuesday morning, about twenty-four hours after the *Titanic* had taken the last plunge, the hopeless truth was becoming clear. . . .[14]

When the news eventually came through there was fierce and widespread anger at some of the circumstances of the disaster and many accusations were made against companies, officials and private individuals. Subsequent enquiries showed that these accusations were only too often well founded, although occasionally ordinary human weakness or unfortunate coincidence turned out to be to blame rather than dereliction of duty or culpable cowardice.

An enquiry was held in New York and another, more formal, in England. From these there emerged a string of items, many of them contributing to the loss of life. There were insufficient lifeboats carried on the *Titanic* and there had been no lifeboat drill. Ice warnings received by wireless had been ignored; the last of them being from the *Californian* which at 10.30 p.m. told the *Titanic* that she was stopped and surrounded by ice. The only wireless operator on the

Californian got an acknowledgement of this message from the *Titanic* whose operator then told him to 'shut up' because he was interfering with messages from America. Having done a long spell of duty, he then went to bed and thus never picked up the *Titanic*'s SOS just over an hour later, although members of the *Californian*'s crew saw rockets from the *Titanic*, only about ten miles away, but their Captain did not believe that they were distress signals and ignored them. The *Californian* might have been alongside *Titanic* an hour before she went down and would perhaps have saved almost everyone. Instead, those who were rescued owed their lives to the whim of the wireless operator on the *Carpathia*, about sixty miles off. He had actually gone off watch, meaning to turn in, but decided to return to the wireless cabin to deal with a few more messages and consequently heard *Titanic*'s distress call. Sixty-four per cent of the first-class passengers survived but only twenty-seven per cent of the third-class passengers, and accusations were made that the latter were not given a fair chance to escape. Amidst the welter of wireless messages – urgent, well meaning and stupid – it was alleged that there were some sent deliberately to influence falsely the salvage market, deeply concerned with the ability of the *Titanic* to reach port, or the ordinary stock market which was depressed by the news. Other messages were alleged to have been sent with Marconi's authority to the *Carpathia* to ensure that the Marconi Company kept a monopoly of the news stories which the wireless operators could give the Press. Marconi denied that he had authorised these messages when they were produced in the American Court of Enquiry.

The *New York Times* for Friday 19 April 1912 carried a long story under the headline 'Marconi Pays Visit to the Rescue Ship'. It said that when the *Carpathia* carrying the survivors was nearing her dock in New York, Marconi was dining with John Bottomley, the Managing Director of the American Marconi Company. He had not intended to go to the Cunard Pier but a reporter called at the house seeking letters of introduction to the wireless operator of the *Carpathia* and Bride, the second operator of the *Titanic*, who was a survivor.

'It sounds so interesting I think I'll have to go down

myself,' Mr Marconi suggested. 'I might as well see the thing through now that I have been such a witness of the preliminaries.' It was suggested that the quickest route to the dock would be by the elevated railway and Marconi and the reporter rushed off. The *New York Times* continued:

At 42nd everybody else got off the elevated train and there was a crush through which Mr Marconi made his way with difficulty. At the foot of the elevated a taxicab was waiting which had been ordered from the *Times* office. Mr Marconi himself had purposely avoided asking for passes as he had no wish to swell the crowd about the pier. A kindly police sergeant suggested that no taxicab would be allowed through the lines without a pass and the taxicab was dismissed. The chauffeur fairly wept as he was told he must go, declaring he was an Italian and the honor of carrying Marconi to the pier was one he would have cherished all his life. A police lieutenant was found. He personally escorted Mr Marconi through the lines into the front of the Cunard pier where weeping women in the arms of relatives were being carried out. It was then 9.45 o'clock and a constant stream of survivors of the wreck was being escorted to the front door of the pier to be put into automobiles. 'A weird and uncanny sight,' said Mr Marconi. 'How can it all be true?'

A policeman invited him to come quickly through the door and past the long line of the suffering. Mr Marconi stopped a moment to observe a young woman who sat on an older woman's lap. The older woman was kissing the younger constantly on the forehead and waving back her hair. Tears from the eyes of both attracted Mr Marconi until he shook his head thoughtfully and spoke with choking sobs between his words. A long staircase led to an upper floor and up this Marconi made his way past sufferers coming down. One girl had a broken leg and two men were carrying her. . . . Mr Marconi caught a sputter of a wireless. He smiled broadly. 'A tenacious operator I should say,' he remarked. He almost ran aboard and threw back the door of a tiny cabin. One lamp was burning and a young man's back was turned to him and between two points of brass a blue flame

Marconi and d'Annunzio in Fiume

Marconi with King Victor Emmanuel III and Mussolini

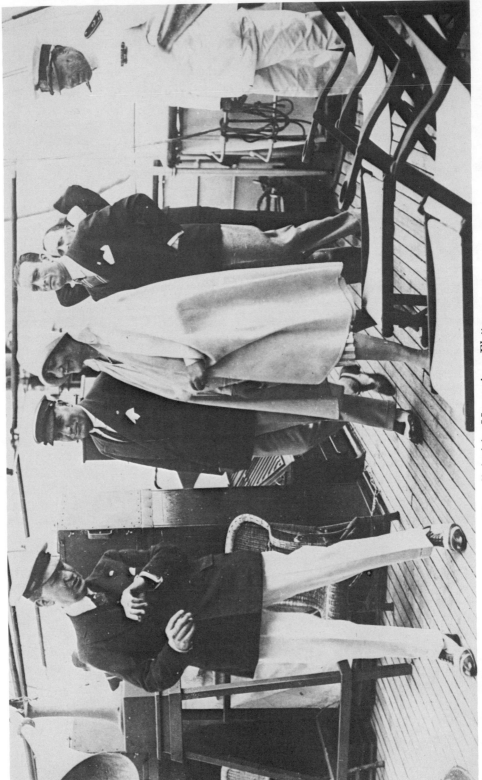

Mussolini visits Marconi on *Elettra*

leaped incessantly. Slowly the youth turned his head round, still working the key. The hair was long and black and the eyes in the semi-darkness were large, staringly large. The face was small and a rather spiritual one which might be expected in a painting. It was clear that from the first tragic moment the boy had known no relief.

'Hardly worth sending now, boy,' said Mr Marconi, hoping to cause the youth to stop.

'But these poor people, they expect their messages to go,' and the boy caught Mr Marconi's face and saw his hand extended. He recognised the man who had discovered the wireless system although he had never seen him before. He glanced from Mr Marconi to a little picture up above the wireless instrument. It was a picture of Marconi. They shook hands long and without saying a word. The boy's face changed in expression gradually, the strain of his long trial was just beginning to break and he smiled.

'You know, Mr Marconi, Phillips is dead,' were his first words.

Mr Marconi asked the operator how his feet were. Both were in bandages and he was working seated on the edge of the bed. A plate of food at his side told how he had eaten.

'I haven't been out of the cabin,' he said, 'since the night after the *Titanic* went down.'

Asking him to talk freely and slowly Mr Marconi led the young man through a complete recital of his experiences from the moment the *Titanic* approached the icefield until the *Carpathia* had touched her dock at the foot of West 13th St. When it was all over Mr Marconi asked many questions.

'How had it ever happened that you didn't feel the shock? I should have thought that it would upset you all terribly.'

'No, Mr Marconi, neither I nor Phillips felt that there had been a collision until the Captain told us.'

'Did the batteries ever stop on you? Did the wireless give out?'

'No sir, the wireless worked right up to the last minute,

as long as there was a wireless cabin to work in. We had to rig up the storage batteries toward the end. But we did it and when we hooked them on the sending kept right up. They were getting weak at the end but were not exhausted. The trouble was water coming in, not the wireless.'

'And the cold in the water? Did Phillips freeze to death'?

'I think he did, sir. I had on my extra jacket and my boots, and that made a difference to me. If only I could have slipped more clothing on Phillips. I slipped on his overcoat and a lifebelt, but I ought to have put on still more. It would have saved him then. My thick clothing saved me I am sure.'

'Some wireless men said they got messages from you – that is, some newspaper correspondents.'

'Not a word, sir, not a single word. Whenever I started to take their queries they sounded so out of keeping with the suffering, so curt and so demanding in tone that I shut them off and went ahead sending our personal messages.'

An ambulance man called at the door demanding that the second wireless man of the *Titanic* come with him at once to hospital as everyone else had gone and he was the last man left. Young Mr Bride introduced the ambulance man to Mr Marconi and the surgeon kindly agreed to wait. The conversation was then concluded and the operator said he was ready to be put on the stretcher.

'A fine boy that, a fine boy,' Mr Marconi said time and time again as he made his way off the ship and back into the throng on the pier. He walked into West 14th St. and then was speeded rapidly in a waiting automobile to the *Times* office where he glanced over the latest dispatches by wireless from overseas and went to his rooms at the Holland House.

Marconi's presence in the United States at this time was in connection with the takeover by the American Marconi Company of the United Wireless Telegraph Company. 'United', successor to the American de Forest Wireless Telegraph Company, had been forced into liquidation in unsavoury circumstances and some of its directors had been sent to prison.[15] In the *New York Times* of 19 April 1912 which carried the eyewitness account of Marconi's visit to the rescue ship *Carpathia* there were reports that on the previous day a special shareholders' meeting authorised an increase in capitalisation of the American Marconi Company, to ten million dollars, in order to acquire the many assets of the bankrupt company and to develop them. This capital was raised by a rights issue to existing shareholders in the American Marconi Company. The newspaper reported sensational advances in the price of the old shares which carried rights to the new issue, and corresponding advances in English and Canadian Marconi shares in an otherwise depressed market.

With his business completed, Marconi returned to England in time for the formal British enquiry into the loss of the *Titanic*. Some of the evidence and some of the questions at this enquiry were sharp enough but the wording of the report was rather bland:

> It has been suggested that the 3rd Class passengers were unfairly treated, access to the boats had been impeded, and when at last they reached the deck 1st and 2nd Class passengers were given precedence in getting places in boats. There appears to be no truth in these suggestions. It is no doubt true that the proportion of 3rd Class passengers saved falls far short of the proportion of 1st and 2nd Class but this is accounted for by the greater reluctance of the 3rd Class passengers to leave the ship, by their unwillingness to part with their baggage, by the difficulty in getting them up from their quarters which were at the extreme end of the ship, and by other similar causes.[16]

In spite of the disappointment of those who hoped for a sensational and damning report, there were many improved safety measures gradually put in hand after the disaster: the fitting of wireless was made compulsory in most vessels and the larger ships had to maintain a continuous watch and also carry emergency wireless equipment; unrestricted transmission by amateurs was stopped and frequency bands were allocated to special purposes so that there should be no repetition of the jamming which occurred after the *Titanic* sank; an Ice Patrol was organised in the North Atlantic to seek out and report by wireless the position of dangerous icebergs in or near the shipping lanes, and since it was set up no ship has been sunk by collision with an iceberg.[17]

The Old Palace in Richmond Park, centre of Bea's social life which had ostensibly caused the near collapse of her marriage during the previous year, had now been given up. Marconi was thirty-eight years old and if he and Bea, with their two children, were ever to have any sort of stable family life then it was time for them to recognise that this needed positive thought and application and the sacrifice of a certain amount of the independence which both of them cherished. Friends suggested getting away from London so Marconi rented Eaglehurst, a country house in Hampshire, and Bea chose furniture, engaged staff, and set about establishing a proper home.

Eaglehurst was near Fawley, on Southampton Water, reasonably accessible to Poole and London where much of Marconi's work in England was carried out. It was a long low building with taller wings at each end, rather ornate, with grounds running down to the beach and a folly near the water in the shape of a romantic tower with battlements and underground passages. In many ways it was an excellent choice for a family home and Marconi's daughter wrote with great affection of the years she spent there as a child.[18] She and her brother had ponies to ride, the beach for digging and paddling, and several different boats to play about in. They had a pet Pekinese too, but unfortunately he took against Marconi, who came so infrequently that the dog did not recognise him as 'family' and set upon him whenever he visited the nursery. The dog was got rid of, and Degna wrote that she and Giulio 'were bereft and mourned him for days'. Most of the children's days were simple and happy ones: picnics with relatives who often stayed at the house, boat trips to the Isle of Wight, Sunday drives to the village church by pony and trap sometimes accompanied by their father. Often when Marconi arrived at Eaglehurst in his magnificent

Rolls-Royce he brought one of his engineering colleagues for the weekend, and in the folly tower he had got the faithful Kemp to rig up a laboratory into which he disappeared for hours when he was at the house.

The tower was out of bounds to the children but on the morning in April 1912 when the *Titanic* left Southampton on her maiden voyage Bea took Degna to the top to watch the great vessel pass so close inshore that they could wave to the passengers on the sunlit decks. Marconi and Bea should have been on board as guests of the White Star Company but business had demanded that he sail a few days earlier on the *Lusitania*, and then at the very last moment Giulio had been taken ill and Bea had cancelled her visit to New York in order to stay at Eaglehurst and look after her baby son.

Having missed their intended holiday together in New York, Bea and Marconi arranged to go to Italy when the *Titanic* enquiries were over. Marconi had work to do in Italy but it was planned to combine this with a car touring holiday designed to foster the rehabilitated married life based on the new country home at Eaglehurst. The high spot of the tour was an invitation in September to dine with the King and Queen of Italy at their hunting lodge near Pisa and during the evening Queen Elena paid Bea the very great compliment of asking her to become one of her ladies-in-waiting. It was a proud and happy evening soon to seem cruelly remote when in a few days Bea saw the King and Queen again, and Marconi heard their voices coming out of the empty darkness which surrounds a man who has just lost his sight.

On the road from Pisa to Genoa, in the new car specially obtained for the tour, Marconi was driving, with Bea beside him and the chauffeur in the back. At a sharp bend in the narrow road they collided with another motor car travelling in the opposite direction. It was a serious collision but no one was killed, most of the injuries being bad cuts and bruises. Marconi received a hard blow on the right side of his face and the doctors at the Spezia Military Hospital where he was taken feared that the damage to the eyeball and the optic nerve would cause him to lose the sight in his right eye. An Italian eye specialist from Turin was at the hospital by evening, and he sent for Fuchs of Vienna, the most eminent European oculist. After a few days it was obvious that the hoped-for recovery in the right eye was not taking place and there was an increasing danger that the left eye, already weakening, might become permanently affected. The specialists decided that the right eye must be removed. When he went to the operating theatre he walked, with Bea on one side of him and his old friend Solari on the other.

Soon he was back in his bed with his eyes bandaged but free now of the pain which he had borne since the accident. Waiting for the bandages to be removed he was reconciled to losing an eye and thankful that his sight had not been altogether destroyed. Sympathetic and encouraging messages were sent to him from all over the world and the King and Queen visited the hospital. Just over a week after the operation the bandages were removed and to Marconi's horror he could see nothing.

But the operation had been a success and the vision in the surviving eye slowly improved over the next few weeks. During this time Bea was almost constantly at his side, reading aloud hour after hour to entertain him and keep him informed of world events. The shared experience of the accident, the weeks of close companionship with one common objective, and the final triumph when he left hospital with his sight restored, did much to renew the old lost affection and respect between them.

Marconi always took great care over his personal appearance, and consciousness of the missing eye, and perhaps too the shock of having come near permanent blindness, possibly added to his natural reserve, indeed coldness, which so many acquaintances remarked upon. But, ever practical and expecting and seeking only the best, he went to Venice and was there fitted with such an extremely well-made artificial eye that casual observers rarely saw that it was not real, and few noticed that he had from time to time to wipe his good eye with a handkerchief because it watered. By November 1912 his sight and appearance were practically completely restored and now the messages sent to him in Italy were of congratulation and good wishes. Kemp wrote from Eaglehurst:

You will be glad to know that your dear children are in splendid health and making wonderful progress in every possible way.

You will be delighted to know that I have erected the 180 foot mast in the field. With your permission I will hoist the ensign belonging to the *Carlo Alberto* to the top of this mast on the day you return to Eaglehurst and the other two Italian ensigns to the two smaller masts on top of the tower. . . .[19]

It was December 1912 when Bea and Marconi returned to the family home and the welcome of their children and friends. Marconi was now fit and eager again for work, and in particular to push forward the Imperial Wireless Scheme now almost at the point of being put into operation, and paid for, by the British Government.

189

CHAPTER 12

TORY CRIES OF SCANDAL

By the end of 1912 Godfrey Isaacs had been Managing
Director of the Marconi Company for nearly three years
and the effects of his energetically pursued policies were
now clearly evident in the Company's affairs. He set out
first to consolidate the Company's hold on the key wireless
patents. Then he sought to increase turnover: by offering
new technical services, by using aggressive salesmanship
to capture business from rivals in established markets, and
by building up the financial interest of the parent company in
associate companies abroad.

Isaacs brought many actions in Britain and abroad against
competitors alleged to have infringed Marconi's patents
and two of these actions were particularly important in
the long run. These were concerned with the Lodge–Muirhead
syndicate in Britain and with the United Wireless Company
in the United States. In Britain it was ruled that Sir Oliver
Lodge's 1897 tuning patent was complementary to the famous
Marconi 7777 patent of 1900 and Isaacs acquired the Lodge
patents for the Marconi Company in October 1911. Lodge was
paid a thousand pounds per year for the seven years the
tuning patent had still to run and he also became scientific
adviser to the Marconi Company, a condition of the deal being
the closing down of the Lodge–Muirhead syndicate which had
installed wireless in India among other places.[1] In the United
States the action against the United Wireless Company had
been instrumental in bringing about the liquidation of that company and the greatly increased capitalisation of the American
Marconi Company arranged, with the help of Isaacs, to finance
the taking over of the assets and activities of 'United'.

The Marconi Company's greatest competitor was without

doubt the German Telefunken Company. Godfrey Isaacs spent much of his first three years in office scheming to win trade from Telefunken, or trying to thwart German efforts to do the same to the Marconi Company, and during the long running battle he used a variety of tactics.[2] He gave up any attempt to compete in Germany itself where the Imperial Government so strongly supported its own national company that opportunities in wireless for foreigners were negligible; he brought patent actions in courts outside Germany to restrict Telefunken's foreign activities; he negotiated a merger of Marconi and Telefunken interests in maritime wireless into the Debeg Company; but, above all, he fought Telefunken for new contracts to build and operate long-distance stations in Spain, Portugal, Turkey, Greece and other countries. The policy of the German Government was as fiercely expansionist commercially as it was politically and when Telefunken sought foreign business they were given considerable diplomatic assistance by German embassies in the countries concerned. Isaacs arranged an interview with the British Foreign Secretary, Sir Edward Grey, and secured an assurance that in future the Marconi Company could rely on similar assistance from British embassies. Between the end of 1910 and the middle of 1912 Isaacs, assisted by Marconi and Solari, brought off a great coup against Telefunken in Spain where by a well-marshalled combination of diplomacy, demonstrable technical ability and business acumen they successfully put to the Government a plan for a large chain of high-power stations covering Spain and the Canary Isles and joining them by wireless to Italy, England and America. This Marconi success was all the more remarkable because Telefunken were already well represented in Spain, with military and naval contracts, before the Marconi Company put forward its grand plan. When the system was ceremonially inaugurated by King Alfonso in May 1912, Marconi and Isaacs were present at the celebrations in Madrid and Marconi was invested by the King with a high-ranking Spanish decoration to add to those which he received from many sources, particularly after the widely publicised success of wireless in the *Titanic* disaster.

191

In England the Imperial Wireless Scheme, which Isaacs had submitted to the Colonial Office soon after he became Managing Director, had been favourably received and negotiations took place between the Post Office and the Marconi Company for the erection of half a dozen large stations throughout the Empire. A tender was finally submitted in March 1912 and on 19 July 1912 the Postmaster General, Herbert Samuel, agreed with the Marconi Company the detailed terms of a contract for this work.

Meanwhile Godfrey Isaacs had gone to New York with Marconi in March 1912 to help raise capital to extend the activities of the American Marconi Company. The new American Marconi share issue was successfully floated, the English Company taking up a large fraction, and Godfrey Isaacs being personally responsible for another big block. Of this block Isaacs placed some with American institutions, some on the New York and London Stock Exchanges, and kept about a hundred thousand shares for private disposal. Marconi himself took ten thousand shares.

When Marconi reviewed the state of his Company in the summer of 1912 he could feel well pleased with the importance and variety of the successes achieved by the Managing Director whom he had chosen after being introduced to him through Bea's family. Godfrey Isaacs was forty-four when he joined the Company in 1910, having had considerable experience in the family business and in general financial affairs in the City. He was one of nine children and the family business interests were most extensive, including a connection in the 1890s with Horatio Bottomley's publishing companies which brought Sir Henry Isaacs, an ex-Lord Mayor, into court in a remarkable case of conspiracy to obtain money from shareholders. The proceedings against Bottomley and others, including Henry Isaacs, were instituted in 1893 by Sir Edward Clarke, Solicitor General in the Unionist Government. Isaacs retained the Liberal QC Sir Charles Russell for his defence, but there was an election, and before the case came to court the Unionists were out of office and replaced by a Liberal Government in which Russell became Attorney General. Russell now prosecuted Isaacs instead of defending him, and Isaacs retained for his defence Clarke, the Unionist ex-Solicitor General who had instituted the proceedings. Confusing the case still further, Russell the Attorney General left in the middle for another appointment and the prosecution was taken over by the new Liberal Solicitor General. Perhaps not surprisingly, the case against Bottomley and the other defendants failed. Much later, in 1903, when Godfrey Isaacs himself was chairman of a committee which exonerated Bottomley after investigating the affairs of one of his companies, the earlier friendly relations of the Isaacs family with Bottomley were recalled.

The ingredients of Godfrey Isaacs' successful first three years with the Marconi Company might have been judged to be his business background, his aggressive commercial instincts, even his connection with Government through his brother Rufus Isaacs the Liberal Attorney General – although the Company had not lacked the entrée to Whitehall in Cuthbert Hall's time. Such matters were soon to come under the closest scrutiny because when Marconi, eager to be active again, returned to England at the end of 1912 after his motor accident, the gossip of intrigue and corruption in the matter of the Imperial Wireless Scheme had become so loud and public that it was to be known internationally as the 'Marconi Scandal'.

To understand the sensation created by the 'Marconi Scandal', the violent political explosions, and the passionate moralising of non-politicians, it is helpful to note that in the affair there were three main strands of reputable opposition to the Government giving the Imperial Wireless contract to the Marconi Company. There was commercial opposition from rival firms whose supporters stated their case in the newspapers and in Parliament. There was ideological opposition from those who believed that such a vital public service should be run by a department of State rather than a private company. There was political opposition from the Unionist Party in Parliament to this Liberal proposal. Interwoven with these three principal strands were dozens of minor threads of dissent, malice and self-interest, springing from motives varying from the worthy to the despicable. Parliament and its adjuncts provided the stage for most of the violent scenes, with the particularly bitter antagonism which existed at that time between the Liberal and Unionist parties over more important matters exacerbating a situation which, although unpleasant enough, hardly justified the almost hysterical national response.

It has been suggested[3] that if there had not been such a harsh vendetta between the two main parties, the Marconi affair would have been played down and the Tories would have co-operated with the Liberals in order to reassure the public. But, ironically, Lloyd George had himself contributed to the stream of abuse between Liberals and Conservatives as long as ten years before, when he joined in a campaign alleging commercial dishonesty against Joseph Chamberlain.[4] It had been said in Parliament that a Government contract was awarded to Kynochs because their chairman was Chamberlain's brother. The insinuations were repeated later during the election campaign, with *Punch* printing a quip that, 'the more the Empire expands, the more the Chamberlains contract'. When the new Parliament met, Lloyd George moved an amendment to the Address to the effect that 'members ought to have no interest, direct or indirect, in any firm or company competing for contracts with the Crown'. During the years after the Liberal 'landslide' victory in 1906 there was plenty of controversial legislation to keep red hot the Conservatives' hatred of the Liberals. There was Lloyd George's battle with the House of Lords, and the Act curbing their powers; the Insurance Bill for which the Liberal Chief Whip, Lord Murray, secured Ramsay MacDonald's promise of Labour support provided the Payment of M.P.'s Bill went through;[5] but protracted and fierce controversy raged most of all over Irish Home Rule and the fate of Ulster. The supporters of Ulster were desperate to get rid of the Government and eagerly sought any issue which might be used to bring down the Liberals and turn them out of office. At the end of 1912 the political fervour was such that the Unionist leader, Bonar Law, was escorted from a meeting to the railway station by a cheering crowd of supporters and a hundred torch bearers.[6] Meanwhile in the Press, Law was having a violent controversy over Home Rule with Winston Churchill whom the Liberals had made First Lord of the Admiralty with the task of creating an efficient Naval Staff organisation so that the defects in planning revealed by the Agadir incident should be quickly remedied[7] before what most people regarded as the imminent and inevitable war with Germany.

Even in this feverish political atmosphere it is remarkable that the relatively trivial actual substance of the Marconi affair should have created such a great and lasting disturbance. Indeed it was not so much the misdemeanours of the Liberal Ministers which made the 'Scandal' as the shifty and politically inept way in which those involved first concealed, and then suffered to be dragged out of them, the originally innocuous facts. These facts as ultimately revealed were comparatively simple.[8]

Godfrey Isaacs brought back from New York the hundred thousand American Marconi Company shares which were his personal responsibility. The day after his return to England he lunched at the Savoy with his two brothers: Rufus, the Attorney General, and Harry who was in the family fruit business. Over lunch Harry arranged to take half Godfrey's shares, and that evening he took another six thousand because his wife asked him to get some for her family. Rufus took none on this occasion but a few days later he met Harry and was persuaded to take ten thousand of the fifty thousand shares which Harry had obtained from Godfrey Isaacs. That same evening Rufus had a meeting with Lloyd George, the Chancellor of the Exchequer, and Lord Murray, the Liberal Chief Whip, and he let them each have a thousand of his shares.[9]

In these transactions the price paid for the shares was well below that at which they were being unofficially traded in London. When dealings opened officially on April 19th all three Ministers sold half their holdings and recouped about three quarters of their total cash liability, thus leaving themselves with a good paper profit on their original investment.

The fundamental question in the subsequent hullabaloo was the propriety of these transactions, and the principal characters in the drama were the three Liberal Ministers, although there were many complexities in the story and very many other people became involved.

The first part of the route taking Rufus Isaacs to the post of Attorney General was very unusual.[10] One or two of the steps were slippery and his early career was unsympathetically scrutinised by opponents and enemies during the scandal. His father took him away from school before he was fourteen and put him into the family business. At sixteen he went to sea as a ship's boy and visited South America and India before returning once more to work for his father. A married sister then got him a job as a clerk in her husband's stockbroking firm and when he was nineteen he applied for full membership of the Stock Exchange, although the application form which he signed stipulated that he should be over twenty-one. He was accepted for membership and left his brother-in-law's firm – which was hammered a few months later – and set up on his own. In August 1884 he was himself hammered, but because all his liabilities of about £8000 were within the Stock Exchange he was not made officially bankrupt. After this setback he planned a fresh start in Panama and had actually left the house on the way to the station when his mother had him brought back. He was put to the Law in Middle Temple and called to the Bar in November 1887, becoming a Queen's Counsel in 1897. By 1904 when he took his seat in Parliament as Liberal M.P. for Reading he was an enormous success at the Bar with a huge income, a house in Park Lane and one in the country, and a gay and influential circle of friends. In March 1910 he was made Solicitor General in the Liberal Government and as such led for the Crown in the famous 'Winslow Boy' case brought by the young naval cadet who had been accused of theft. One of the witnesses cross-examined by Isaacs during this case was a half-brother of the 'Winslow Boy' and later, as a Conservative M.P., played a part in the campaign against the Marconi contract. In October 1910 he became Attorney General, and in 1912 he was given a seat in the Cabinet[11] after Haldane had been made Lord Chancellor – a post which traditionally went to the Attorney General. Rufus Isaacs was the first Attorney General to sit in the Cabinet and he was given this responsibility as an acknowledgement of his standing in the Liberal Party after complaining to Asquith at not getting the Woolsack. It was while the discussions about his Cabinet post were taking place that the first rumours of the Marconi Scandal became public.

The Marconi Company's tender for the Imperial Wireless Scheme had been provisionally accepted by the Postmaster General, Herbert Samuel, in March 1912 and the contract had been signed in July, subject to Parliamentary ratification. In the interval between March and July the only information publicly available about the terms of the contract was contained in a circular issued by the Company which gave only some of the details, and created an impression that the terms were particularly advantageous. The result was a boom in English Marconi shares and complaints that the Government had favoured the Company. There was a corresponding boom in the newly issued shares of the American Marconi Company which were floated just after the acceptance of the Imperial Wireless tender became known. When the boom in English and American Marconi shares was quickly followed by a slump, the complaints of Government favouritism were supplemented by uglier accusations that the market had been rigged by Godfrey Isaacs, Marconi, and others, and these rumours were given extra spice when it was suggested that prominent Liberal Ministers had themselves been speculating in Marconi shares. In July 1912 certain journals published attacks upon the Marconi Company, the terms of the contract, and the Government. Hilaire Belloc and G. K. Chesterton were concerned in the publication of one of these journals, the *Eye Witness*, edited by Cecil Chesterton (G.K.'s brother), in which appeared the following:

Isaacs' brother is chairman of the Marconi Company. It has therefore been secretly arranged between Isaacs and Samuel that the British people shall give the Marconi Company a very large sum of money through the agency of the said Samuel and for the benefit of the said Isaacs.

Samuel and Isaacs considered legal action against the

197

Eye Witness and consulted the Prime Minister, but Asquith, in a letter from Balmoral in August, dissuaded them, saying that such proceedings would only secure notoriety welcome to such a journal.

With so much genuine opposition and wild rumour there was no question of the contract being ratified when it was laid before the House of Commons in August. The matter was deferred until after the Summer Recess and a debate arranged for October on a motion to set up a Select Committee of Enquiry. The Committee had a technical and a political task to perform, and to help it with the first part of its duties, reporting on the relative merits of the Marconi and other wireless systems, there was a technical advisory committee under Lord Justice Parker with the President of the Institution of Electrical Engineers and a number of other eminent scientists. This advisory committee conducted a searching enquiry, visiting wireless stations and taking evidence from witnesses, including an indignant Marconi who denied statements that the Admiralty was not using the Marconi system:

> I am at a loss to understand on what grounds this statement can be made. I have on many occasions in different parts of the world intercepted the signals transmitted from many of His Majesty's ships, and, in my judgement, there is nothing to suggest that these signals were transmitted by means in any way differing from that of our principal system, and, finally, I would state that in September 1911, one of my engineers was invited to inspect the wireless apparatus on one of His Majesty's ships. I accompanied him, and I declare that the system installed upon that ship was the Marconi system pure and simple.

The Parker Committee's report gave unequivocal support to the Postmaster General in his choice of the Marconi system: 'The Marconi system is at present the only system of which it can be said with any certainty that it is capable of fulfilling the requirements of the Imperial Chain.'

The political part of the Committee's task was inevitably

less straightforward and its difficulties were summed up by a senior Conservative member of the Committee, L. S. Amery, writing his political memoirs forty years later:

> I found myself involved in the most unpleasant and exasperating experience of my political life. A Parliamentary Joint Select Committee was set up in October 1912 to enquire into the Marconi Contract and the rumours flying about of ministerial speculations in Marconi shares, and I was appointed a member of it. . . .
>
> A Select Committee of the kind appointed is obviously a most unsatisfactory body to examine into a question affecting the conduct of Ministers or the character of a Government. The Opposition members are inclined to make the most of the case against Ministers, while the Government supporters are tempted to whitewash. But, never, I think, in the whole course of our political history, has there been a worse Select Committee than this one. The Conservative members, led by Lord Robert Cecil, were no doubt eager to get to the bottom of the rumours. The chairman, Sir Albert Spicer, an amiable but weak personality, was genuinely anxious to be impartial. But the Government majority, led by Mr Falconer and Mr Handel Booth, were quite shamelessly determined to burke all inquiry that could possibly elicit facts damaging to Ministers. Embarrassing questions were vetoed, the American dealings deliberately kept dark for weeks; and when Ministers at last appeared they were not allowed to be examined by counsel.[12]

In the Commons debate in October 1912 Lloyd George, Rufus Isaacs and Herbert Samuel denied all the rumours and the charges made against them. In particular they declared that they had never held any shares in the Company. But the form of words chosen for these denials was such that the listening M.P.s and the public reading the Parliamentary reports believed them to refer to shares in *any* Marconi Company, although in the case of Lloyd George and Isaacs the denials were only true in respect of shares in the English Marconi Company. It seems possible that the

Prime Minister had been told about the American Marconi shares owned by his Chancellor and Attorney General when he discussed with Isaacs the question of a libel action against *Eye Witness*. If this is so then Asquith connived at, or at least condoned, the misleading of the House of Commons and the public. Certainly Bonar Law and most of the Tories thought the denials repudiated the whole affair.[13]

The Select Committee met for the first time in October 1912 and the rumours and speculation continued in private and in the Press. A number of journalists who had been prominent in writing about Marconi affairs were called as witnesses and in February one of them, Maxse of the *National Review*, stated in evidence that the Ministers should be brought before the Committee and asked whether they had dealt in the shares of *any* Marconi Company. A French newspaper, *Le Matin*, printed a garbled version of Maxse's evidence and although it published a withdrawal a few days later, Rufus Isaacs and Herbert Samuel decided to sue. Isaacs proposed to make the case an opportunity to reveal publicly that he and Lloyd George had bought American Marconi shares. This fact had apparently already been made known privately in January to Falconer and Booth, two Liberal members of the Committee, so that they might fend off dangerous questions.[14] But in view of Maxse's evidence, disclosure to the Committee was now inevitable and it was considered that the impact of the revelation would be considerably reduced if it trickled out first in a foreign court. The *Le Matin* case was much more a political exercise than a legal one.

The first that Bonar Law knew of the trouble[15] about to strike the Liberal Party was when Campbell, one of his own members, asked whether it would be in order for him to accept a brief for *Le Matin*. Bonar Law agreed and was subsequently angry when he heard that, without consulting him, Carson and F. E. Smith were to appear for Isaacs and Samuel against *Le Matin*. Samuel would much have preferred non-political counsel but he allowed his solicitor and Rufus Isaacs to persuade him otherwise.[16] It was Winston Churchill who arranged that these two most prominent Tory lawyers should defend the Liberal Ministers.

Churchill was particularly active behind the scenes in support of Lloyd George and the others, and he did everything he could to reduce the harm that the affair did to them and to the Liberal Government. At this time he and F. E. Smith were both interested in an agreed political programme on major issues, like Ireland and the House of Lords, leading to a coalition government, and indeed they pursued the matter with Lloyd George after the Marconi affair was over.[17] Perhaps this common political ground helped Churchill to secure Smith and Carson for the *Le Matin* case, a coup which not only ensured that the difficult case would be well handled in court but also had the effect of preventing them from taking an active part in Tory attacks on the Government which must now be expected. As Samuel wrote just before the trial:

> The fact has to be stated, and although there was nothing dishonourable in what they did, it was certainly unwise, and the statement which Rufus Isaacs will make in the witness-box on Wednesday will undoubtedly give rise to a great deal of hostile comment. However it can't be helped, and the Government must stand as best they can.[18]

Churchill also did another very useful job for the Liberal cause by persuading Northcliffe to treat the Marconi case sympathetically in his newspapers. When Lloyd George thanked him for the way he had handled the affair, Northcliffe replied:

> I adopted my line about this Marconi business because five minutes' lucid explanation showed me that it was the fairest one. Moreover, I am neither a rabid party man nor an anti-Semite.
>
> I was particularly glad to do so, in as much as I feel that you will now know that I am not personally hostile to you, as was twice suggested last year by mutual friends. You gave me some shrewd blows, and I replied to them. So far as I was concerned that was the end of it. A week-end glance at the French and German newspapers convinces

201

me that this country has before it more urgent business than personal or party issues.[19]

Writing more informally to Winston Churchill, Northcliffe stated bluntly what he thought of the way Isaacs and Lloyd George had behaved: '. . . Your Marconi friends stage-manage their affairs most damnably. For a couple of really clever people I cannot understand such muddling. . . .'[20] He also firmly refused to be co-operative in treating a new twist in the story: Lord Murray, who had resigned as Liberal Chief Whip, left the country for South America 'on business' before the investigations were completed. Northcliffe wrote:

When you came to ask me to treat the Marconi matter on non-Party lines, I accepted your word that there was nothing more than what you told me about the Attorney-General and George.

Their transactions do not seem to me to be of any particular demerit, except for the way in which they have been slowly dragged out before the Public. This morning I read of an entirely fresh crop of developments, of which I know you were unaware. They do not appear to affect Sir Rufus or George, nor to be particularly noxious in themselves, apart from the fact that they have been ferreted out by newspapers. I kept my promise to you most gladly, but I must express my opinion that steps should be taken to ask Lord Murray to come back. His absence gives the impression, probably quite erroneous, that there is what newspapers call 'a big story' behind the whole of this matter, and I have no intention of letting my journals remain silent on his abstention. . . .[21]

Lord Murray, Master of Elibank and Liberal Chief Whip, had been present at Lloyd George's house when Rufus Isaacs called that evening in April 1912 and he, like the Chancellor, had taken a thousand American Marconi shares. As a member of the House of Lords his enquiry was in the hands of a special committee of the Upper House. In a note to Lloyd George headed 'Secret. Burn' he wrote:

202

Rufus and I agreed that while my enquiry was 'on' it would be wiser if we were not seen together in public or known to be together as it would only be said that we were concocting my evidence, or that I was being primed or some such rot.

Under the circumstances therefore I think that the precaution which applies to him and me should for *a few days longer* apply to us two, and that I had better breakfast here instead of in the 'old spot', as a reporter has been known to hang about in Downing Street. . . .

You have been having difficult times. I think I can feel so well how it all happened: you and I used to scent some these dangers [*sic*] together once upon a time.[22]

A clerk in the office of Murray's stockbroker revealed[23] that the Chief Whip had made a further investment of nine thousand pounds in the shares on behalf of the Liberal Party Fund and to a certain extent in the public mind this implicated the whole of the Party in the affair. When Murray went off to South America in the middle of the scandal, hecklers at Liberal meetings shouted not only 'Marconi' but 'Bogota'. He wrote from Bogota on 20 August 1913 with news of Lloyd George's son who was also out there, working for Murray's company:

In the midst of all the suffering which singular ill-fortunes and venom have brought upon us let me cheer you with a little note regarding Dick. . . . [He went on to say how well Dick was doing in his work, arranging oil contracts in South America].

These Yankees know a thing or two! My difficulties have not been lessened by the trouble with which Reuter and the Tory Press took care to keep the South American Press informed of my iniquities. It was very ungrateful of Reuter, because I subsidized him heavily when I was Chief Whip to cable the speeches of Liberal Cabinet Ministers throughout the world and otherwise give fair play to the Liberal Party, and miserable as I have been throughout all this business I could not help smiling to think that I

203

should find myself the victim of a system I had tried to eradicate, and at the hands too of an agency that had but a year ago fawned at my door, and might even have been quite willing to take payment in American Marconi shares for their useful services. Of all this wretched business I shall write nothing and I shall come and see you on my return home.[24]

Murray went on to refer to Winston Churchill's speech on the Marconi affair at the Liberal Club: '*It was just like him. I have always regarded him as a really true friend who will always stand by one in foul or in fair weather*' and he ended the letter with 'my love to dear old Rufus'.

Relations between Murray and Lloyd George were, surprisingly, unaffected by the former's flight to South America and friendly letters passed between them during the next year or two. Writing from Brooks's Club in 1914 to Lloyd George, Murray says:

I am sending you 100 Corona Corona Cabinet as I know you like them. I go this afternoon to Sunningdale.

If you are able to get away and want to sleep in the country today, tomorrow, or Monday, with some motoring thrown in, you know where to come.[25]

The date of this trifling note strikes a particular note of bathos: it was 1 August 1914.

Lloyd George did not feel obliged to return the friendship and loyalty shown to him during the scandal, particularly by Churchill and Asquith. Certainly he attacked rather than defended Churchill over Gallipoli[26] and it was suggested that the campaign about Asquith's excessive drinking emanated from Lloyd George and his circle.[27]

Three women recorded some of Lloyd George's less widely publicised activities during the Marconi hearings. Frances Lloyd George in her autobiography[28] tells how Lloyd George had given her a book on Parnell by Kitty O'Shea and how she went to Scotland to think over her future. While she was there she received a proposal of marriage from a 'suitable' young man. Lloyd George wrote that the decision must be hers but he followed this almost immediately with an urgent letter saying that something terrible had happened and that he needed her in London. Although there had been rumours for some time Lloyd George had felt justified in treating the matter lightly, she said, because he was innocent of the dangerous accusation brought against him in connection with the Marconi shares which Rufus Isaacs had persuaded him to buy. He tormented himself with how he had let down his non-conformist supporters and what his fond old Uncle Lloyd would think of him. She returned from Scotland to London soon after Christmas 1912 and placed herself unconditionally in Lloyd George's hands. Probably at the suggestion of Masterman, Financial Secretary to the Treasury, she visited newspaper offices to try to find out if there had been any public mention of American Marconi shares which would have made them available to the general public. This would have exonerated Lloyd George and Rufus Isaacs, but after many weary but hopeful days nothing could be found. She said that the personal relations between Lloyd George and Isaacs were never quite the same after the Marconi affair.

When it came to outlook Lloyd George and Rufus Isaacs parted, for the latter had what might be called the 'cafeteria' mind – self-service only. Ambition was his ruling quality, quietly he sought and obtained advancement until he became Viceroy of India – he, a Jew!

It was suggested[29] that when Lloyd George was giving evidence before the Select Committee he did not fully understand the share transactions made by him and in his name (like Murray he had later bought more shares after getting the thousand from Isaacs). His evidence was interrupted by the weekend, during which he met Rufus Isaacs and Masterman, who was closely concerned with the Chancellor and Attorney General while they were appearing before the Committee. Mrs Masterman described a tense scene between the three men. Lloyd George was still in a 'fog' about his transactions and was using 'technical terms' and he became sulky when Masterman and Isaacs impressed upon him that he must tell his story in ordinary language.

Immediately before the final debate in the House of Commons, which was to consider the findings of the Select Committee, Lloyd George had the benefit of several notes from Margot Asquith giving very positive advice on how he should conduct himself. The style was very much her own: the writing a hurried scrawl covering the paper both horizontally and, in the margins, vertically, while the message itself did not make it absolutely clear whether the instructions it contained were from the Prime Minister or from Mrs Asquith. On 13 June 1913 she wrote from 10 Downing Street:

> I dined alone with my husband last night – he was in *Derby form* – He said he wanted to see you and Rufus to have a careful talk over the speeches: 'If Lloyd George and Rufus play their cards *well*, show the proper spirit, *I* will let the opposition HAVE IT!!' . . . Committee have proved nothing but great indiscretion. The points are these. This debate must show that nothing of this kind can ever happen again and that when you realised the folly you apologised (That part of your speech should be broad and simple in *no* way rhetorical it will have more effect) and did your best. Henry is in *just* the right mood, a man stirred by the caddish behaviour of Bonar Law, Lord Bob Cecil, etc. *Do* see him today. You and Rufus will be in high spirits I bet after the debate but *do* see Henry today or Monday. Talk it closely over also with Rufus so that the three speeches shall cover like a miniature mosaic *all* the ground.[30]

The day before the debate Mrs Asquith dashed off a note while on the train telling Lloyd George not to attack the Opposition – she was sure Henry would do this.

> . . . but don't do it tomorrow – you could even anticipate that silly *Spectator* by saying that the Prime Minister would not have done what you did because he had more foresight. He wouldn't be our Prime Minister if he hadn't a little more of everything than some of us and ALL OF YOU.

The report laid before the House by its Select Committee reflected the strictly party lines of its constitution and was in accord with the way it had conducted the enquiry. There were in fact three reports: one from the Liberal majority, one from the Unionist minority, and another one from the chairman. Amery, a Unionist member of the Committee, described these reports:

> The Unionist members submitted a report drafted by Robert Cecil and myself. It cleared Ministers of any charge of corruption, but found them guilty of grave impropriety in making an advantageous purchase of shares in the American company while the contract was still under discussion. It also described the 'reticence' of Ministers in the October debate as 'a grave error of judgement and as wanting in frankness and respect for the House of Commons'. This was, of course, incontinently voted down. The chairman's report, while accepting the strange ministerial contention that the rumours published in the Press had no connexion with the American share dealings, concluded with a mildly worded, but unmistakable, censure both on the transactions of Ministers and on their subsequent reticence. We were not surprised when this, too, was turned down and a fantastic report substituted, as the report of the Committee, by Mr Falconer, which made the rumours antecedent to the American share purchases, and treated the latter as in every way blameless. This was too strong a dose for the public, and even for the most obedient sections of the Liberal Party in Parliament and in the Press. The defiant attitude which Ministers had maintained before the Committee could obviously not be sustained in the debate which was opened on June 18th and the two errant Ministers were told that they must frankly express their regret at what had occurred.[31]

In their characteristic styles Rufus Isaacs and Lloyd George had given their evidence, answered the questions, and made their statements. Isaacs said: 'I say solemnly and sincerely it was a mistake to purchase those shares.' Lloyd George declared: 'I acted thoughtlessly, carelessly, mistakenly, but I acted openly, innocently, honestly.' There were conflicting opinions of their performances. Amery thought that they were 'each strikingly effective', but Sir Edward Cadogan wrote[32] that after hearing Rufus Isaacs before the Committee, he and Waley Cohen agreed that they had never heard evidence so badly given, and that Lloyd George's apologia on the floor of the House was no more reassuring.

But two men survived the months of enquiry with untarnished reputations. Herbert Samuel, the Postmaster General, never bought shares in any Marconi Company and it was agreed that his department had negotiated the contract with nothing else in mind but the public interest. Marconi himself, an unwilling participant in what the *Daily Telegraph* called the 'farcical proceedings', had the sympathy of the general public who felt that he had been unfairly drawn into the machinations of politicians and scandalmongers. The *Telegraph* voiced the general feeling, 'To him at least a word of apology is due. We are sure the British public regrets the manner in which his name has been dragged through the mire of personal allegations and partisan recriminations.'

In his own evidence Marconi said:

I wish to state most emphatically that I have never at any time speculated in any of the shares of my companies. I have always supported them whenever money has been required, and frequently to very large sums. I have occasionally sold shares, not in consequence of markets or circumstances connected with the company's business, but only when I have required moneys for business in which I am interested other than that of the Marconi companies. During the whole of the period of the boom in shares in the parent company or the American company, or any of the companies with which I am associated, I have never bought or sold a share. . . .

I do not wish to conclude without expressing my resentment at the reflections which have been made upon my company and upon me for having innocently entered into a contract with His Majesty's Government. I resent the inquiry into and publication given to the affairs of my company, which have no relation whatsoever to the contract entered into with His Majesty's Government, and I would in this respect particularly express my regret that the services which my company and I have for so many years rendered to the Post Office, the Admiralty, the merchant marine, and in fact the whole nation, should not have been deemed worthy of higher consideration.

The June 1913 debate in the House of Commons ended with all charges of corruption against Rufus Isaacs and Lloyd George being repudiated, but the Government was forced by the Opposition and some of its own backbenchers to accept an amendment taking notice of the fact that the Ministers had expressed regret that they had bought shares and that they had not mentioned these purchases in the earlier debate in October 1912. The Select Committee was wound up by the Liberals on 2 July 1913, a move which some considered premature and calculated to stifle further investigation.

On 1 July a banquet was given for Rufus Isaacs and Lloyd George at the National Liberal Club and the Chancellor referred to the now ended Marconi affair in a speech which attacked his critics for humbug and self-righteousness and referred to himself as being persecuted for trying to 'lift the poor out of the mire and the needy out of the dunghill'. Amery found this more than he could stomach and spoke out very strongly against the Liberal Ministers in a speech ending:

Now that the truth – or at any rate a substantial portion of it – has come out, Ministers are attempting to bluff the country into believing that while they have done nothing that is not wholly admirable and worthy of imitation, they have been the victims of a cruel campaign of slander invented by the sheer devilish malignity of their political opponents. Really that won't wash. The cruel campaign is largely a figment of their own imagination. No serious journal or responsible person has ever charged them, or charges them now, with corruption. The fact remains that they did speculate improperly, and that they did for months mislead the House of Commons and the public. Most men, I think, in such circumstances would realize that they had made a serious mistake and would keep quiet. Lord Murray wisely chose the seclusion of Bogota. Mr Lloyd George prefers to crow brazen defiance to the public conscience from his own dunghill at the National Liberal Club. We can afford to leave him there.[33]

There were a few more shots in the battle. The Unionists published in the Press the comments they had been unable to make to the Select Committee before the Liberals ended its meetings. Cecil Chesterton, author of the notorious article in *Eye Witness*, had never appeared before the Committee but he was found guilty of criminal libel against Godfrey Isaacs. An offshoot of this case was an action by a Unionist M.P. and another shareholder in English Marconi against Godfrey and Harry Isaacs, Marconi and others including jobbers in the American Marconi shares, asking for a fraction of the profit alleged to have been made in dealing in these shares. The case was settled out of court with one of the jobbers paying a large sum of costs.

There was still some opposition to the granting of a new contract for Imperial Wireless to the Marconi Company and on 17 July 1913 the *Electrical Times* stated:

We hold no brief for the Marconi Company but the American Marconi affair should not be allowed to influence sane men's judgement to such an extent that they should use all their efforts to oppose anything with which the name of Marconi is associated.[34]

A revised contract containing some protective clauses for the Crown was debated and ratified by Parliament in August 1913 and by the summer of 1914 work was well advanced on several of the stations. But once again the great scheme was delayed by a political rather than a technological failure, and this time the delay was not the twelve months of the Marconi Scandal but nearer twelve years. This time the political failure was the ultimate one and the Post Office cancelled the contract and all work was stopped soon after the outbreak of the Great War.

Assessments of the effects of the Marconi Scandal have differed widely. The delay in the Imperial Wireless Scheme was an identifiable and undeniable effect. The formulation of 'rules of obligation' and 'rules of prudence' governing Ministerial conduct and a review of the function of the Select Committee were two less concrete political effects. Perhaps most significant were the effects the Scandal did not produce. It did not bring down the Liberal Government nor destroy Lloyd George's career and deny the country his wartime leadership, although Winston Churchill believed that this might have been done if some of the Tories had not been too stupid to handle it properly but 'frankly some of them were too nice'[35] and he considered that Carson and F. E. Smith rescued Lloyd George.[36]

The moral consequences of the Scandal were widely discussed. G. K. Chesterton in his autobiography suggested that because of it 'the ordinary English citizen lost his invincible ignorance; or, in ordinary language, his innocence . . .' but Rufus Isaacs' son, writing of his father, considered the whole thing to have been a molehill. Petrie, describing the early history of the Labour Party,[37] said that it attracted many idealists because 'there was much genuine idealism about the ILP and the Fabian Society while there was precious little about a Conservatism dominated by big business and Whig Irish Landlords or Liberalism in the grip of the men of the Marconi Scandal'. But, if it existed, the moral effect had no practical consequence when such an issue was raised only a few months after the Scandal had supposedly run its course. In October 1913 there was surprise verging on sensation when Asquith offered Rufus Isaacs the office of Lord Chief Justice of England and he accepted, becoming Lord Reading. All the outcry had no effect and two English poets demonstrated the range of feelings about the appointment. Kipling wrote his poem about Gehazi, Elisha's swindling servant, one verse of which goes:

> Whence comest thou Gehazi
> So reverend to behold
> In scarlet and in ermine
> And chain of England's gold?

In quieter style Rupert Brooke, on the way to Fiji, wrote from across the world to a friend saying he was thinking of giving up the National Liberal Club 'because I hate the Liberal Party and the Marconi affair and the whole mess and Rufus Isaacs as Lord Chief Justice'.[38] The attacks on Reading continued for years, one of the campaigners being an organisation called the Society for Upholding Political Honour, and particular efforts were directed at getting him removed from the British delegation to the Peace Conference in Paris after the war.

A final comment on the Scandal from Marconi's daughter reveals that, whatever the general effects of the Scandal, Marconi himself never forgot how the carefully cultivated friendly links with the world of politics which had so often eased the progress of his big technical schemes had on this occasion dragged him into a squalid brawl between the parties which stopped the Empire Wireless Chain, cost his Company money, and threatened his own good name. 'To the end of his life Father was racked with anger at this abuse of his name. It seemed a denial of everything he had accomplished, an intolerable injustice.'[39]

So exclusive was the attention focused upon the Marconi Scandal and the delay in the Imperial Wireless Chain that the public might easily have been misled into thinking that the Marconi Company had abandoned technology for investment and litigation. On the contrary, much was going ahead in Britain and abroad. The Marconi Company was now producing standard wireless equipment in large numbers on factory lines, particularly for merchant vessels and warships. To improve the transatlantic telegraph service and make it more reliable and competitive with the cable, newly designed

Marconi stations had been erected in Wales and in America, near New York. A fundamentally new wireless technique of great potential had been developed by the Marconi Company and its competitors: this was telephony using thermionic triode valves to generate a continuous electrical oscillation of a single high frequency which was transmitted after having impressed upon it the lower frequencies of the spoken words in the message. With great perception, looking ahead to a lucrative new field of application for wireless, the Marconi Company was now beginning to make significant progress with aircraft communications in which it had been interested since the first air-to-ground transmission had been made in 1911 in America from an early Curtiss machine using Marconi apparatus.

Grahame-White, the aviation pioneer, lived at Orange House, Kingsbury, near London, and his wife liked to entertain lavishly. Among the social 'lions' who came to the house was Marconi[40] and there was a certain piquancy about this meeting when, no doubt, Grahame-White discussed the experiments in air-to-ground communication that were being carried out at his Hendon aerodrome in conjunction with the Marconi Company. But he probably had more than technical thoughts on his mind when he talked to Marconi. Here was a man who had cultivated and found support for a scientific idea until it had grown into a great group of companies. The English air pioneer had similar ambitions, and although he expected to hear something interesting from Marconi the scientist, he would have had high hopes of useful advice from Marconi the promoter.

Grahame-White had prepared a complete scheme for a British civil aviation service, and by the autumn of 1912 he had a backer, Sir Edgar Speyer, who was prepared to put up the two million pounds needed to start. The financier had attached one proviso to his offer: the British Government must show its confidence in the future of civil and military aviation by a token contribution of a hundred thousand pounds.

The task of securing such a comparatively trivial sum from the Government must have seemed an easy final step to

213

Grahame-White. He had a well-worked-out scheme, and solid financial backing. He had access to the Chancellor of the Exchequer, Lloyd George, a radical who was likely to be sympathetic to Government participation in an industry of national importance. By the greatest good luck of all Lloyd George was personally extremely interested in the aeroplane and had visited the air display at Hendon.

But if Marconi's success in a similar venture had been an inspiration and a source of hope to Grahame-White, Marconi's name – or rather the scandal labelled with his name – queered the pitch for pre-war civil aviation. When Grahame-White met the Chancellor, Lloyd George was almost completely distracted by the Marconi Scandal and the threat it posed to his political future. He took no interest in Grahame-White's project and referred it to Jellicoe, the Chairman of the Imperial Defence Committee. After a recent trip in a Zeppelin, Jellicoe was enthusiastic about airships and had no faith in heavier-than-air machines. He gave no support to the scheme, which therefore lapsed, and it was seven years later before British civil air services were inaugurated. The aircraft which made the first commercial flight from London to Paris was a de Havilland machine: the wireless equipment fitted in it was Marconi's.

When the newspapers were at last free from reports of the Marconi Scandal there was, for Marconi, a welcome re-appearance of a front-page story in the old style – a rescue at sea, a triumph for wireless, and acknowledgement of humanity's debt to Marconi. In October 1913 the *Volturno*, sailing to America with a full load of emigrants, caught fire in mid-Atlantic and lay disabled and blazing fiercely in a terrible storm. The wireless SOS brought ten rescue ships to the scene by the next morning, but so heavy were the seas that their boats could not hope to fetch over six hundred to safety. But time was short, for the fire had now taken such hold that the *Volturno*'s Captain feared he might have to abandon ship, and indeed a panic among the passengers resulted in the loss of over a hundred who jumped into the water or tried prematurely to launch boats. Fortunately the storm abated slightly and one of the ring of vessels was a tanker which pumped oil on to the

water so that a fleet of small boats was able to ferry more than
five hundred people to safety.

The story of the *Volturno* rescue, and the part played in it
by wireless, was featured in many newspapers. *Punch* published a cartoon[41] showing Marconi receiving the gratitude of
the world, and the *Daily Telegraph* went further and declared
that England had not sufficiently rewarded him:

> the country on which he has showered such untold benefits
> has been content to single him out as an unwilling partici-
> pant in an unsavoury scandal. . . .
>
> Surely the time and occasion have arrived when the
> State may well revive, if that be necessary, its standard of
> honour, and grant to the wizard who enabled such a
> triumph to be achieved in the name of humanity some
> fitting token of England's gratitude for the great permanent
> addition he has made to what may be described as our
> armoury of mercy.[42]

A few months later, in July 1914, Marconi received an
honorary GCVO from the King at Buckingham Palace.
It was fitting that the decoration he received was of the
Victorian Order which is the personal gift of the Sovereign,
unlike the majority of comparable British awards which
are distributed through the office of the Prime Minister.

In March 1914 Marconi added to the Italian honours he
already possessed the special distinction of Senatore – life
membership of the Italian Upper House – a title bestowed on
mature and distinguished men of science and arts. Marconi
was just forty, the minimum age, when he received this
honour, and it was in accord with the generally greater
recognition, financial and honorary, given to him in Italy than
in England – a fact on which he had remarked bitterly during
the Scandal. The Italian public, too, were generous in their
adulation, although some of their demonstrations were not
entirely welcome: Marconi had his coat ripped during one
encounter with an enthusiastic crowd in Rome. Woodward,
Marconi's expert on signal reception, described a similar
occasion:

My personal experience of Mr Marconi was that he could be most friendly and affable to those whom he knew intimately but he was somewhat reserved towards comparative strangers. Although he was naturally appreciative of the interest taken in himself and his work he was without side and was embarrassed by undue attention. Although most of his early work was carried out in this country he was, I think, better known and esteemed by the general public in Italy than over here. I remember an occasion when he visited a music hall in Rome with the Marchese Solari, his secretary, and myself. We were rather late in going in but apparently a few persons recognised him on entering. Someway through, later in the programme, a comedian came on and in his patter mentioned his name. Immediately those around us stood up and shouted the name Marconi with the result that within a few seconds the house was on its feet shouting and cheering. It was rather embarrassing and we beat a hasty retreat and I learned afterwards that the comedian apologised for the embarrassment occasioned and for causing him to miss the rest of the show. Such an incident could not have occurred in this country, not only because we are less demonstrative than the Italians but he would not have been so well known or acclaimed.[43]

Another piece of continental hero-worship, or perhaps just collector's zeal, is shown in a letter to Marconi from a young woman in Budapest:

I wrote you just a month ago and begged you to be so kind and sign an enclosed leaf of a fan on which the signature of Mr Edison was. Though I should have been very, very glad and happy if I could have possessed also your precious signature on the side of Mr Edison's I beg you instantly to be so kind and to return me the fan leaf because I never hope to get once more the signature of Mr Edison. I beg you, dear Sir, to sign the fan leaf on the same side where Mr Edison signed it or to return me the fan leaf without your signature. I hope you cannot be so cruel to do the latter.[44]

Nestling pathetically in the Marconi archives among a little sheaf of similarly worded letters from the same Elisabeth is the flimsy wooden fan leaf, carrying Edison's wasted signature, but not Marconi's, and now broken into three pieces. The dates of the letters are 1912, a busy time for Marconi when he was much abroad. Perhaps he never saw the letters or the fan leaf.

It was just like the old days of wireless, when Marconi visited Italy to receive the honour of Senatore in March 1912. He gave a lecture to a distinguished audience in Rome including the King and Queen and, typically, he seized the opportunity of carrying out some successful experiments on radio telephony at sea with the Regia Marina. But his principal technical interest at this time was in the improvement of the transatlantic wireless telegraph service. The greatest cause of interruption in this service was the failure of the land lines between the remote Glace Bay and Clifden stations and New York or London, the destination or origin of most of the messages. New stations were under construction near New York and on the British mainland in Wales with the advantage of shorter, more reliable, land lines. The extra distance the wireless signals had to travel was no longer important now that the original apparatus had been so much improved. A special feature of the new stations was that each would have receiving and transmitting aerials separated by some miles, with a cunning method of combining signals from the directional aerials so that the powerful signal leaving the transmitting aerial did not swamp the weak signals coming into the receiving aerial. Duplex working was now possible on both sides of the Atlantic and the speed of handling messages considerably increased. Marconi was particularly concerned with the station being erected at Caernarvon in Wales, and his letters to Woodward who was also involved suggest what his attitude was to the relative importance of work and domestic affairs. On 3 December 1913 he wrote from Marconi House, London:

Thank you for your letter of yesterday in reply to which I have to tender to you my most hearty congratulations on your engagement. I hope that I may have an early opportunity of again meeting your fiancée. I shall be very glad for you to come back to work now and shall speak to Mr Gray with a view to arranging that you get the remaining two or three weeks of your holiday which I understand are due to you in about a month's time when you say you would like to have it. I take it this is for the purpose of getting married.[45]

On 1 April 1914 Marconi wrote again on the same subject:

I have no objection to you commencing your leave on the evening of April 7th, but in view of the fact that I intend shortly visiting the Welsh station I should be glad if then you did not take more than one week, or possibly ten days as I note that you are desirous of getting married on the 14th. In consideration of your not taking from the 7th the three weeks which are due to you I should be prepared to let you have a few extra days when you take the remainder of your leave at a later date which would be more convenient to me.

Marconi's own married life did not prosper during 1913 and 1914. Eaglehurst in Hampshire was still the family home, although Bea spent most of the winter of 1913 in Rome, taking the children and Lilah with her. Bea took up her place in the Italian Court as lady-in-waiting to the Queen and entered enthusiastically into the social life her duties entailed. In England, Marconi mixed work with a social life of his own among the bright and brittle people of the London theatre. He had first been introduced into such company by Bea's sister Moira, a theatrical designer, at whose London flat he and Bea often stayed. Marconi's daughter recorded that her mother spoke of his recurring fits of jealousy during these years:

She gave up the parties she loved, knowing that the subsequent accusations would rob her of her pleasure. . . .

If jealousy were justified it was Mother who had every right to be jealous. This theatre world was no part of her world, neither as to its morals, which she knew were deplorable, nor its manners, which could hardly conform with her upper-class conventions. At a time when a single standard of behaviour for men and women was inconceivable, her flirtations were limited to come-hither glances from behind a fan. His affairs were doubtless outrageous, but she was bound to accept them as long as she remained married. . . . One reason why Father enjoyed his theatrical friendships was that they were so frankly superficial they did not impinge on his inner heart. At the same time he longed for the warm, human love of which he believed his wife capable but which he never wholly won from her. In her way she failed him because she was incapable of expressing her feelings. The gap between them widened.[46]

Marconi was in Italy in March 1914 when he was made a Senatore, and he and Bea came back to England with the children soon afterwards. He was in Caernarvon in May for the opening of the new transatlantic wireless station, at a theatre party arranged by Tree at His Majesty's in June, at Buckingham Palace in July to receive his GCVO, and later that month he and Bea were entertained by Beatty aboard his flagship H.M.S. *Lion*, one of several hundred vessels gathered at Spithead for the Naval Review.

After the Review the Fleet sailed off for the annual training exercises and manoeuvres which for economy reasons were this year on a restricted scale. At the end of July the manoeuvres were over, the Fleet about to disperse and discharge all its naval reservists back to their homes. Instead, a wireless message from the Admiralty ordered the vessels to their war stations and they were all deployed ready for action by 3 August 1914 when the great Telefunken station at Nauen in Berlin, now under the control of the military authorities, ordered all German shipping at sea to run for the nearest port. Next day Marconi House, London picked up a German broadcast[47] that war had been declared against France, Russia, and England. The message was passed to Godfrey

Isaacs who telephoned it to a British Cabinet Minister. At 11 p.m. that night the British ultimatum to Germany expired without direct answer and the Grand Fleet received from the Admiralty the wireless message: 'Commence hostilities against Germany'.

CHAPTER 13

GREAT WAR DIPLOMAT
AND SUBALTERN

WHEN Britain declared war on Germany Marconi's position became difficult. For all his British blood and connections, he was an alien, and moreover a citizen of a country which was bound to Germany in the Triple Alliance, although on 2 August 1914 Italy had declared her intention of remaining neutral. An alien living in a house overlooking the sea, and known to have there wireless equipment capable of communicating with the Continent, naturally attracted a certain amount of suspicion in the early months of the war when rumours of spies and enemy agents circulated freely. In November 1914 the Home Office refused to grant him the pass he had asked for to enable him to travel about the United Kingdom on business, and he was told that he could be given no exemption from the provisions of the Aliens Restriction Order.[1] But in a short while the attitude of the authorities changed and he was able to leave Eaglehurst and go to Rome, where with the good offices of the British Ambassador he arranged for the return home to England of Lilah, his sister-in-law.

Marconi took his seat in the Italian Senate in Rome in January 1915 and he was probably then given the first of many diplomatic missions he subsequently undertook for his country. Among his political papers is a memorandum concerning the possibility of Italy entering the war on the side of the Allies. It is likely that he was intended to use this to influence friends in British Government circles when he returned to England early in 1915. The long document shows considerable prescience and is headed 'Very Private' but bears no evidence of origin or date, although the indications are that it was prepared at the end of 1914 or the beginning of

221

1915 by the pro-war party in Italy, worried that the German, von Bülow, might succeed in preventing Italy from joining the Allies.

Sig. Giolitti's public statement that Italy could obtain much without war, his interviews with von Bülow etc., have considerably improved the chances of German diplomacy and raised the hopes of non-interventionists. Von Bülow is reported to be endeavouring to persuade Austria, now conscious of her precarious position, and under strict German military control, to give way before it is too late. The lesson of '66 when, had she surrendered Venice some weeks earlier, she might have averted Königgrätz, and the present feverish military preparation of Italy should aid the efforts of von Bülow.

Should the effort to persuade Austria fail, von Bülow will approach Italy directly with a view to Italy dissociating Germany from Austria and declaring a war against Austria alone. He will point out that Germany has done nothing to justify Italy declaring war on her, but on the contrary the existence of the Triple Alliance since '82 has safeguarded the peninsula from aggression either from France or Austria and that thereby Italy had been able to consolidate her favourable position and develop her trade and industry. Moreover a victorious France would be a serious menace to Italy and only with the help of Germany could it be resisted. With true German methods von Bülow will suggest that hostilities against Germany will be regarded as rank treachery and lead to inextinguishable hatred.

It is not impossible that these arguments will have weight with the Italian Government. In such conditions Austria could not put up serious opposition, merely making a show of resistance, and Italy would with little difficulty annex unredeemed Italy without attempting more serious hostility against Austria. It is easy to see that Germany would regard this solution of the difficulty with equanimity. It would not to any appreciable extent impair the efficiency of Austria in a military sense and it would enable the Central Powers to continue with their premeditated plan of campaign. It might even lead Bulgaria to take similar action against exhausted Serbia and in any case would make it possible for Italy to take sides with Germany at a Peace Congress and probably at a later date to make a new alliance with Germany against possible French pretensions. Nor would the Austrians be unwilling when in extremis to put up with this solution. They are now so bound up with the future of Germany that considerations other than those affecting Germany are no longer of interest to them. This solution would also find much favour in Italy. Much as Austria is hated, Germany still enjoys a good deal of sympathy, especially in the South where Tunis, and the Tariff War which followed, are not forgotten. The result would please the man in the street and would be a feather in the cap of the Government to have accomplished the last step in the unity of Italy with an insignificant loss of life and a comparatively insignificant loss of capital.

No responsible ruler of Italy could risk the future enmity of Germany unless Italy were guaranteed the complete goodwill and support of France, and this could only be assured by France's recognition of Italy's rights in the Mediterranean. The possibility of an aggressive France, and Poincaré's speech is not forgotten, is a menace Italy must keep in mind. It would be madness for Italy to join in crushing Germany unless she can be safeguarded against such a menace. The democracy of Italy – one may say of Europe – would view with pleasure the complete discomfiture of Germany, but it would not ensure enduring peace unless it were accompanied by some grouping similar to the Bismarckian Triple Alliance – say an alliance of the liberal western powers which would protect the new settlement from any attack from a regenerated Germany. For it should not be forgotten that the more Austria is crushed – and that Austria will go is now practical politics – the more certain it is that the German-speaking Austrians will enter the German Empire, and no one can prevent them doing so. As a result one may say that the more serious the defeat of the Central Powers the more certain it is that, in population at any rate, the new Germany will be far stronger than present

223

Germany. There will certainly be a population of over eighty millions, and absolutely homogeneous, compact and bound with a sentiment of a common disaster. There may be a new dynasty, and parliamentary government may be introduced, but the patriotism of Germany will remain, and if France annexes Alsace-Lorraine that patriotism will be nursed on a grievance and be looking out for revenge as soon as the nation is ready for it. France no doubt intends to annex Alsace-Lorraine but if she does, she should prudently consider the means necessary to retain them against a revengeful Germany.

They can only be retained by a new political grouping which must involve a complete change in Franco-Italian relations. This change can only be brought about by the transfer of Tunis to Italy. It should not be forgotten that the entrance of Italy into the Triple Alliance was due to the acquisition of Tunis by France. . . . Tunis geographically should belong to Italy, and the bulk of the white population is Italian. Moreover France with her stationary population has more colonial possessions than she can really manage, whereas to Italy with her ever increasing race Tunis would have real value. So far as British interests are concerned they would in no way be affected by the transfer of Tunis to Italy. Britain has nearly as much interest as France in desiring Italy to annex unredeemed Italy, but also to throw her whole might on the side of the Allies which would certainly be the case if France offered Tunis to Italy. . . .

What is suggested is that England should tactfully put the proposal to France. England could do so honestly as it would not be affected by the transfer, but it might be able to suggest a recompense elsewhere. If England could bring about the cession of Tunis, it would lead to a rapid conclusion to the war and a lasting peace, and it would be a glory to British diplomacy.[2]

Soon after taking up his Senatorial duties Marconi left Rome to visit France, England and America. He saw at first hand some of the early effects of large-scale modern war between the great nations: the enthusiasm of the civil population not yet oppressed by wartime controls nor stunned by endless casualty lists; the cool, fluid manoeuvres of long-term diplomacy; the highly paid slavery in factories doubling and redoubling their output of war equipment; the first bomb stories when Zeppelins raided London in April 1915; the thrills of shared fear and relief in transatlantic liners slipping past the waiting U-boats.

While he was in London Marconi was presented with the Albert Medal of the Royal Society of Arts at a meeting on 13 April 1915 and at the end of April he sailed for America in the *Lusitania*. On the voyage a U-boat periscope was sighted[3] off the Fastnet Rock but the Cunarder used her speed to get away before torpedoes could be fired at her. It was in the same waters, on 7 May 1915, when she was on the return trip from America, that the *Lusitania* was torpedoed with the loss of nearly 1200 lives. The resulting outcry, particularly from America, at this unprecedented barbarity in sea warfare was partly responsible for a temporary suspension of the U-boat 'sink anything' tactics.

In New York Marconi gave expert evidence in a patent case between the American Marconi Company and an American associate company of Telefunken. But he did not remain long in America, not even until the end of this case. On 26 April 1915 Italy had signed with England and France the secret Treaty of London promising to enter the war within a month, in return for which she was promised Tyrol, Trieste and North Dalmatia, but not Fiume. Marconi was aware that the Italian Government was soon to carry out its promise, and when he was told by the Italian Ambassador that the declaration was imminent he withdrew from the court case, telling the Judge that he was returning to Italy to serve his country. He sailed from America in the *St Paul* on 22 May 1915 and Italy declared war on Austro-Hungary on 24 May, but not on Germany until 1916.

So soon after the sinking of the *Lusitania* it would under any circumstances have been a nervous voyage for the passengers on the *St Paul*, but added to this it was strongly rumoured that the Germans might make an attempt to capture Marconi. His name was not included in the passenger list, although his travelling companions were aware of his identity and were prepared for elaborate subterfuges in the event of the ship being searched by a boarding party from a U-boat. However, the *St Paul* got across unmolested and Marconi was in London on 31 May, in Paris on 4 June, and then back in Italy to offer his services to the armed forces.

Marconi was commissioned in the Italian Army in June 1915 with the modest rank of Lieutenant and given a roving mission to inspect the mobile wireless stations used at the Front and suggest how communications might be improved. His role was soon extended to include the task of procuring the wireless equipment he thought was needed, and in July 1915 he came to England on a mission to obtain not only wireless but other war stores. His brief was apparently sufficiently wide for him to make a plea to the British Government for a reduction in the shipping freight charges which had so alarmingly put up the price of coal which Britain was supplying to Italy now that she was an ally.[4] His liaison duties also took him to Foch's headquarters in December 1915 and he lunched there with Foch, French, Joffre and Haig, an engagement which presumably arose more from his name than his military rank. In April 1916 Bea came up to London for the birth of their daughter Gioia, and as soon as she was well enough returned with the baby to join the other two children at Eaglehurst.

Marconi had been working since the end of 1914 with an Italian services team, incuding Solari, looking at the possible military applications of wireless in aeroplanes. In September 1915 the first Marconi apparatus was fitted in an Italian two-seater military biplane[5] and Solari flew as radio operator and carried out successful experiments transmitting Morse from air to ground. Aeroplanes fitted with wireless transmitters were used mostly in spotting fall of shot for artillery units, and Marconi himself witnessed a battle between the big guns when he was flying over the Front. Early in March 1916 Marconi was sent back from his duties to hospital in Genoa with a septic throat. While he was there Solari visited him[6] and found that he was much less concerned with his tonsillitis than with the decision he had just made to turn his wireless researches from long waves, with their huge aerial systems, to ultra short waves with correspondingly small aerials and metal reflectors only a few feet square. Such an aerial with reflector was made in the Marconi works in Genoa and brought to the hospital, where Marconi and Solari carried out the first experiments in a long corridor.

Soon afterwards the experiments were transferred to sea, and with the co-operation of the Regia Marina Marconi, who had Franklin, a senior engineer from the English Company, to help him, established ultra short-wave communication between two battleships at a range of six miles.[7] The ultra short waves were not suitable for very long-range communication but, because they could be directed at the chosen receiving station very much like a light beam, they were ideal for tactical communications between warships where security of information was essential and where it was important that there should be no interference when signals were passing between many ships in a task force.

While Marconi and Franklin were working with the Italian Fleet on this new application of wireless the British Grand Fleet fought the Battle of Jutland on 31 May 1916 as a result of another new wireless technique: that of direction finding.

A directional aerial is one which transmits or receives signals better in one direction than any other and these aerials greatly improved the efficiency of signalling between two fixed stations. On the powerful long-range wireless stations such aerials were enormous structures permanently pointing in the required direction, e.g. from Caernarvon to New York, but smaller directional aerials which could be rotated were devised and used with sensitive receivers to determine the direction from which any particular signal was coming. The most famous of such aerial systems was due to Bellini and Tosi and their patents were taken over by the Marconi Company. A Marconi–Bellini–Tosi DF station was able to determine the direction in which a particular transmitter lay, and two such stations could, in principle, fix the position of the transmitter at the point where the two bearings crossed. In practice the accuracy of the fix was determined by the distance apart of the two DF stations and their position relative to the transmitter. Bearings from as many stations as possible were taken to improve accuracy.

One of the Marconi Company engineers, Round, developed stations which were used in great numbers by the British Army and Navy. Army Intelligence used them to determine the position of enemy wireless stations and where possible to eavesdrop on the messages passed, or at least to monitor the volume and character of the traffic, and thus attempt to predict the enemy's intentions. In a tactical role the stations had some success in fixing the position of enemy spotter aircraft so that RFC scout planes could be sent to destroy them. A chain of stations around the British coast was used by the Admiralty to find the position of enemy U-boats, surface vessels, and Zeppelins.

Naturally the Germans were aware of the possibility of their transmissions being picked up by DF stations and they took precautions, but they had no idea that Round had developed such sensitive stations. In particular they did not know that the stations in Britain could detect and obtain fixes on transmissions between German warships in home waters. Throughout the war a stream of valuable information was fed to British Intelligence by Round's stations, and he was awarded the Military Cross. He refused it on the ground that the award was inapplicable since the medal was awarded for gallantry. Eventually it was sent to him through the post.[8]

In May 1916 Marconi's old friend, the British wireless pioneer Henry Jackson, now Admiral Sir Henry Jackson, was First Sea Lord, the professional head of the Royal Navy. He described the circumstances leading to the Battle of Jutland:

> We have heard much about the use of direction finding for minor tactical movements of all arms, but this is a case of a major strategical operation which brought about the historical meeting of the British and German fleets at the Battle of Jutland on 31 May 1916. I was First Sea Lord at the time, and so was responsible for the disposition of the Grand Fleet.
>
> Our wireless direction-finding stations, under Captain

Round, kept careful and very intelligent watch on the positions of German ships using wireless, and on the 30 May 1916 heard an unusual amount of wireless signals from one of the enemy ships which they located at Wilhelmshaven. This was reported to me, the time was a critical and anxious one in the War, and I also had some reasons for expecting the German fleet might put out to sea during the week. Our fleet was ready at short notice, and had arranged, unless otherwise prevented, to put to sea on the following day for a sweep of the North Sea. But if the German Fleet got to sea first, the chance of our meeting in waters not unfavourable to us was remote; our object was to try to get to sea before or shortly after the Germans, and hitherto we had not succeeded in doing so. Later on in the afternoon it was reported to me that the German ship conducting the wireless traffic had changed her position a few miles to the northward. Evidently she and her consorts had left the basins at Wilhelmshaven and had taken up a position in the Jade River, ready to put to sea. This movement decided me to send our Grand Fleet to sea and move towards the German Bight at once and try to meet the German Fleet and bring it to action. . . .[9]

The two Fleets did meet but the decisive action expected did not take place. A combination of chance, indifferent equipment and tactical failures deprived the British public of the clear-cut victory they had been led to expect. The British Fleet lost more ships than the Germans and more than twice as many men, but the Germans had broken off the action and run for home. There was much argument about whether Jutland was a victory or a defeat, and English newspapers published uncensored accounts of the action which upset the Admiralty who referred the matter to the Director of Public Prosecutions. A letter from the Admiralty Chief Censor to Jellicoe's Secretary complained of the Attorney General, F. E. Smith, as being a man without principles.

While we have to go to men like FES – in the last resort – we cannot expect a conviction, or even a prosecution, because he must keep one eye on his political future – he can't afford not to – hence he thinks many times before tackling the pestiferous Harmsworth papers. . . .[10]

Marconi was in London while this argument about Jutland raged (he was an impressive uniformed figure at the Company's annual meeting in July) and he must have been stirred by the thought that all the ships engaged had carried wireless, which he and his old friend Jackson, so closely involved, had first taken to sea in warships twenty years or so before. Particularly satisfying must have been Jellicoe's statement in his formal despatch that wireless telegraphy had worked well in the battle; there was of course no public word of the part played by wireless direction finding before the action.

While he was in England during the summer of 1916 Marconi arranged with Bea that they should give up Eaglehurst and move the family to Rome, no easy task in wartime. Bea and the three children with a couple of servants and a mountain of luggage crossed the Channel in a ship blacked-out as a precaution against U-boats and went by rail through France and Switzerland to Rome where Marconi had booked an enormous suite in a luxury hotel.

Life in wartime Rome was very different from that at Eaglehurst. Everywhere was excitement and activity. The hotel was crowded, the public rooms bustling with officials, businessmen and politicians, many of whom were as keen to have a few words with Marconi as he was to avoid them. Unlike an ordinary lieutenant in wartime, his military duties were not all-engrossing. Staff work in connection with military wireless, and official discussions as a Senatore with influence in England and America, kept him in Rome for long periods, and he had enough spare time to make it worth while setting up a laboratory in one of the rooms of the hotel suite. There was time and opportunity too for an active social life, which pleased Bea greatly. Both she and Marconi were welcome in the drawing rooms of Rome's fashionable hostesses and they became close friends of artists, writers and politicians, including d'Annunzio the poet and Nitti the politician who both played strange parts later in Marconi's life.

Marconi and Cristina

Marconi at opening of Vatican radio station
with Pope Pius XI and Cardinal Pacelli

The United States declared war in April 1917 and Italy at once organised a mission to visit America to foster goodwill between the two countries and to discuss economic agreements, war aims, and the prizes of victory. Marconi was specially qualified to be a member of this mission because of his excellent knowledge of the United States, which he had visited forty times in twenty years, and his scientific and business standing in the country. It was even rumoured at this time that he might become Italian Ambassador in Washington. The mission was headed by an Italian nobleman who was a kinsman of the King and one of the other delegates was Nitti. The programme was exhausting with a special train to carry them on a long tour of the States.

Marconi was immensely popular. He made speeches at dinners, at Washington's Tomb, at the University of Columbia where an honorary D.Sc. was conferred upon him. He described, rather generously, Italy's contribution to the Allied cause, claiming for instance that Italy's declaration of neutrality in August 1914 had allowed France to move a million men away from the south and throw them against the German advance on the Marne thus probably altering the course of the war. He emphasised his own special ties with America and America's special links with Italy. Indeed in these sections of his speeches there was a hint of coldness towards England and France perhaps implying that a special relationship should exist between Italy and America. Referring to the dispute at the time of his claim to have sent wireless signals across the Atlantic, he spoke of the helping hand extended to him by America 'when there was much galling scepticism in all Europe except Italy',[11] and he referred to Italians and Americans as peoples who had both had to fight hard for independence.

When Marconi came back from his patriotic mission in America he seemed to feel the need to return to the Italian countryside of his childhood. He gave up the hotel suite in Rome, opened up Villa Grifone again, and installed his family there hoping to visit them when his military duties permitted. The winter of 1917–18 when the Marconis returned to the country was a bad one for Italy with a disastrous

231

defeat at Caporetto. Civilian transport in rural areas was disorganised and on the occasions when Marconi had leave he found it almost impossible to reach Villa Grifone. So the Marconi family accepted the invitation of one of Guglielmo's old school friends, called Gregorini, to stay with him at his house near Bologna. Gregorini had an American wife and two pretty daughters who worked locally for the Red Cross. There was not so much entertainment for Bea as in Rome but life was pleasant enough there, and they had the ultimate social triumph of an informal visit from the Prince of Wales who was touring the Italian Front with two ADCs who knew Bea.[12]

From early in 1918 Marconi's duties became almost exclusively political and diplomatic. In April he was in London as the representative of the Italian Parliament at the Allied Parliamentary Conference on Commerce. He was no doubt speaking with conviction in his voice and Telefunken in his mind when he said that one purpose of the Conference was to consider 'the methods necessary to prevent the recurrence of any unfairly obtained German preponderance in the commercial field'.[13] He was in London in connection with the Conference until July 1918 and his engagements included a summons to Buckingham Palace, and banquets at the Guildhall and the House of Lords, at all of which he assiduously pressed Italy's case in speeches and private discussion.

Bea and the children moved into a villa in Rome in the summer of 1918 and during the short periods when Marconi was in Italy the family saw quite a lot of him. He even had a laboratory in one room in the villa where he apparently toyed briefly, privately and unfruitfully with an idea he had for a novel source of industrial power.

In September 1918 Marconi was back in England, this time for a festival of Anglo-Italian goodwill promoted in London.[14] The principal Italian representatives at the celebrations were Marconi and Prince Colonna the Mayor of Rome, but there were other Italian officials, representatives of Italian workers' movements, who held a joint demonstration in Hyde Park with British Trade Unionists, and a detachment of the Royal Regiment of Carabinieri whose band and colourful full-dress uniforms made a bold show in the parades. The celebrations lasted nearly a week with official luncheons and banquets and other less formal parties. Italian flags decorated many buildings and Marconi himself was greeted with cheers and applause by crowds in the streets. He and Prince Colonna were received by King George at Buckingham Palace and the Prince invested with a decoration in the newly constituted Order of the British Empire.

By early October 1918 when Berlin made its first overtures for peace, Marconi was at home in Rome. With a sensitive wireless receiver installed in the villa he picked up the news broadcasts from Berlin, Paris and London, and Bea and the children were thus among the first to know about the steps in the negotiations based upon President Wilson's Fourteen Points which led to the armistice. In the ecstatic relief at the ending of the slaughter and the misery, few thought of the difficulties which would arise in the interpretation of the peace terms. Marconi and Bea could hardly have foreseen that the Peace Treaty would not only hasten the break up of their marriage but also provide the means of its final dissolution.

233

CHAPTER 14

THE GREAT WHITE YACHT
AND DIVORCE IN FIUME

In 1919 Marconi was able to gratify the highest flights of
dreams and ambitions which grew when he first darted among
the larger vessels in Leghorn Harbour in his sailing dinghy
with his cousin Daisy as an admiring passenger. The little
boat, which old Giuseppe had given him, kindled the boy's
love of the sea although it did not lead on to a naval career as
he and his father had hoped. During the years of his increasing
affluence Marconi had owned and sailed a succession of boats of
increasing size, and in 1915 he kept the *Zut*, a modest two-ton
sloop, at moorings in Cowes.[1] But he had long been acquainted
with craft of a very different class: the great ocean racers whose
contests he had reported by wireless in Britain and America;
and the large and elegant steam yachts which attended the
big regattas and cruised round the Mediterranean coast.
Marconi had seen something of the social opportunities of
the millionaire-style steam cruising yacht when he was entertained aboard Sir Thomas Lipton's *Erin* in New York, and
other possibilities of such a vessel were revealed to him when
Empress Eugénie, wife of Napoleon III, loaned him her yacht
Thistle for wireless experiments between Nice and Corsica.
Eugénie, exiled in England, was interested in science, and
during her wide travels in *Thistle* before the 1914 war the
Germans suspected her of spying because she was believed to
have influence in Anglo-French affairs and her yacht was
fitted with Marconi's wireless. But it was the long cruise on
the *Carlo Alberto* which impressed upon him the scientific
advantage of a mobile laboratory in which equipment could
be set up for long periods and easily taken wherever experimental requirements dictated. By 1919 Marconi's new work on
short waves had reached a stage which justified extensive

234

tests over long ranges. Such tests would be of exactly the same general type as those carried out with the original long wave system years before, using temporary facilities in passenger liners and crude field stations with balloons and kites. This time Marconi had more experience, more influence, and more available capital, and he was able to buy from the British Admiralty a vessel which had been commandeered for war service in the North Sea.

The vessel, which he renamed *Elettra*, had been built in Scotland for an Austrian nobleman and was therefore confiscated as enemy property during the war. She was large, displacing over seven hundred tons and being more than two hundred feet long, and had two main staterooms with several smaller guest cabins. With a crew of about thirty she had the range and was seaworthy enough to cross the Atlantic or sail to most parts of the world. For Marconi she was more than a convenient mobile laboratory for a coming series of experiments: she was a new version of the attic at Grifone where he could get away from the world and work on his own. But it was a more congenial seclusion than that of his boyhood. He could fill the guest cabins as he wished with old friends, favoured relatives, attractive women, who in their various ways could enliven his leisure time, but from whom he could at any time escape to the sacrosanct wireless cabin. Marconi regarded the *Elettra* as his private kingdom where he ruled as positively as his father had done at Villa Grifone. The rules of conduct for the guests on *Elettra* were considerably more free and easy than old Giuseppe would have liked, but he might have been amused to see that his son insisted on meals being served punctually to the very second. Apart from close personal friends who came as cabin guests, Marconi entertained at luncheon and dinner parties influential people associated with the steam-yacht society to which he now belonged. He pointed out these advantages in a letter to Godfrey Isaacs from Cowes:

> The King came on board my yacht yesterday afternoon and remained over an hour looking over the wireless apparatus and the yacht generally. I was able to show him my good

signals arriving from America and discuss more matters of interest. Last night I dined with the King and Queen on the Royal Yacht. Tomorrow I am expecting the Prince of Piedmont. . . . I have met more people here who may be of use to us. . . . As you probably know I have been elected a member of the Royal Yacht Squadron. . . .[2]

For guests in *Elettra* the entertainment had an extra dimension to that on other yachts. There was the feeling of important and mysterious activities going on behind the scenes, and Marconi's aloof manner and occasional disappearances from the party suited well the role of high priest in which his visitors tended to cast him. He enjoyed this role, fostering it from time to time with a scientific party trick. As a man who had often seen a Royal Yacht lying impressively offshore, and had visited foreign ports in the *Carlo Alberto*, he was thrilled with the idea that when the *Elettra* steamed into a bay and dropped anchor the 'marvellous white ship', as d'Annunzio called her, could lie there remote and insulated from people ashore, and yet the focus of tremendous interest and attention because Marconi was on board and probably talking by wireless to the other side of the world.

While negotiations for the purchase of the *Elettra* were going on in 1919, Marconi was heavily engaged in diplomatic and political work. He and Nitti, the Italian Prime Minister, visited London and tried unsuccessfully to arrange a British loan to Italy, and then later he was appointed by the Italian Government as a Plenipotentiary Delegate to the Paris Peace Conference.

Lloyd George, Clemenceau, Orlando and Wilson were the four principals at the negotiations in Paris to reach a settlement satisfactory to Italy and the three Great Powers in the matter of Tyrol, Dalmatia and the Adriatic coast.[3] This problem was made more difficult by the fact that the concessions promised to Italy by England and France in the 1915 Treaty of London were not the same as those proposed by President Wilson, who favoured an ethnic settlement in terms of population and national interest. Orlando tried hard to get for Italy the best of both sets of proposals which were much complicated by the creation of the new state of Yugoslavia. Marconi himself had a long private discussion in Paris with President Wilson[4] and was distressed at what he regarded as Wilson's failure to recognise the sacrifices which Italy had made in the war. The great bone of contention was Fiume, and in spite of long, embarrassing wrangling between Wilson and the Italians the future of this city was never settled by the Peace Conference. Diplomatic embarrassment became extreme when in September 1919 Marconi's friend, the Italian patriotic poet d'Annunzio, repudiated the Paris negotiations and, in a characteristically romantic gesture, seized Fiume and declared it an independent State fiercely loyal to the Italian mother-land.

Marconi was not lucky in his international political missions during and after the war. He felt keenly that Italy was treated less than generously and he resented intensely being associated with the diplomatic failures. In all sorts of ways the 1920s started badly for him. The British Imperial Wireless Scheme had been resurrected after the war but this vital part of his dream of world wireless communication had been soured beyond recovery by the 'Marconi Scandal' and an unpleasantly familiar pattern of bickering between the Government and the Marconi Company held up the post-war plans. Marconi's mother, Annie, died in London while Guglielmo was away in Italy and he was not present at her funeral in Highgate cemetery where Alfonso the elder son, and always the less favoured one, completed the devoted care he had given his mother all her life, while her more famous son had sent her money but visited her less and less. The few threads still hold-ing Marconi's marriage together were strained near to breaking by his casualness towards his own family and his too ready attachment to other women. Often during the 1920s when the world was unsympathetic, the yacht *Elettra* provided a refuge for Marconi where he could withdraw and work on his new ideas for long-range wireless communication using short waves.

The handing over of the *Elettra* by the Admiralty, and the repairs and refitting necessary to make her once more into a cruising yacht, were carried out during January and February

1920 at Birkenhead. Marconi's old ex-Navy assistant, Kemp, was sent to stand by the vessel, and he regularly wrote letters, often on successive days, keeping Marconi informed of progress and setbacks in the work and, on one occasion, trying to persuade him for the benefit of his health to come up from London to the Mersey and join the yacht for her sea trials. As soon as the work was completed and she was accepted as satisfactory by her newly appointed Italian captain, Marconi set about planning his first cruise for the spring of 1920. It was from England to the Mediterranean coast of North Africa and Italy, with a long stop at Seville in Spain where Bea's childhood friend Ena was now Queen and where Marconi's friend, and sometime patroness, ex-Empress Eugénie was spending her old age at the palace of the Duke of Alba. Bea was told of the planned route and sent for from Italy, leaving the children with friends, but when she joined Marconi on the yacht in England she found that the guest list, which she had not seen, was much less to her liking than the itinerary. Among the guests was Marconi's latest flame, a most tenacious one, invited with her husband for the whole cruise.

It seems remarkable that under these circumstances Bea should have joined the cruise and stuck it out until the end. But, as her daughter wrote, 'There had always been women in Marconi's life but Beatrice had held her own, tolerating his adventures because they ended in homecomings.'⁵ Even after this cruise when she had such a miserable time, in part neglected by Marconi for his lady guest and in part shutting herself away in her own cabin, she could still write, from Houlgate in France where she was staying with the children, to 'Dearest Guglielmo' sending him 'Kodaks' of the children who had won prizes in a beach competition, and signing 'Fond love, Bea'.⁶ Perhaps there had been yet another reconciliation, or perhaps these were the words used semi-automatically by a wife who had, if not condoned, recognised and accepted a long-established marital situation and who saw no point in letting pointless bitterness intrude into the simple mechanics of family life at the risk of making a private problem into a public spectacle. At any rate, Bea once more accepted an invitation to cruise in *Elettra* in the second summer of Marconi's ownership. This time she had seen the guest list and it was truly a family gathering. Her children were there, and her two sisters Lilah and Dorrien. But at the end of this family cruise Dorrien discovered that the 'other woman' was waiting to join Marconi in Venice and she rushed indignantly to tell Bea, who was little surprised. Marconi's daughter wrote:

> Father had, of late, been anything but a model of discretion. His affair was no longer a secret, anywhere. . . . Even the newspapers made insinuations of the Marconi-and-a-certain-lady variety. The blatancy of the adventure robbed Mother of her last line of defence – the pretence of ignorance.

Equally portentous was the fact that just after this cruise Bea met a man who wished to marry her.

These two cruises must have been disagreeably tense at times even to someone like Marconi who could switch off at will his sensory connections with those around him. But between the two cruises he was able to use *Elettra* on a mission which gave him great satisfaction. In September 1920 he was asked by the Italian Government to go to Fiume and have personal discussions with his friend d'Annunzio about the future of the city. There was a tumultuous reception for Marconi when he sailed into the harbour in his great white yacht, and the next few days of patriotic fervour and romantic speeches demonstrated to the world, as no doubt they were intended to do, that whatever the politicians decided about d'Annunzio's city, its allegiances were firmly to Italy. In November 1920 Italy and Yugoslavia agreed about the division of Istria and Dalmatia, and signed the Treaty of Rapallo under which Fiume became a Free City.

Marconi's scientific interest was now concentrated on short-wave wireless, and he and Franklin were working hard in England on experiments which pushed up towards a hundred miles the range of reliable communication using such waves. The wavelength used in these experiments was of the order of fifteen metres, whereas that used for the established transatlantic and other long-range stations was some hundreds of metres. Ultra short waves, which Marconi, Solari and

Franklin had also investigated briefly, have a wavelength of about one metre or less. The three systems: long wave (hundreds of metres), short wave (tens of metres), and ultra short wave (metres), were distinguished from each other in practical terms by the size of the aerial and its directivity. Long-wave aerials were enormous structures and even the comparatively recently developed directional types did little more than concentrate the sensitivity of the aerial from an all-round, 360-degree, field into a sector of perhaps nearly a hundred degrees pointing in the requried direction. Short-wave aerials could be made much smaller and their directivity much sharper so that the field of sensitivity was perhaps only thirty degrees wide and now looked much more like a beam pointing towards the other station. With ultra short waves there was again a corresponding decrease in the aerial size and the directional properties began to approach those of a searchlight beam and it was feasible to communicate with one rather than the other of a pair of ships a mile or two apart on the horizon. Although the *minimum* size necessary for the aerial decreases with reduced wavelength, so that something a metre square might suffice for ultra short waves, the directivity and general efficiency of an aerial at any wavelength is improved if its size is increased above the minimum. Thus the extremely efficient and highly directive receiving aerial of the Jodrell Bank radio telescope is two hundred and fifty feet in diameter although the wavelength of the signals it receives may be well under a metre.

There was no Mediterranean cruise for *Elettra* in the summer of 1922. Instead Marconi sailed her across the Atlantic by way of the Azores and Bermuda to New York where he addressed a meeting of the American Institute of Electrical Engineers and saw for himself something of the boom in entertainment broadcasting which was taking place in America.

In 1916 David Sarnoff, who started as an office boy with the American Marconi Company and rose to be head of the great Radio Corporation of America, had suggested the manufacture of a 'radio music box' which would receive several different wavelengths at the throw of a switch and 'be supplied with amplifying tubes (valves) and a loud-speaking telephone, all of which can be mounted neatly in a box'. No one was greatly interested in the idea then, and in any case during the war there was no question of it being developed. But after the armistice American and British engineers designing radio telephony systems used gramophone records in their test transmissions and their 'programmes' were picked up by amateur wireless enthusiasts who encouraged them to be more ambitious.[7] In England the Marconi Company transmitted a number of modest chamber concerts, and Northcliffe, with an eye to publicity, sponsored a *Daily Mail* broadcast from Chelmsford by Dame Nellie Melba on 15 June 1920. When the singer arrived at the Marconi works and was told that her voice would be sent out from the aerial slung high in the air, she declared that she had no intention of climbing the masts.[8] In America, by this time, entertainment broadcasting had grown very fast and the possibility of a huge new market for domestic radio equipment was now recognised. The rate of growth was much slower in Britain where a Post Office licence was required for any transmission, but this control did at least prevent a repetition of the chaos which arose in America with a multitude of unrestricted private stations tending to interfere with each other and with established radio communication and navigation services to shipping and aircraft. Furthermore the circumstances surrounding early broadcasting in Britain – with an unimaginative, or even antagonistic, Government department constantly chivvied by the radio manufacturers and the amateur wireless enthusiasts among the general public – provided conditions favourable to the formation of the British Broadcasting Company in December 1922 and its successor the British Broadcasting Corporation in 1926.

Marconi's stay in New York in the summer of 1922 was only a short one, but while he was there Bea, who had been visiting friends in Boston, met him for a few days. Their lives were now almost entirely separate and indeed the fact that they travelled back to England together in the *Mauretania* was only due to urgent business which forced Marconi to abandon his plan to sail home in *Elettra*. During the remainder of 1922 he was mostly in England, attending Cowes Week in *Elettra* in August, while Bea was mostly with the children in Italy at holiday resorts, returning with them in the autumn to the home she had made in Florence. The closing months of this year brought events which were to reshape Marconi's public and private life. In October 1922 the Fascisti marched on Rome and Mussolini was invited to form a government. In Florence the man who had earlier asked Bea to marry him continued to court her to such effect that in 1923 Bea would ask Marconi to give her a divorce.

In England during 1922 and 1923 Marconi was working on the use of short-wave radio for long-distance communication. He and Franklin and the associated Marconi staff achieved big improvements in aerial design, and in the valves and associated circuits which presented special difficulties when carrying the very high-frequency currents needed to generate short wave radiation. Meanwhile long waves were being used by the transatlantic and other commercial stations and the renewed discussions about the Imperial Wireless Scheme were all in terms of such long-wave signals. As soon as the war was over the Marconi Company had offered a direct radio service between England and Australia, but the idea, although well received in Australia, was turned down by the British Government. The subsequent protracted negotiations were a thinly disguised conflict between the Marconi Company and the Post Office, who wished to build and operate the stations themselves. Dissatisfaction with the communications within the British Empire was expressed by many and:

> . . . the attitude of the Dominions was somewhat different after the war and they frequently expressed their disgust at the expensiveness of, and the delays involved with, existing means of communication . . . less willing to subject their policies to the overriding wisdom of the Imperial Government. They felt that the British Government had not, so far as radio communications were concerned, played a distinguished role in the pre-war years.[9]

In 1919 the Government appointed a Committee to consider

and prepare a scheme for Imperial communications. The chosen chairman, Sir Henry Norman, was however known to be antagonistic towards the Marconi Company who submitted a scheme to the Committee but refused to give evidence before it. The report of the Committee[10] recommended a chain of stations each separated by about two thousand miles from its neighbours. It was an old-fashioned scheme differing from pre-war ideas only in that it used valves. The Marconi scheme was much more ambitious and there is little doubt that it could have been realised, but the Norman Committee rejected it as impracticable financially. The *Electrical Review* commented:

> We have seen so much of the effects of State operation, especially during the War, that we have the gravest misgivings as to the desirability of placing the wireless chain in the hands of Government departments. On the other hand, there is one bright, if solitary, example of efficiency to the credit of the State – the management of the Pacific Cable by a Commission. In this connection we can hardly ignore the ambitious scheme put forward by the Marconi Company which was curtly turned down by the committee; without discussing the merits of the rival schemes, we must express the opinion that the decision of the Marconi Company, owing to a personal quarrel between its managing director and the chairman of the committee, to abstain from giving evidence before the committee was a strategical blunder of the first magnitude. In the past we have defended the company against unjust political and other attacks, but in this case we must admit that if it is cut out of the Imperial scheme, it will only have itself to thank. . . .[11]

However, Australia was not willing to accept the delays consequent on being at the end of the chain proposed by the Norman Committee when they knew that they could have a direct link with England. They took action independently of the Imperial Scheme and, when other Dominions followed suit, the British Government dropped the Norman proposals and in March 1923 Bonar Law announced in the House of

Commons that the principle of a state monopoly in Imperial communications was abandoned. The Marconi Company at once applied for a licence to operate a wireless service to the Dominions but it was turned down as too monopolistic, and counterproposals by the Post Office that they and the Company should work jointly included conditions unacceptable to Marconi interests. Quarrelsome negotiations dragged on into 1924 with the possibility of agreement fading as the Company and the Post Office became more firmly entrenched in their opposing positions, with different Postmasters General, and even different governments, unable to produce a bold stroke to break the deadlock. Yet another committee was appointed to review the matter.

In 1923 Marconi not only faced the fact that his Imperial Wireless Scheme was hopelessly bogged down, but also that Bea wanted a divorce. This is the order of precedence he would surely have allocated to the two problems. His divorce appeared not to touch him deeply, indeed the marriage now ending seemed to have involved him only superficially compared with his dedication to technical and business ambition. Even his affairs with women somehow lacked any hint that he would consider the world well lost for them. Certainly he spent time and money on his affairs – writing, telephoning, giving jewels from Cartier – but his diaries, in which he wrote sparsely and irregularly, suggest that he ran more than one affair at a time, and during them all he wrote to Bea in mildly affectionate terms about family matters. A draft of one of his letters to a woman friend, at what was clearly a crisis in the affair, certainly lacks spontaneity because it is roughed out with many phrases crossed out or amended, but it also lacks the feeling, indeed passion, which other men might have revealed in similar circumstances:

. . . imagined I had been run over, or I had been with you, which in her eyes is worse. I have never seen her so upset – instinct perhaps – she could not know . . . had been waiting for me for hours. I did not deny it but told her nothing, but she knows. She makes me feel very ashamed of myself. It will mean a great deal for me to give you up. . . . I feel each

time I come to you less able to resist . . . if I did give way as
I feel I might I should despise myself in consequence as
I know if in London it will be me, not you, who will ring up
and arrange to meet. . . .

Looking back to Miss Holman of SS *St Paul,* and forward to
Miss Paynter of Cornwall, it seemed that even when Marconi
became engaged, and subsequently disengaged, there was
little passion or despair on his side.

He did not forgo his summer cruise in *Elettra* in 1923
but apart from enjoying the congenial company – not Bea's –
he carried out meticulous tests on the ranges at which short-
wave signals could be received from the experimental station
which had been set up at Poldhu with an aerial system
designed to direct the radiation in a relatively narrow beam
out across the Atlantic towards the west coast of Africa.
The results were good enough to justify feverish activity for
the rest of 1923 and the first months of 1924. In the spring of
1924 Marconi exploded a mine under the Imperial Wireless
negotiations. On the strength of the success so far achieved the
Marconi Company proposed a new Imperial Wireless Scheme
based upon short-wave beam stations. The proposals were
sensational and in one blow the cumbersome structure of the
old negotiations was destroyed, and so advantageous were the
technical and financial terms of the beam scheme that further
bargaining was pre-empted. This was Marconi's favourite way
of resolving a technical dispute: with an impressive demonstration of a new discovery. Equally characteristic in its own
way was his solution to the personal problem of his divorce, a
delicate matter for a prominent Italian citizen.

Influential and well-informed friends in politics had often
played their part in Marconi's enterprises. Now his own
knowledge and his own influence in a special political area
helped him to find a clever solution to his divorce problem.
He and Bea each went to the Free City of Fiume and established residential qualifications there. In September 1923
Italy annexed Fiume, and in January 1924 Yugoslavia
acknowledged this annexation. The legal anomalies and
uncertainties inherent in this fluid situation allowed Marconi's

petition for divorce to be granted by the Tribulane di Fiume in February 1924 and later confirmed by the Italian Court of Appeal. With the transfer of Fiume to Italy, Bea and Marconi recovered full Italian citizenship, without ever having effectively lost it. In April 1924 Bea was married to the Marchese Liborio Marignoli.

Marconi with short-
wave aerial

Marconi, with
Cristina and Elettra,
leaves a London
nursing home

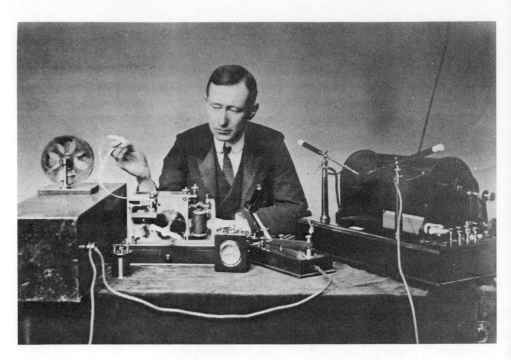

Marconi and early apparatus

Modern Marconi satellite station

CHAPTER 15

IMPERIAL GAMBLE
AND ECCLESIASTICAL MANŒUVRE

THE springing of the mine under the seemingly endless Imperial Wireless discussions gave a certain malicious satisfaction to Marconi and his colleagues within the Company, but the decision to put forward a short-wave beam scheme early in 1924 was a dangerous one which put the solvency of the Company in jeopardy.

The old long-range stations using long waves were very large and needed hundreds of kilowatts of power to force their signals thousands of miles. In 1924 the Marconi Company had lucrative orders from Australia and South Africa for the erection of very high-power stations of this type. But if Marconi and Franklin were right about the significance of their short-wave beam experiments, then communication over such very long distances would be possible using only a few kilowatts of power from much smaller and cheaper stations. The beam of short waves was directed towards the receiving station thousands of miles away and the beam was also elevated so that the signals were sent up over a hundred miles into the ionosphere and then bent back again to the Earth's surface. Marconi wrote to Solari in June 1923 giving detailed results of his work on short waves, especially that carried out on the *Elettra* during the recent cruise to Cape Verde. He ended:

The results of these experiments have convinced me that I am at the beginning of a revolution in our ideas about the validity of the theory upon which long distance telegraphy depends.

I believe that with short wave stations of only moderate power it will be possible to obtain an excellent commercial service between Italy and the Argentine.[1]

247

He went on to say that he expected the signalling speeds possible with such short-wave stations to be much in excess of those currently being achieved with the conventional long-wave system. In concluding he asked Solari to communicate these findings to 'His Excellency the Head of Government', and Solari records that, 'the above findings were sent by me to Il Duce'.

But great promise is a very long way from a reliable commercial service. No one appreciated this better than Marconi who still remembered bitterly the fiasco of the first commercial transatlantic service into which he had been prematurely and unwillingly pushed by his Board of Directors in 1902. The pleasure of thumbing the nose at the latest of the Imperial Wireless Committees weighed little compared with the technical, and indeed moral, considerations when the Marconi Company decided to announce the short-wave beam scheme.

> The issue resolved itself into one of principle. The easy way out would be to engineer the new system at comparative leisure and in secrecy, letting the existing long-wave situation take its course. Then after a few years, when the giant Australian and South African stations (and perhaps others) had been built, the short-wave system could be unleashed. All would be perfectly legal; at the time the long-wave contracts had been placed, the super high-power stations were the only certain means of achieving the desired ends.
>
> But such a course was considered as breaking faith with the customers concerned, namely the Australian and South African Governments. . . . The decision to inform all interested parties was taken. It was done in the full awareness of the serious consequences it could have for the Company. Performance specifications and guarantees would have to be given based on theoretical calculations alone, and the penalty for failure would probably be bankruptcy.[2]

Once the decision was taken and the Marconi Company presented its proposals for a short-wave beam system, the new scheme was quickly accepted by the Government – the newly elected first Labour Government – and Ramsay MacDonald defended this action against the inevitable Parliamentary critics, in particular those who stated that a project of such enormous strategic importance to the Empire should not be in the hands of a company directed by a foreigner. The contract between the Marconi Company and the Government was signed on 28 July 1924, apparently in the face of opposition from the Post Office.[3] But even if the Post Office officials were disappointed that their new political masters had granted a contract, they must have been gleeful at the severity of its terms. The first beam link was to be between England and Canada, and only if it were successful would others be commissioned. The station had to be completed, ready for stringent tests by the Post Office, six months after the site was available. The cost of the work would be paid to the Company in instalments spread over a year, subject to satisfactory operation during all this period. Failure in operation at any time during that period would entail the return of all payments to the Government, and the Company would have to clear the site at their own expense.[4]

While sites were being selected for the beam stations, the experimental and development work was pushed forward with utmost urgency. A fundamental point still to be established was the best wavelength to use in the short-wave band. Tests from Poldhu to *Elettra* and to temporary experimental stations in Canada, the United States, Australia and South America showed that about thirty metres wavelength gave the best reception, this information being obtained only a little before the construction of the aerial systems was due to begin. The general design of these complicated aerials and reflectors, and the associated feeder system to carry the very high frequency currents from the transmitting valve circuits, had been worked out by Franklin, but everyone expected that much more development and modification would be needed when the apparatus and the aerial were completed and the system first switched on. This certainly proved to be the case, and the many problems which arose required solutions ranging from the major design effort of producing novel liquid-cooled transmitting valves to ingenious but relatively minor innovations in transmitter and receiver circuits. In all this Marconi played a large part, stimulating and encouraging the engineers who were working at great pace and under considerable strain to meet dates. He told Solari at the time, 'When I am allowed to work in my own technical field I am the happiest man in the world.'[5] In the autumn of 1926 the Post Office engineers were due to carry out on the Bodmin station their rigorous tests to confirm faultless operation for some sixteen hours out of every twenty-four, at a very high signalling rate. In May when the apparatus was assembled, tested, and put into service, there was a general sense of sickening worry when no signals of any sort were detected in Canada. However much Marconi shared this worry he did not show it. Nancarrow, a senior engineer in charge of the station, remembers how this period revealed to him 'the true nature and spirit of Marconi'.

From the first period of shock when it was found that the expected communication to Canada did not materialise, to the successful outcome, I never saw Marconi other than calm, quiet spoken, and apparently unaffected by the set-back which had overtaken this quite new venture in long distance radio communication.

Quite quickly we established what I like to recall as mutual confidence and respect, and when he made a visit he was quite happy to let me know what he wished to do and leave it to me to see that that was duly arranged. Thus when he was accompanied by visitors from his ship I would see that they were looked after by my staff and he was freed for conversations with Franklin.

Two memories remain of lunch with him and his captain on the *Elettra* which illustrate his good nature and charm. One, when at lunch, he asked me if I liked spaghetti because that was the basis of the main course, and I said that if he would give me a lesson on the handling of the stuff I would make the attempt. He smiled (I never heard or saw him laugh) and when the time came charmingly complied. The other, when I went to sign the visitors

250

book – I was going to sign after some names half-way down a page when he restrained me with the remark that I was a very special person and that I should sign on the top of a new page, which I did.[6]

The 'successful outcome' was in October 1926 when the Bodmin station, transmitting to Canada, and the corresponding receiving station at Bridgwater, were tested and accepted by the Post Office. In the next few months other short-wave beam stations were accepted and services established with South Africa, India, Australia, New York and South America. All these stations showed performances greatly superior to the contract requirements, an indication that the Marconi Company had been so concerned about the punitive clauses which might be invoked by the Post Office that they were forced to the expense of designing for the highest performance because they had so little information available upon which a closely calculated economic design could prudently be made.

The success of the beam system was a realisation of the dream of world communications which Marconi had had as a boy at Villa Grifone. Once more he was acclaimed throughout the world, and Mussolini, always keen to acknowledge an Italian success, sent him a telegram congratulating him on his '*sistema onde corte a fascio*'. The well-defined bundle of radio waves, called a 'beam' in English, had been named '*fascio*' by Marconi early in his experiments, and he jokingly claimed later to have been the 'first fascist in Italy'.

The frequent long voyages in *Elettra* to carry out short-wave experiments were no hardship to Marconi. He said that he regarded the yacht as his home, and he certainly sailed in her at least as often for pleasure as for scientific work. The vessel was very much a bit of Italy. The crew of thirty were nearly all Italian and their appearance, manner and voices established the atmosphere, as did much of the food on board, although Marconi's breakfast always consisted of boiled eggs, bread and butter, marmalade and tea, served on the stroke of eight. A guest who was watching the Schneider Trophy races from *Elettra* recalled[7] his embarrassment when he excitedly

251

cheered the victory of the British sea-plane only to realise immediately that most of those around him were supporting the Italian entry. Apart from his cabin, Marconi had two retreats on board: the wireless room and his study. The largest item of furniture in the study was a piano which Marconi would play, sometimes to entertain guests, but often alone for an hour or more at a time. The most striking feature of the room, giving it the air of a theatrical pub, was Marconi's collection of inscribed photographs of distinguished visitors: the King of Italy and the Queen – '*yours affectionately, Elena*' – Alfonso of Spain, King George V and Queen Mary of England, d'Annunzio, Mussolini – '*to Marconi, Magician of the Spaces, Conqueror of the Earth*' – Mary Pickford – '*don't forget to visit us when you are in California*'.

The dining room would seat a dozen or more guests and, particularly at Cowes, there were many parties attended by the distinguished and the famous as well as close personal friends. Entertainment broadcasting was just beginning in the twenties, and *Elettra* was well known for providing music from London for the entertainment of her guests, with the dance band of the Savoy Orpheans occasionally coming over a little too loud for taste of the owners of other yachts nearby. A luncheon guest on one occasion was Lord Mountbatten whose own interests and recent naval training had made him an expert on radio communication. He recalls:

I was present in my own yacht at Cowes and the invitation from Marconi was a purely social one. I do not think he had any idea that I was a specialist in radio and after lunch when he was showing guests round his ship he took us into his main wireless office which of course absolutely fascinated me being full of the latest developments. He gave a very general description of what was going on in the office and when I started going round and asking specific questions about various sets he expressed great surprise at my interest and knowledge and then sent for his Senior Radio Officer to answer my questions.

The impression I had was that at this stage, which I think was about 1926, he had lost close contact with all the developments although they were being carried out under his aegis.[8]

This perspicacious observation was an early identification of the fact that Marconi began to disengage from the Company's interests in radio communication once the Beam System of Imperial Communications had been achieved.

After their divorce in 1924 Bea was never a guest on board, but their two older children, Degna and Giulio, spent several summer holidays with their father, enjoying themselves hugely although discipline was sometimes strict.[9] If Giulio was late for breakfast his father would make it an uncomfortable meal and hardly speak to him for the rest of the day. Of the experimental work on the yacht, Giulio remembered that his father 'did not show the slightest outward sign of satisfaction or otherwise at the result', an observation echoed on another occasion by Marconi's colleague Paget who said:

He was never unduly elated and never unduly depressed. When the twenty masts erected at Poldhu for the transatlantic transmission collapsed in a gale Marconi looked at the wreckage and said quietly to me: 'Well, they will be built again.' That was all.[10]

Marconi corresponded frequently and affectionately with Bea about the children and other matters.[11] He was able to tell her that Queen Mary had asked after her at Cowes, and he even wrote saying how worried he had been about her confinement with the first child of her new marriage. He told her how disappointed he was that Giulio had written to him saying that although he had passed all the necessary examinations he did not wish to enter the Regia Marina. So disappointed was Marconi that he went specially to Italy to talk to Giulio. When he returned to London he had persuaded the boy to change his mind, but Giulio's naval career was short and he resigned his commission in 1933.

Marconi was in London a good deal during the mid-1920s and he usually stayed at the Savoy. He could walk there conveniently from the Company offices in the Strand and he generally had his own special suite and a favourite table reserved for him in the dining room. He is said[12] to have been something of a trial to the staff: fussy about his food, complaining if he had to wait for the lift, and, at the barber's, insisting that no towel be placed round his neck and then getting angry if hair fell on to his suit. He gave parties at the Savoy and was invited to many fashionable private parties and public functions. Often he was the guest of honour of some association connected with radio or the Press. In the manner of the time, the initial letters of the principal courses on one such menu spelled MARCONI, and at another dinner there was entertainment: Argo the French Clown; Colleen Clifford, Songs and Impressions at the Piano; Gordon Marsh and the Marshmallow Girls. His affairs with women still continued, and the fact that London tradesmen could send one lady's unpaid bills to him at his office indicated that the relationship was well known. There was now, however, no fundamental reason why Marconi should not indulge his liking for attractive women. He was a single man, but in 1925 he set out to enter once again, less than two years after leaving it, the married state which appeared to have meant so little to him before. There were many names on his list of social engagements, which read like the dramatis personae of a society magazine – Lady Cunard, Cynthia Mosley, Lord Birkenhead, Constance Bennett – but he was now over fifty and perhaps he was lonely for something more stable and comfortable than the planned luncheon and impersonal hotel luxury. *Elettra* was a home of a sort but a yacht could not offer the many amenities of a family house in the country, like Eaglehurst.

Marconi liked Cornwall. His work had first taken him there before 1900 and while finding a suitable site and making the early experimental tests from Poldhu he travelled over the Lizard promontory, down the peninsula towards Land's End, and across the water to the Isles of Scilly. During the years before the Great War he was often at Poldhu working on the long-wave transatlantic service and he made many friends in the county. In 1920 and afterwards, similar experimental work, this time with short waves, brought him again to Cornwall for long periods and the *Elettra* became a familiar sight in the ports and coves along the coast from Falmouth to Land's End. Later, when there was no longer any experimental requirement for the yacht to work near Poldhu, Marconi often went for pleasure cruises along the Devon and Cornwall coasts. It was in April 1925 that a local newspaper, the *Cornishman*, printed a report from the *Daily Express*, headed 'Marconi's Love Romance: Engagement to a Cornish Girl Expected'.

It is understood that an announcement of the engagement of Senatore Marconi, the world famous wireless genius, to Miss Elizabeth Narcissa Paynter, only daughter of Lt. Col. Camborne H. Paynter and Mrs Paynter, is likely to be made in the course of the next few days.

Senatore Marconi is at present on his yacht *Elettra* at Gibraltar, and but for illness would have been with Col. Paynter and his family for the celebration of Miss Paynter's eighteenth birthday on Tuesday.

Senatore Marconi and Col. and Mrs Paynter have been the closest friends for many years. Miss Paynter has known Senatore Marconi since she was a child of fourteen. He was a visitor at Christmas and with Miss Paynter attended a ball in Penzance.

A wonderful wireless receiving set, one of Senatore Marconi's latest inventions, known as the supermarine, is installed at Boskenna, and it is possible to talk from the yacht *Elettra* to the house.

Miss Paynter is one of the debutantes to be presented to court this summer. All Cornwall will send congratulations to her as soon as the engagement is formally announced. It is, I understand (says the *Express* correspondent) Senatore Marconi's intention to make a home in London.

A telegram wishing many happy returns has been received by Miss Paynter from Senatore Marconi. His yacht will moor in Penzance harbour on Saturday evening and he will spend Easter as the guest of Col. and Mrs Paynter at Boskenna.

All the friends of the Paynters and the country folk from Penzance to Land's End have known about the regard

which has obviously been growing up between Senatore
Marconi and Miss Paynter, and the expected engagement
has been freely talked about. Senatore Marconi has been
frequently at Boskenna, the delightful, centuries old,
Cornish manor house, with its wooded estate running to the
margin of the sea a short distance to the west of Lamorna
Cove with its colony of artists.[13]

Not all 'the country folk from Penzance to Land's End'
took to Marconi, and many felt that his romantic activities
in Cornwall were not exclusively centred on Miss Paynter.
A girl who attended a ball at Boskenna, where Marconi was a
guest, recalled,[14] over forty years later, that his presence
brooded unpleasantly over the whole evening and she disliked
him even though she did not speak to him. The following
morning there was a lawn meet at Boskenna, the stirrup cup
being dispensed in the pouring rain. 'Marconi and Betty
Paynter went round in a Rolls'. The Press were anxious to find
out all about the engagement and, in the words of another
local resident, 'Photographers kept popping out of the
hydrangeas and trying to snap Marconi, until Colonel Paynter
put his foot down.'[15] (The hydrangeas in the grounds of
Boskenna are up to nine feet high, and the Colonel was late of
Skinner's Horse, an Indian Regiment.) The group of artists
who worked in the district included Laura and Harold Knight,
Stanhope Forbes and Lamorna Birch, whose daughter shared
lessons with Betty Paynter. Some time before the engagement,
one of Marconi's women friends had taken a cottage at
Lamorna Cove and she was greatly excited when the *Elettra*
steamed around the headland into the cove and she was rowed
out to the yacht by Lamorna Birch for a party.[16]

A family into which Marconi proposed to marry usually
needed to be persuaded that this was an acceptable notion.
A week after publishing the account of the conjectured
engagement the *Cornishman* had two items.[17] The *Elettra* was
reported to have attracted a crowd of onlookers and one
cinema photographer when she put into Penzance floating
dock, but Marconi was said to be unwell and busy and could not
give press interviews. In an adjoining column it was noted that

Col. C. H. Paynter, Boskenna, St Buryan, Cornwall had written to the Press contradicting statements that his eighteen-year-old daughter Elizabeth was engaged to be married to Senatore Marconi the wireless expert.

Marconi's relationship with Bea had always been unusual – too free-ranging when they were married and unsuitably close after they were divorced – but in August 1925 he pushed self-delusion too far. He wrote to Bea:

> Don't be surprised or upset if you hear I have become engaged to Betty Paynter. I care for the girl an awful lot, more than I ever thought I could, and she for me. I have been fighting against myself over this for a long time, but I am afraid it's no use. After all, even you know how lonely I am. . . .

Bea's reply was clear, logical, and crushing,

> I am surprised to hear you have decided to take the step you write me of in your last letter and create new ties and most probably a new family. I would like to wish you every happiness but this news distresses me for I wonder after all the years we were together when your own desire expressed continually was for freedom to concentrate on your work as your family impeded and oppressed you, why you should suddenly feel this great loneliness and need of a home – this craving for fresh ties!![18]

But the marriage of Marconi and Betty Paynter never took place. In a few months they grew apart and Marconi was a 'free' man again.

In July 1926 Marconi was accorded an honour which gave him particular pleasure. His home town of Bologna gave itself over for a day to the celebration of the thirtieth anniversary of his first successful wireless demonstrations at Villa Grifone. He was received in great style at the University, where he had failed to matriculate, and he delivered there a long speech giving an account of his work over the thirty years. In this connection he produced an impressive list of the companies with which he had been associated,[19] in order, he said, to demonstrate to the Government and the people the vital part played by the technical and commercial skill of an Italian citizen in the principal world-communication organisations. It was on this occasion that Marconi produced his pun on *fascio* – a beam – and declared himself to have been the first fascist in Italy. He had in fact enrolled in the Fascist Party in 1923. A few days after the Bologna celebrations Mussolini adroitly manipulated a demonstration by the Italian Senate whose members greeted with cheers and the Fascist salute the entry of Il Duce who skilfully directed the applause to Marconi whom he had brought into the Chamber with him.

In Marconi's private life 1926 was notable as the year he decided that he wanted to marry Cristina Bezzi-Scali, a beautiful Italian girl less than half his age. Her family was of the Roman nobility, her father highly placed in the Vatican, and approval was unlikely for her marriage to a middle-aged Protestant, divorced with three children. Marconi felt that he could overcome any personal objections – he had, after all, some proven expertise in winning over reluctant potential relatives-in-law. He addressed himself therefore to the *sine qua non* of the whole enterprise, the securing of an annulment of his first marriage. Informed opinion would have given him as little chance of success as it had of sending signals across the Atlantic, and the Ecclesiastical Law of the Roman Catholic Church upon which the matter would depend was almost as complicated in its workings as the ionosphere.

Of the limited number of grounds recognised by the Roman Catholic Church for the annulment of a marriage the only one which Marconi's lawyers thought could be of use to him was that which involved lack of proper consent. Consent, that is, in the sense of absolute commitment to the married state with no question of it being ended by anything but death. If any case was to be made out in the Ecclesiastical Courts it would be necessary to produce witnesses who would swear that Marconi or Bea had said, before their marriage, that if it were a failure they would consider divorce.

Marconi met Bea in Rome to put the matter to her, and she promised her co-operation. He wasted no time and assembled witnesses – relations and friends from over twenty years ago – to testify before the Roman Catholic Ecclesiastical Commission at Westminster Cathedral in July 1926. Bea was in Italy and her examination was to be conducted there. All through the summer and autumn Marconi wrote her long letters with details of what he and other witnesses had said in London, and gave her minute instructions on how she should give her own evidence. He counselled her not to show his letters to anyone, and, indeed, they were irregular to say the least:

> When you are called at Spoleto, do try and confirm all I have said, otherwise we may lose, and our position will be worse than before . . . the Ecclesiastical Court has got copies of the divorce decree of Fiume, so don't say anything different to it if you are asked. . . .[20]

Eventually he was able to write to her that the annulment had been granted by the Westminster authorities but that this decision would now have to be approved by the Vatican Court, and he instructed her on how she might possibly avoid appearing before this court and so not run the risk of cross-examination on her evidence. At last, in April 1927, the annulment was confirmed by the Tribunal of the Sacra Rota in Rome on the grounds of 'defective intention', and Marconi and Cristina Bezzi-Scali were married the following June.

Marconi had planned a honeymoon which was to be very different from his first, when he and Bea had returned prematurely to London after a week of isolation and tension in Ireland. He was ready for a long holiday after the sustained pressure of bringing the Empire Beam Radio Scheme to a successful conclusion. Added to this had been business worries caused by the fact that Godfrey Isaacs had been forced by ill-health to retire in 1925 and had died almost immediately afterwards leaving the Board to disentangle all sorts of schemes and financial arrangements which only he had fully understood. There had, too, been the undeniable strain of marshalling witnesses and presenting the case for the annulment. Marconi wanted a long holiday now, and, as later events showed, he certainly needed one, although perhaps not of such a tiring nature as he and Cristina undertook.

They spent a few months in Italy and in England, with many social engagements and parties in London and aboard *Elettra*. Then in October 1927 they sailed for the United States to a great round of entertainment, ceremonial and general adulation of the great inventor, who was happy enough to join in the celebrations, the more so because his young wife was so proud to be at his side sharing it all. He spoke at banquets and receptions, to reporters and to scientific societies. He wore his Fascist badge in his buttonhole and praised Mussolini's achievements in Italy but would not discuss the desirability of Fascism in America. His political opinions were bland and so too were his scientific speeches: all history, anecdote and crystal gazing, with no hard core of new information. Marconi was having a holiday, a period of retirement which turned out to be longer than he had expected.

When Marconi and Cristina returned to England he was not well, and after complaining of pains in the chest he suffered a heart attack in their suite at the Savoy. Angina was diagnosed and he spent some weeks under care in a nursing home before returning once more to the Savoy. But almost at once he had another attack, and this time a severe one. His recovery was very slow and it was months before he was able to undertake the journey back to Italy, and not until about January 1930 did he resume a full programme of work, although he had been able to cruise in *Elettra*. Meanwhile his own country had been generous with honours: he had been created an hereditary Marchese, elected a member of Mussolini's newly formed Royal Academy, and made its President.

After his long respite Marconi's life changed in one major respect. In the few years before his second marriage, and during the honeymoon and his subsequent period of ill-health, Marconi had become disengaged from the two activities which had made his name famous – the development of long-distance wireless communication and direction of the affairs of the Marconi Company.

In 1922 Kellaway, an ex-Postmaster General, became a director and later succeeded Isaacs as Managing Director. Subsequently other directors were appointed who were skilled committee men and negotiators rather than the experts in engineering, finance or foreign languages of the old days. When the Board was reconstituted in 1927 Marconi was the only member with technical or linguistic ability, and immediately after his wedding to Cristina he resigned his chairmanship and became an ordinary director. His influence over the affairs of the Company was now much reduced, and in 1928, when the Cable and Wireless merger was brought about by Act of Parliament, the Marconi Company itself was shorn of all its interests in the handling of messages and left as a manufacturer of equipment.[21]

The principal driving force of Marconi's life had been the ambition to cover the world with a wireless system of his own and to found a great company to manage and exploit that system. Twice he had linked the major countries of the world with his wireless: first with the high-power long-wave system, and then in 1926 and 1927 with the greatly more efficient short-wave beam system. He had no driving ambition left in this field. His Company had grown great and spread throughout the world, but now he was out of sympathy with a cost-conscious Board who would not automatically subscribe to research and innovation and who did not take kindly to the expensive grandeur of their foreign founder who was so rarely present at their meetings. In particular he could not forgive the Board for being outmanœuvred in the merger negotiations by the Cable interests. When Marconi had first mentioned publicly the possibility of such a merger[22] it had been from a position of great strength, with the cable companies in a panic about the new Beam Wireless Scheme. When the merger terms were announced the Cable group had 56 per cent of the voting power of the new company and the Marconi Company had 44 per cent.[23]

Marconi's marriage to his Italian bride marked the start of a spiritual withdrawal into his home country. He travelled abroad still, but his interests were in Italy. He had administrative work in Rome in his government posts as Senator, President of the National Research Council, and President of the Royal Academy; his research interests moved towards radar and television which are systems of relatively short range so that experiments did not require him to move many miles from home; and his new family life bound him closely to Italy and also prompted him to push his old family further away – after the first two years of his marriage to Cristina the children of his first marriage were no longer invited to spend summer holidays with him. On 20 July 1930 Cristina gave birth to a daughter who was christened Maria Elettra Elena Anna by Marconi's friend Cardinal Pacelli. Maria was Cristina's first name, Elettra was after the yacht, Elena in honour of the Queen of Italy who was godmother, and Anna after the two grandmothers who, fortunately for the child, shared a single name.

CHAPTER 16

SICKNESS, POLITICS,
AND THE END IN ROME

CRISTINA was not a wife to tolerate being left alone while her husband travelled the world on business. She went with him on most of his trips, whether they were to the United States and beyond or just short voyages in Marconi's yacht. Countess Bezzi-Scali, Cristina's mother, was happy to look after the child while her son-in-law and daughter were away. When he had returned to Italy from his honeymoon, so unexpectedly prolonged by illness in London, Marconi's convalescence, and then his official duties, had kept him in, or close to, Rome for some time. Surprisingly for such an independent man, Marconi seemed to a certain extent to be assimilated by his wife's family. He and Cristina and the child now made their home in an apartment in the Bezzi-Scali mansion in Rome, and they no longer used Villa Grifone as a country house but went instead to Civita Vecchia, a seaside town convenient to the capital. Since his marriage Marconi had turned to Roman Catholicism into which faith he had been baptised, although under his mother's influence his active religious observances, such as they were, had always been in the Protestant Church.

In 1930 Marconi's friend Cardinal Pacelli, Secretary of State to Pope Pius XI, was engaged in a comprehensive reorganisation of the working methods of the Vatican secretariat,[1] among his reforms being the introduction of typewriters and an efficient telephone system. Pacelli approached Marconi and arranged for a powerful short-wave radio station to be constructed in the Vatican City so that Roman Catholic opinion, and the voice of the Pope himself, could be broadcast directly to most parts of the world. When the station was opened in 1931 it gave the Vatican a means of world com-

263

munication independent of the Italian Government. This was a matter of particular concern because Pius XI was at this time preparing his anti-Fascist encyclical and it was very probable that the Government would jib at allowing the Italian telegraph system to be used to publish it to Catholics abroad. The encyclical condemned the systematic attempt of the Fascist Party to direct the spirit of the country's youth towards what was tantamount to exclusive devotion to the State. Cardinal Spellman took the document secretly to Paris and it was published there in June 1931. Mussolini was much interested in the possibilities of broadcast propaganda and he could not have welcomed the initiative of Pacelli and Marconi in providing facilities for this in the Vatican at a time when the enormous influence of the Pope was being exerted against certain Fascist activities. It is ironical that Marconi should later have been criticised for too strongly supporting Mussolini, and Pacelli condemned for not strongly enough denouncing Nazi behaviour when he himself was Pope Pius XII during the 1939–45 war.

Just two years after the opening of the Vatican short-wave broadcasting station Marconi again offered his services to the Pope and provided him with one of the first applications of his experiments with microwaves. He installed a microwave link between the Vatican City and the Pope's summer residence fifteen miles away, giving instant and private telephone communication between the Pope and his staff at all times.

Marconi's driving passion was the discovery of new techniques. When he had solved one great technical problem he wanted to push on to the next big step and he was happy to leave colleagues to reproduce and extend any system he had invented, once he was satisfied of its fundamental reliability. He only gave his attention to duplicating a system already known to work when the time involved was clearly defined and short, and when the return in terms of money or publicity was likely to help, if only indirectly, with future major projects. Into this category fell the reporting of the America's Cup races, the wireless link between Osborne House and Prince Edward in the Royal Yacht, the Vatican City radio station and the microwave telephone link for the Pope. For this reason Marconi was not greatly interested in the use of radio to broadcast entertainment and news to the millions, nor did he wish to devote time to the improvement of television, already invented and demonstrated by someone else. When the objective was a new technology, Marconi focused it sharply to the exclusion of all else, and he gathered everything which would help him towards his goal: scientific principles old and new, gifted men of ideas, skilled artisans, and men of influence who could make available capital and facilities for major projects. Whatever organisation was willing and best able to support him was welcome to receive the benefits of his invention: a commercial organisation like Lloyd's or a newspaper; a Government department like the Post Office or the Board of Trade; any country, Britain, Canada or the United States – although his patriotic inclination was naturally to his own country, and Italy had on the whole been more consistently loyal to him and appreciative of his work than any other nation.

The major project which concerned him in the 1930s was the development of microwaves: radiation with a wavelength of less than a metre. This was a strange reversion to the work he had done as a boy at Villa Grifone. The small spark which was then the only available source of electromagnetic energy for the transmitter had produced very short waves, and much of the work of investigators before Marconi had been concerned with showing how these waves were reflected and refracted just like light. All Marconi's early efforts to improve the range of his wireless system had led him to increase the wavelength of the signals. The high-power transatlantic system had used a wavelength of hundreds of metres. Then had come the short-wave beam system, with wavelengths measured only in tens of metres, using the ionosphere, at first unwittingly, to obtain equally long ranges with very much less power than the long-wave systems. In turning back again to wavelengths less than one metre, Marconi was particularly interested in their highly directional properties, but he now had the advantage of thermionic valves and generally improved circuits in the transmitters and receivers he used.

The extremely narrow beam directed from a microwave transmitter to the chosen receiving aerial meant a high degree of privacy in communication. This property had been used by Marconi in the Pope's microwave radio telephone system where the aerial in the Vatican 'looked' directly at its companion fifteen miles away at Castel Gandolfo. A further application Marconi made of the narrow and well-defined microwave beam was to provide a marked path into a harbour for ships in fog or foul weather. In fact two separate transmitters each sent a microwave beam seaward from the harbour. The two beams overlapped slightly along a central line which led precisely to the harbour entrance, and if the receiving vessel was to the left of this line then it detected a note of one pitch, while to the right of the line a different note was heard. When exactly on line neither note was audible, precautions being taken to avoid a breakdown in the apparatus being mistaken for this situation.

On a number of occasions when experimenting with his microwaves, Marconi had observed that if an object such as a motor car passed through the transmitted beam then a hissing noise was sometimes heard in the receiver. He considered this phenomenon while working on other microwave experiments, and in the summer of 1933 he told Solari[2] that he believed that an object in the microwave beam would reflect enough energy for a receiver placed near the transmitter to detect it. He recognised the military implications of such a system and proposed to the authorities that experiments should be undertaken under his direction as President of the National Scientific Research Council. Marconi was on the track of radar, an application of microwaves to the detection of ships and aircraft, which was just the type of important technological innovation to attract his interest. Experiments were put in hand during 1934 and 1935, Marconi and Solari working together with assistance from the Italian Navy and the Italian Marconi Company. The preliminary results were successful enough, and the military application sufficiently obvious, for the Italian Government to require all further experiments to be carried out in secret, and for Mussolini to insist that foreign assistants – in particular English ones – be replaced by Italians. Tests with aircraft are particularly difficult to conceal, and such tests, combined with the secrecy surrounding the work, gave rise to the almost inevitable rumours of 'death ray' experiments. But Marconi could not, or at any rate did not, give to the radar project that single-minded attention which he had devoted to his wireless when he was a young man. His health was deteriorating, he had official duties in Rome, he travelled abroad for pleasure and business, and in the autumn of 1935 Italy went to war in Abyssinia.

Marconi's frequent visits to London in the early 1930s were for a variety of reasons: business, scientific meetings, memorial celebrations, and social occasions. In 1931 he took part with old colleagues in a BBC broadcast on the thirtieth anniversary of the transmission of the S's across the Atlantic. Earlier in the same year he was presented with the Kelvin Medal by Rutherford. These two names recalled his earliest days of wireless when established scientists, Kelvin and Rutherford among them, had doubted the young inventor's claims and argued about priority of invention. The 'inventor' was however in impeccable academic company at a memorial concert in honour of Faraday at the Queen's Hall, when his companions on the platform to give tributes included Zeeman, de Broglie, Debye and Rutherford. Sir Henry Wood who conducted the orchestra recalled[3] how interested Marconi was in the musical part of the programme.

Now that he was sixty, Marconi was no less reserved. He still resented sharing the lift at his London office with anyone he did not know personally. Low, the cartoonist, surely an expert at penetrating the barricades of person-ality, recorded in his autobiography[4] that Marconi was nervous and would not talk and was one of a small number of people who sat for him of whom he 'got only their appearance'.

The most ambitious of Marconi's trips abroad was his world tour between the late summer of 1933 and early 1934. Cristina, of course, came with him, their daughter remaining in Rome with her grandmother. The journey was a triumphant progress, with parties and celebrations of every kind. They spent some time in New York, attended 'Marconi Day' at the Chicago Exposition, and toured on through America to San Francisco, being entertained in surroundings as diverse as Roosevelt's White House, a cowboy gathering, and Pickfair, Mary Pickford's estate in Hollywood. They sailed across the Pacific to Japan, where they met the Emperor. Then on to China, India and Ceylon, and back at last to Italy to a backlog of work which kept Marconi busy in Rome all through the summer, apart from a hurried trip to England. In retrospect it is hardly surprising that in the September, when in Venice to address a conference on possible medical applications of microwaves, he had another severe heart attack. When he had recovered, his doctor brought him back to Rome, but in November he went to England with Cristina to attend the wedding of Princess Marina of Greece and the Duke of Kent. Friends in London thought he looked tired.

He made no attempt to take life easy, and while he was in London in the cold November of 1934 he had the usual press of engagements including one or two which must have taxed him unreasonably. He made a quick journey to Scotland and back to attend the lively election for Rector of St Andrews University, where he came top of the poll. He went with the Italian Ambassador in the fog to an international soccer match at Highbury. Once more he was taken ill, and in December he was under treatment in a London nursing home while Cristina, left alone in her hotel, sent to Rome for her mother and daughter to come and join her. It was February before they returned to Rome, and Marconi was still far from well, his doctor ordering a long rest. But this did not suit him and he frequently visited the Senate and his office at the Italian Royal Academy, and went on with the supervision of the radar experiments. That summer he again visited England and attended the Naval Review of 1935, showing a keen interest in demonstrations of the remote control of aircraft by radio. In his own country final preparations were being made for the war in Abyssinia and the opposition Mussolini expected from England, France and the League of Nations.

As President of the Royal Academy of Italy, Marconi was

also a member of the Fascist Grand Council. He met Mussolini often and was flattered by the dictator's attention, while the Duce was glad to have had such a famous international figure as a convinced member of the Fascist Party since 1923. Marconi had declared that he was a Fascist by conviction and not for convenience. Now with the Abyssinian conflict about to start and all Italy in a ferment of patriotism, Marconi spoke out for his country against her critics and in particular against the decision of the League of Nations to impose sanctions against Italy. He broadcast from Rome to the United States a justification of Italy's claims, and then at Mussolini's request he undertook a last long journey on his country's behalf, to South America, England and France. As a scientist with a lifetime spent in identifying cause and effect he could have had little doubt about the consequences to his health of such a journey. But, whenever his country had gone to war – in 1911, in 1915 and now again in 1935 – he had always responded with the instant unquestioning patriotism which was perhaps never again evident in generations born after the 1914–18 war. His doctor was insistent that it would be folly to travel, but in October 1935 he set out for Brazil to rally to their country's cause the large colonies of Italians there. Possibly his task in South America involved more than propaganda. There was a suggestion that he was also trying to raise money for the Italian Government whose economic position was far from sound, particularly with the application of sanctions. After some weeks in Brazil he sailed to England where he had a meeting with Edward VIII, the uncrowned King deeply involved in the constitutional crisis. He also saw John Reith who refused to allow him the facilities of the BBC to make a broadcast putting the Italian point of view to the British people.

I took him to lunch and we had a pleasant talk. He said he expected to be told that he could broadcast about anything under the sun except what he wanted to broadcast about. Quite right. I asked if Mussolini had put him up to this and he did not deny it; a clever move. [5]

This refusal aroused considerable protest in England where much private and Government opinion at the time was in favour of placating Mussolini. A letter to the *Times*[6] pointed out, for instance, that Abyssinia had flagrantly violated the principal condition of her admission to the League by not taking any steps to abolish slavery within the country. Furthermore Laval and the British Foreign Secretary were formulating the Hoare–Laval plan for dividing Abyssinia. This was favourable to Italy, and acceptable to England and France, but thwarted by premature revelation in the French Press and a consequent storm of protest which resulted in Hoare's resignation and Eden's appointment to the Foreign Office.[7] Marconi's time in London and his subsequent visit to Laval in Paris coincided with the period of the Hoare–Laval negotiations and it is not impossible that he played some diplomatic role for Italy.

Returning home to Italy from Paris he spent the night on the Rome express. At lunch on the train on 15 December he had yet another bad heart attack, but with the help of injected stimulant which he always had near him he recovered and was able to walk from the train in Rome. He would not set out again on any great enterprise. There were just eighteen months of life left to him and these were not happy months.

His brother Alfonso died in London and Marconi was now too ill to leave Italy for the funeral. A succession of heart attacks greatly limited his activities, even in Rome, but he still went to his office as often as he could, and even took some part in the microwave experiments. He was worried too that his personal finances were not as sound as he would have wished. But in his dying months he did draw consolation from the fact that he had moved towards ending the estrangement between himself and the children of his marriage to Bea. He saw his daughter Degna frequently in Rome during 1936 and they reminisced happily together over old family memories. On 17 July 1937 Marconi had an audience of the Pope, and on 19 July a consultation with his lawyer, which events aroused speculation that he might have planned some change in his affairs. But there was no time now for any material change to be made.

His last day was scorching hot in Rome and he went to the station to see Cristina and their seven-year-old daughter off to the seaside where he planned to join them the next day for the child's birthday. He did some work in his office in the morning and then called on Solari before returning to his apartment to prepare for an appointment with Mussolini that evening at six o'clock. But at five o'clock he was taken ill and in the early hours of 20 July 1937 he died.

Wireless carried the news of Marconi's death all over the world, and the most eminent scientists and men of affairs paid tributes and attended memorial services. But, unique, for this man only, was the most impressive gesture of all: wireless stations everywhere closed down, and for two minutes the ether was as quiet as it had been before Marconi.

There were thousands of obituary notices and editorials in newspapers and scientific journals everywhere. Two matters of speculation and comment raised in many of these obituaries can be looked at again now in the context of events which occurred after they were written in 1937.

Marconi's friendship with Mussolini and his speeches in support of Italian Fascism have, since the 1939–45 war, been criticised, overlooking the great change in opinion about Mussolini which has taken place since Marconi's death. A contemporary judgement was given in an editorial in the *Electrician* on Marconi's death:

the BBC refused to allow him to broadcast a statement on the Italo-Abyssinian conflict. Had he been permitted to do so, it is possible that a better understanding would exist today between Great Britain and Italy than is, unfortunately, the case.[8]

Even if Italian Fascism had been generally identified as reprehensible in the 1930s it would be unwise to take Marconi's speeches as expressions of deeply felt sympathy with an evil cause. When he was asked to make a speech he did not approach the task with enthusiasm, but rather with a dispassionate desire to assemble and present the available material in a manner best calculated to match the occasion and please his audience. It is unlikely that he had given much thought to the mission work of the Salvation Army before he was asked to introduce General Booth to an audience of fellow passengers on a transatlantic liner, but his speech was most moving. He was more concerned with making a good speech than with considering whether he should, in fact, be speaking at all. He never questioned why he was chosen to make a speech or undertake a mission. He was not a modest man and he could usually believe that he was the best person available to do the job, or the natural choice because of his eminence. His unyielding standard was that there were certain duties he would accept without question: the demands of his work no matter how menial or arduous; the call of his native land in time of war. He would not refuse the summons of a King or a Queen, perhaps he could not resist the call of a Prime Minister or a Duce.

The other matter for speculation in the 1937 obituaries was on the further work Marconi would have done if he had lived longer. Perhaps if he had lived until 1945, in good health, the Italian Navy would have fought the war in the Mediterranean with first-class radar, and perhaps Marconi would have played a diplomatic role in the armistice negotiations after Mussolini fell. Certainly it is unlikely that his yacht *Elettra* would have lain, as she did in 1944, beached after being bombed in the waters of Yugoslavia where d'Annunzio had called her 'the great white bird'.

But the speculation, and the evaluation of Marconi as a politician, a husband, a businessman, are secondary issues. The world must judge Marconi as a wireless man, because this was what he chose to be. All other roles were to him minor ones, taken up lightly because of circumstances, convention, or a lesser passion than that which drove him to create great communication systems. As *The Times* put it:

What other men had been content to prove impossible, he accomplished; and this is surely greatness. The history of wireless communication has been a history of miracles;

272

but the true miracle, as Carlyle remarked, is the life of a man – the vision and the faith, the patient labour illuminated by the unshakable resolve, which surmount all the barriers and in the end confound the wise.[9]

SELECT BIBLIOGRAPHY

AMERY, *My Political Life*, Heinemann 1967

BAKER, *A History of the Marconi Company*, Methuen 1970

BLAKE, *The Unknown Prime Minister*, Eyre & Spottiswoode 1955

DONALDSON, FRANCES, *The Marconi Scandal*, Rupert Hart-Davis 1962

DUNLAP, *Marconi the Man and his Wireless*, Macmillan, New York 1937

FOREST, DE, *Father of Radio*, Follett, Chicago 1950

HYDE, MONTGOMERY, *Lord Reading*, Heinemann 1967

JACOT AND COLLIER, *Marconi, Master of Space*, Hutchinson 1935

LLOYD GEORGE, FRANCES, *The Years that are Past*, Hutchinson 1967

MARCONI, DEGNA, *My Father Marconi*, Muller 1962

PESSION, *Marconi*, U.T.E., Turin 1941 (Italian)

PETRIE, *Scenes of Edwardian Life*, Eyre & Spottiswoode 1965

Report of Norman Committee on Imperial Wireless Telegraphy, Commd. 777. HMSO July 1920

SOLARI, *Il Trionfo di Marconi*, Fratelli Bocca, Milan 1942 (Italian)

STURMEY, *Economic Development of Radio*, University College London Survey, Duckworth 1958

WALLACE, *Claude Grahame-White*, Putnam 1960

274

REFERENCES

CHAPTER 1

1 Solari, L., *Sui Mari e Sui Continenti con le Onde Elettriche*, Milan, 1942.

CHAPTER 2

1 *La Tribuna*, Rome, July 1897.
2 *Electrical Engineers and Workers*, Kingsford, Arnold, 1969.
3 Jacot and Collier, *Marconi: Master of Space*, Hutchinson, 1935.
4 *Ibid.*
5 Interview, *McClure's Magazine*, March 1897.

CHAPTER 3

1 *Rivista Marina*, July 1896.
2 *Past Years*, Lodge, Hodder & Stoughton, 1931.
3 Hill, J. Arthur (ed.), *Letters from Sir Oliver Lodge*, Cassell, 1932.

CHAPTER 4

1 Jacot and Collier, *Marconi: Master of Space*, Hutchinson, 1935.
2 *Times*, 11.6.1897.
3 *Electrician*, Vol. 40, 1897.
4 Marconi, Degna, *My Father Marconi*, Muller, 1962.
5 Marconi Historical Archives.
6 *Ibid.*
7 *Ibid.*
8 Public Record Office, ADM 116/523.
9 *Times*, 13.10.1897.
10 Marconi, Degna, *My Father Marconi*.

11 Jackson to C-in-C Devonport; PRO, ADM 116/523.
12 *Dublin Daily Express*, 21.7.1898.
13 MHA.
14 *Dulbin Daily Express*, 22.7.1898.
15 Supplement to *Dublin Evening Mail*, 21.7.1898.
16 Zanichelli, *La Telegrafia Marconi e il Giornalismo*, Bologna, 1898.
17 Marconi, Degna, *My Father Marconi*.
18 MHA.
19 *Electrical Review*, Vol. 43, August 1898.
20 MHA.
21 MHA (Kemp unpublished diaries).
22 *Electrician*, 28.1.1898.
23 *Journal of the Institute of Electrical Engineers*, Vol. 28, 1899.
24 *Times*, 3.3.1899. (Copy of Marconi's paper to IEE.)
25 Marconi, Degna, *My Father Marconi*.
26 Jacot and Collier, *Marconi: Master of Space*.
27 MHA.
28 Marconi, Degna, *My Father Marconi*.
29 Letter of 1.7.1899, PRO, ADM 116/523.
30 *Times*, 17.7.1899.
31 PRO, ADM 53.12.434.
32 *Times*, 22.7.1899'
33 *Navy and Army Illustrated*, 2.9.1899.
34 *Times*, 22.7.1899.
35 *Western Morning News*, 17.7.1899.
36 Parliamentary Proceedings, 14.7.1899.
37 PRO, ADM 53.12.434.
38 *Naval and Military Record*, 10.8.1899.
39 *Times*, 4.8.1899.
40 Letters of 25.7.1899 and 10.8.1899, PRO, ADM 116/523.

CHAPTER 5

1 Marconi Historical Archives.
2 Public Record Office, ADM 116/563.
3 *Ibid.*
4 *Ibid.*
5 Pocock, *Journal RN Scientific Service*, Vol. 20, 1965.
6 PRO, ADM 116/523.
7 *Ibid.*
8 *Ibid.*

9   Watson Watt, *Three Steps to Victory*, Odhams, 1957.
10   MHA.
11   *Ibid.*
12   *Ibid.*
13   *New York Herald,* 30.9.1899.
14   *Ibid.*
15   MHA.
16   *New York Herald,* 30.9.1899.
17   *Proceedings of the American Institute of Electrical Engineers,* Vol. 14, 1897.
18   *Report of Chief Signal Officer to Secretary of War,* Government Printing House, 13.6.1899.
19   *Proc. Am. IEE,* Vol. 16, 1899.
20   *Ibid.*
21   *Electrician,* Vol. 44, 1899.
22   *Electrician,* Vol. 44, 1899.
23   *Electrical World,* November 1899.
24   Marconi, Degna, *My Father Marconi,* Muller, 1962.

CHAPTER 6

1   Public Record Office, ADM 116/523.
2   *Times,* 24.2.1900.
3   Marconi Historical Archives.
4   *Ibid.*
5   PRO, ADM 116/570.
6   MHA.
7   *Ibid.*
8   *Times,* 14.12.1900.
9   MHA
10   *Times,* 9.10.1900.
11   MHA.
12   MHA.
13   *Étoile Belge,* 11.3.1900.
14   MHA.
15   *Marconi Book of Wireless,* Marconiphone, London, 1936.
16   Baker, *History of the Marconi Company,* Methuen, 1970.
17   *Times,* 5.2.1900.
18   PRO, ADM 116/523.
19   MHA.
20   Solari, L., *Sui Mari e Sui Continenti con le Onde Elettriche,* Milan, 1942.

CHAPTER 7

1 Marconi Historical Archives (Dowsett MS.).
2 *New York Times*, 15.12.1901.
3 *Times*, 18.12.1901.
4 *Times*, 19.12.1901.
5 *Ibid.*
6 *Times*, 20.12.1901.
7 Jacot and Collier, *Marconi: Master of Space*, Hutchinson, 1935.
8 MHA.
9 Marconi, Degna, *My Father Marconi*, Muller, 1962.
10 Jacot and Collier, *Marconi: Master of Space*.
11 *Punch*, 22.1.1902.

CHAPTER 8

1 *Nature*, 19.12.1901.
2 *Times*, 20.12.1901.
3 *Times*, 19.12.1901.
4 *Times*, 24.12.1901.
5 *Saturday Review*, April 1902.
6 Vyvyan, *Wireless Over Thirty Years*, Routledge, 1933.
7 Thompson, J.S. and H.G., *Sylvanus P. Thompson: His Life and Letters*, 1920.
8 *Electrical Times*, 15.5.1902.
9 Solari, L., *Sui Mari e Sui Continenti con le Onde Elettriche*, Milan, 1942.
10 Jacot and Collier, *Marconi: Master of Space*, Hutchinson, 1935.
11 Solari, L., *Sui Mari e Sui Continenti*.
12 *Ibid.*
13 Marconi Historical Archives (De Sousa MS.).
14 Solari, L., *Sui Mari e Sui Continenti*.
15 *Ibid.*
16 *Nature*, 9.10.1902.
17 Solari, L., *Sui Mari e Sui Continenti*.
18 Vyvyan, *Wireless Over Thirty Years*.
19 MHA (De Sousa MS.).

CHAPTER 9

1 *Electrician*, 12.6.1903.

2 Marconi Historical Archives (Lamb to Secretary of Marconi Company, 31.12.1902).
3 MHA (Marconi to Postmaster General, 2.3.1903).
4 MHA (Austen Chamberlain to Marconi, 4.3.1903).
5 MHA (Cuthbert Hall to Marconi, 18.12.1903).
6 MHA (Cuthbert Hall to Marconi, 8.1.1904).
7 MHA (Cuthbert Hall to Marconi, 5.9.1903).
8 Marconi's Evidence in Chief before Select Committee of House of Commons, 1913.
9 Vyvyan, *Wireless Over Thirty Years*, Routledge, 1933.
10 MHA (Cuthbert Hall to Marconi, 25.4.1904).
11 MHA (Fleming to Marconi, 5.6.1903).
12 MHA (Hopkins/Shaw letters, 19.3.1959, *et seq.*).
13 *Electrician*, 19.6.1903.
14 India Office to Viceroy, 30.6.1905. India Office Library PW 331/1906.
15 MHA (Cuthbert Hall to Marconi, 17.7.1903).
16 Follett, *De Forest: Father of Radio*, Chicago, 1950.
17 *Electrician*, 10.7.1903.
18 Josephson, Matthew, *Edison*, Eyre & Spottiswoode, 1959.
19 Marconi, Degna, *My Father Marconi*, Muller, 1962.
20 MHA (Signora Marconi/Kershaw letters, 28.4.1906 *et seq.*).
21 Baker, *History of the Marconi Company*, Methuen, 1970.
22 Solari, L., *Sui Mari e Sui Continenti con le Onde Elettriche*, Milan, 1942.
23 Follett, *De Forest: Father of Radio*, Chicago, 1950.
24 MHA (Cuthbert Hall to Marconi, 19.1.1904 *et seq.*).
25 India Office Library ZP1872 C.W. Traffic. Prog. 17–8.9.1904.
26 India Office Library P6838 C.W. Tel. 1904.
27 India Office Library PW 331/1906.
28 India Office Library PW1175/05, 17.6.1905.
29 Marconi, Degna, *My Father Marconi*.
30 *Ibid.*
31 MHA (Marconi to Signora Marconi, 9.9.1904).

CHAPTER 10

1 Marconi, Degna, *My Father Marconi*, Muller, 1962.
2 Marconi Historical Archives (Dowsett MS.).
3 MHA (Cuthbert Hall to Marconi, 15.2.1904).
4 MHA (Cuthbert Hall to Admiralty, 24.8.1904).
5 MHA (Admiralty to Marconi Company, 12.9.1904).

6   MHA (Cuthbert Hall to Marconi, 14.9.1904).
7   MHA (Marconi to his mother. Mon 1960 [sic]).
8   MHA (Bea to Marconi, 30.1.1907).
9   MHA (Eileen O'Brien MS.).
10 MHA (Cuthbert Hall to Marconi, 10.7.1907).
11 *Electrician*, 25.10.1907.
12 MHA (Bottomley to Marconi, 11.12.1907).
13 Fessenden, *Scientific American* Supplement, 16.11.1907.
14 *Electrician*, 28.2.1908.
15 *Electrician*, 6.3.1908.
16 MHA (Cuthbert Hall to Marconi, 10.7.1907).
17 Vyvyan, *Wireless Over Thirty Years*, Routledge, 1933.
18 MHA (Bottomley to Cuthbert Hall, 21.5.1906).
19 Follett, *De Forest: Father of Radio*, Chicago, 1950.
20 *Electrician*, 13.3.1908.
21 MHA (Fleming to Marconi, 4.10.1901).
22 MHA (Cuthbert Hall to Marconi, 6.2.1904).
23 O'Neill, *Prodigal Genius*, Spearman, 1968.

CHAPTER 11

1   Solari Papers; Marconi to Solari, 29.1.1910.
2   Hyde, Montgomery, *Lord Reading*, Heinemann, 1967.
3   Solari, L., *Sui Mari e Sui Continenti con le Onde Elettriche*, Milan, 1942.
4   *Nature*, 17.11.1910.
5   Marconi Historical Archives (Marconi letter 26.2.1911).
6   MHA (Marconi letter 4.8.1911).
7   MHA (Annie Marconi letter 21.9.1911).
8   Nicolson, *King George V*, Constable, 1952.
9   Vyvyan, *Wireless Over Thirty Years*, Routledge, 1933.
10 MHA (Marconi to Isaacs, December 1911).
11 MHA (Annie Marconi to Marconi, 10.12.1911).
12 MHA (Marconi to Beatrice Marconi, 10.12.1911).
13 Priestly, J. B., *The Edwardians*, Heinemann, 1970.
14 *Manchester Guardian*, 14.4.1937.
15 Follett, *De Forest: Father of Radio*, Chicago, 1950.
16 Mersey Enquiry into the loss of the *Titanic*. Presented to Parliament 30.7.1912.
17 Baker, *History of the Marconi Company*, Methuen, 1970.
18 Marconi, Degna, *My Father Marconi*, Muller, 1962.
19 MHA (G. S. Kemp to Marconi, 10.10.1912).

CHAPTER 12

1 Hill, J. A., *Letters from Sir O. Lodge*, Cassell, 1932.
2 Marconi Historical Archives (Dowsett MS.).
3 Ensor, *Oxford History of England*, OUP, 1936.
4 Petrie, *Scenes of Edwardian Life*, Eyre & Spottiswoode, 1965.
5 Lord Murray to Lloyd George, October 1911. Beaverbrook Library L.G. Papers C/6/5/6.
6 Owen, F., *Tempestuous Journey*, Hutchinson, 1954.
7 Hyde, Montgomery, *Lord Reading*, Heinemann, 1967.
8 Donaldson, Frances, *The Marconi Scandal*, Hart-Davis, 1962.
9 Hyde, Montgomery, *Lord Reading*.
10 *Ibid.*
11 Blake, *The Unknown Prime Minister*, Eyre & Spottiswoode, 1955.
12 Amery, L. S., *My Political Life*, Hutchinson, 1953.
13 Blake, *The Unknown Prime Minister*.
14 Amery, L. S., *My Political Life*.
15 Blake, *The Unknown Prime Minister*.
16 Hyde, Montgomery, *Lord Reading*.
17 Owen, F., *Tempestuous Journey*.
18 Hyde, Montgomery, *Lord Reading*.
19 Northcliffe to Lloyd George, 24.3.1913. Beaverbrook Library C/6/8/1A.
20 Northcliffe to Churchill, undated. Beaverbrook Library C/3/15/21.
21 Northcliffe to Churchill, undated. Beaverbrook Library, C/3/15/20.
22 Murray to Lloyd George. Beaverbrook Library, Lloyd George Papers C6/5/6–8.
23 Blake, *The Unknown Prime Minister*.
24 Murray to Lloyd George. Beaverbrook Library. Lloyd George Papers C6/5/6–8.
25 *Ibid.*
26 Taylor, *English History, 1914–45*, OUP, 1965.
27 Petrie, Sir Charles, *Scenes of Edwardian Life*, Eyre & Spottiswoode, 1965.
28 Lloyd George, Frances, *The Years That Are Past*, Hutchinson, 1967.
29 Hyde, Montgomery, *Lord Reading*.
30 Margot Asquith to Lloyd George. Beaverbrook Library. Lloyd George Papers C/6/12/2, 3, 4.

31   Amery, L. S., *My Political Life*.
32   Cadogan, *Before the Deluge*, Murray, 1961
33   Amery, L. S., *My Political Life*.
34   *Electrical Times*, 17.7.1913.
35   Cooper, Duff, *Old Men Forget*, Hart-Davis, 1953.
36   Moran, *Churchill: The Struggle for Survival*, Constable, 1966.
37   Petrie, *Scenes of Edwardian Life*.
38   Hassall, *Rupert Brooke*, Faber, 1964.
39   Marconi, Degna, *My Father Marconi*, Muller, 1962.
40   Wallace, *Claude Grahame-White*, Putnam, 1960.
41   *Punch*, 22.10.1913.
42   *Daily Telegraph*, 15.10.1913.
43   Woodward Papers; private communication.
44   MHA (Elisabeth Beck to Marconi).
45   Woodward Papers; private communication.
46   Marconi, Degna, *My Father Marconi*.
47   MHA (Dowsett MS.).

CHAPTER 13

1   Marconi Historical Archives (Home Office to Marconi, 17.11.1914).
2   MHA (Hist 29).
3   Dunlap, *Marconi: The Man and His Wireless*, Macmillan, N.Y., 1937.
4   MHA (Marconi Speech 1915).
5   Solari, L., *Sui Mari e Sui Continenti con le Onde Elettriche*, Milan, 1942.
6   *Ibid*.
7   MHA (Dowsett MS.).
8   Baker, *History of the Marconi Company*, Methuen, 1970.
9   *Journal of the Institute of Electrical Engineers*, Vol. 58, No. 28, January 1920.
10   Jellicoe Papers, Vol. 1. Navy Records Society.
11   Dunlap, *Marconi: The Man and His Wireless*.
12   Marconi, Degna, *My Father Marconi*, Muller, 1962.
13   MHA (Marconi Speech April 1918).
14   Jacot, and Collier, *Marconi: Master of Space*, Hutchinson, 1935.

CHAPTER 14

1 *British Sports and Sportsmen*, 1915.
2 Marconi Historical Archives (Marconi to Godfrey Isaacs, 3.8.1922).
3 Taylor, *English History, 1914–45*, OUP, 1965.
4 Pession, *Marconi*, UTE, Turin, 1941.
5 Marconi, Degna, *My Father Marconi*, Muller, 1962.
6 MHA (Letter from Beatrice to Marconi, 6.8.1921).
7 Briggs, *The Birth of Broadcasting*, OUP, 1961.
8 Baker, *History of the Marconi Company*, Methuen, 1970.
9 Sturmey, *Economic Development of Radio: Survey by Department of Political Economy UCL*, Duckworth, 1958.
10 Report of Norman Committee on Imperial Wireless Telegraphy, Commd. 777, July 1920.
11 *Electrical Review*, 16.7.1920.

CHAPTER 15

1 Marconi Historical Archives (Marconi to Solari, 25.6.1923).
2 Baker, *History of the Marconi Company*, Methuen, 1970.
3 Sturmey, *Economic Development of Radio: Survey by Department of Political Economy UCL*, Duckworth, 1958.
4 Baker, *History of the Marconi Company*.
5 Solari, L., *Sui Mari e Sui Continenti con le Onde Elettriche*, Milan, 1942.
6 Nancarrow; private communication, 18.3.1969.
7 MHA (Memoir by Captain Daly).
8 Lord Mountbatten; private communication, 11.11.1970.
9 Marconi, Degna, *My Father Marconi*, Muller 1962.
10 *The Electrician*, 23.7.1937.
11 Marconi, Degna, *My Father Marconi*.
12 Jackson, Stanley, *The Savoy*, Muller, 1964.
13 *Cornishman and Cornish Telegraph*, 8.4.1925.
14 Mrs A. G. Sparrow; private communication, August 1970.
15 Nancurvis; private communication.
16 Mrs E. Lamorna Kerr; private communication, August 1970.
17 *Cornishman and Cornish Telegraph*, 15.4.1925.
18 Marconi, Degna, *My Father Marconi*.
19 Solari, L., *Sui Mari e Sui Continenti*.
20 Marconi, Degna, *My Father Marconi*.
21 Baker, *History of the Marconi Company*.

22   Paris Telecommunications Conference, 1925.
23   Baker, *History of the Marconi Company*.

CHAPTER 16

1   Hatch, *Apostle on the Move*, Allen, 1967.
2   Solari, L., *Sui Mari e Sui Continenti con le Onde Elettriche*, Milan, 1942.
3   Wood, H., *My Life of Music*, Gollancz, 1938.
4   Low autobiography, Michael Joseph, 1956.
5   Reith, J., *Into the Wind*, Hodder & Stoughton, 1949.
6   *Times*, 6.11.1935.
7   Taylor, *English History 1914–45*, OUP, 1965.
8   *Electrician*, 23.7.1937.
9   *Times*, 21.7.1937.

INDEX